Livestock E
Guidelines and Standards
(LEGS)
Second edition

D0789596

12/2

LEGS Handbook Structure

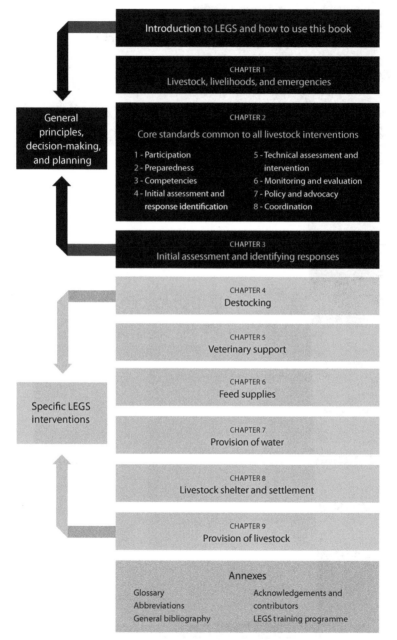

Introduction to LEGS and how to use this book

CHAPTER 1
Livestock, livelihoods, and emergencies

General principles, decision-making, and planning

CHAPTER 2
Core standards common to all livestock interventions

1 - Participation
2 - Preparedness
3 - Competencies
4 - Initial assessment and response identification

5 - Technical assessment and intervention
6 - Monitoring and evaluation
7 - Policy and advocacy
8 - Coordination

CHAPTER 3
Initial assessment and identifying responses

CHAPTER 4
Destocking

CHAPTER 5
Veterinary support

Specific LEGS interventions

CHAPTER 6
Feed supplies

CHAPTER 7
Provision of water

CHAPTER 8
Livestock shelter and settlement

CHAPTER 9
Provision of livestock

Annexes

Glossary
Abbreviations
General bibliography

Acknowledgements and contributors
LEGS training programme

Livestock Emergency Guidelines and Standards (LEGS)
Second edition

Practical Action Publishing Ltd
The Schumacher Centre
Bourton on Dunsmore, Rugby,
Warwickshire CV23 9QZ, UK
www.practicalactionpublishing.org

First published 2009
Second edition 2014

ISBN 978-1-85339-860-5 Hardback
ISBN 978-1-85339-861-2 Paperback
ISBN 978-1-78044-860-2 Library Ebook
ISBN 978-1-78044-861-9 Ebook

LEGS (2014) *Livestock Emergency Guidelines and Standards*, 2nd edition Rugby, UK:
Practical Action Publishing
http://dx.doi.org/10.3362/9781780448602

Since 1974, Practical Action Publishing has published and disseminated books and information
in support of international development work throughout
the world. Practical Action Publishing is a trading name of Practical Action Publishing Ltd
(Company Reg. No. 1159018), the wholly owned publishing company of Practical Action.
Practical Action Publishing trades only in support of its parent charity objectives and any profits
are covenanted back to Practical Action (Charity Reg. No. 247257, Group VAT Registration No.
880 9924 76).

Cover and text design by Messaggio Studios
Indexed by Liz Fawcett, Harrogate
Typeset by Bookcraft Ltd, Stroud, Gloucestershire

Contents

Praise for this book

'Easier to use, expanded response options and more case studies: this second edition of LEGS has surpassed the very high standards set by the first edition. It continues to be the benchmark for best practice in emergency livestock programming.'

Neil Marsland, Senior Technical Officer, Emergency Operations and Rehabilitation, FAO, Rome

'LEGS is an essential part of the toolkit for humanitarians who come in contact with animals through their work. We use LEGS in our disaster assessment work and for training governments in appropriate responses to livestock emergencies. Well thought-through and practical by nature, we endorse these guidelines and standards.'

James Sawyer, Director of Disaster Management, World Animal Protection

'This new edition of the Livestock Emergency Guidelines and Standards, which builds on the 2009 edition and practitioner experience of using it, is an important resource not just for livestock specialists but for everyone engaged in improving the quality of humanitarian interventions. Crucially, the revised book continues to situate livestock support interventions within a wider livelihoods perspective and framework.'

Sara Pantuliano, Director, Humanitarian Policy Group, ODI, London

'I welcome the second edition of LEGS, a practical expression of the core principle of building local capacities to ensure appropriate livestock interventions during times of crisis. Grounded in a commitment to preparedness in order to maintain the coping capacities of livestock keepers the application of the LEGS standards can reduce costs of emergency response in other life-saving sectors. I strongly recommend LEGS for both development and humanitarian actors working in areas where livestock is the main livelihood.'

Joanne O'Flannagan, Humanitarian Programme Coordinator, Trócaire, Ireland

Introduction to LEGS and how to use this book

What is LEGS?

Livestock Emergency Guidelines and Standards (LEGS) is a set of international guidelines and standards for designing, implementing, and evaluating livestock interventions to help people affected by humanitarian crises. LEGS is based on three livelihoods objectives: to provide immediate benefits, to protect livestock assets, and to rebuild the livestock assets of crisis-affected communities. LEGS supports the saving of both lives and livelihoods through two key strategies:

- LEGS helps identify the most appropriate livestock interventions during emergencies.
- LEGS provides Standards, Key actions, and Guidance notes for these interventions based on good practice.

Origins of LEGS and the second edition

The LEGS process grew out of the recognition that livestock are a crucial livelihood asset for people throughout the world – many of whom are poor and vulnerable to both natural and human-induced disasters – and that livestock support is an important component of emergency aid programmes.

The publication of the first edition of LEGS in 2009 responded to the need to help donors, programme managers, technical experts, and others to design and implement livestock interventions in emergencies. At the same time, LEGS recognized the need to plan for climatic trends affecting communities that rely heavily on livestock. The first edition drew on multi-agency contributions, on wide-ranging reviews, and on collations of practitioner experiences of using evidence-based good practice. This second edition builds on the first edition by incorporating new experiences and evidence obtained since 2009 as well as user feedback provided as a result of a broad consultation process. The LEGS Handbook has also been redesigned to make it easier to use.

Who should use LEGS?

LEGS can be used by anyone who is involved in livestock-related projects in emergencies. In particular:

- LEGS is aimed at people who provide emergency assistance in areas where livestock make an important contribution to human livelihoods; that is, aid organizations, bi- and multilateral agencies, and governments.
- LEGS is also relevant to policy and decision-makers in donor and government agencies whose funding and implementation decisions affect emergency response.
- A third audience for LEGS includes educational institutions and community-based organizations.

The scope and approach of LEGS

LEGS focuses on the areas where emergencies, livelihoods, and livestock overlap, emphasizing the need to protect livestock during emergencies as well as to help with rebuilding livestock assets afterwards. LEGS covers all types of livestock, from small species such as chickens to large animals such as cattle or camels, including animals used for transport or draught power. Because livestock are important in many different parts of the world and in many different environments, LEGS covers rural communities (farmers and pastoralists) as well as peri-urban and urban livestock keepers. LEGS also provides guidance on livestock kept by displaced people, including those living in camps.[1]

LEGS is structured around livelihoods objectives, underpinned by a rights-based approach, notably the *right to food* and the *right to a standard of living*, in line with the Sphere minimum standards (Sphere, 2011). The LEGS livelihoods perspective also means that the guidelines are concerned not only with immediate emergency response but also with recovery-phase activities and links to long-term development (*Box I.1*). Preparedness is a significant aspect of emergency response in LEGS, as is the importance of preserving livelihood assets to protect future livelihoods and to save lives.

The challenges of livelihoods-based thinking in emergencies

Taking a livelihoods perspective in emergency response highlights the need to develop close links between relief and development; for example, through emergency preparedness and post-emergency rehabilitation. Some donors and NGOs are moving towards more holistic programming, and new approaches are evolving. Examples are large-scale social protection systems for pastoralists, and insurance schemes to protect farmers and livestock keepers from weather hazards. By harmonizing relief and development programming, development professionals can help their clients become more resilient to disasters.

LEGS's key focus is to improve the quality of humanitarian interventions. However, the vulnerability of livestock keepers to disaster is determined by a range of socio-economic, political, environmental, and demographic factors, and humanitarian work cannot ignore these issues nor the need to link itself with development and with long-term policy changes to reduce vulnerability. Humanitarian work must also take account of the future possible impacts of climate change on livestock keepers, including increased risks of disasters.

While many of these issues are the subject of continued debate, the LEGS livelihoods approach can help to link relief with development; see, for example, the 'LEGS and resilience' discussion paper in the Resources section of the LEGS website: <http://www.livestock-emergency.net/wp-content/uploads/2012/01/LEGS-and-Resilience-Discussion-Paper-final2.pdf>.

While acknowledging that evaluation and impact assessments of emergency livestock projects have been limited (and the same is true of humanitarian projects in general), LEGS follows an evidence-based approach to setting standards and guidelines. Since the publication of the first edition of LEGS, new response options have been reviewed. Cash transfers and vouchers in particular have been recognized as a useful livelihoods-based approach during emergencies (see <www.cashlearning.org/>). Cash and voucher programming options relating to livestock support are therefore described in *Chapter 3 (Initial assessment and identifying responses)* and in the relevant technical chapters (4–9).

Other response options are also evolving for which more information is needed if we are to understand their impacts on more vulnerable households and the contexts in which such approaches can be used or scaled up. As they are still under evaluation and as there is not enough of an evidence base for them as yet, such options have not been included in this edition of LEGS.

Links to other standards and guidelines

LEGS provides standards and guidelines for good practice and assistance in decision-making. It is not intended to be a detailed manual for the implementation of livestock interventions during emergencies. That sort of hands-on guidance is covered by other sources listed in the references at the end of each chapter. In particular, the United Nations Food and Agriculture Organization (FAO) has published a practical manual for livestock interventions in emergencies that is designed to complement LEGS (FAO, 2015).

LEGS and Sphere

The process by which LEGS has developed mirrors that of the *Humanitarian Charter and Minimum Standards in Humanitarian Response* – the Sphere Handbook (Sphere Project, 2011). The content and layout of LEGS are designed to complement the Sphere Handbook, thus ensuring crucial links between protecting and rebuilding livestock assets and other areas of humanitarian response. In 2011, LEGS was designated as a companion to Sphere. Other companion standards include the following:

- *Minimum Standards for Education: Preparedness, Response, Recovery* (INEE, 2010)
- *Minimum Economic Recovery Standards* (SEEP, 2010)
- *Minimum Standards for Child Protection in Humanitarian Action* (CPWG, 2012).

National guidelines

In some countries, national guidelines for emergency livestock responses already exist, and LEGS aims to complement these guidelines. LEGS can also be used to guide the development of new national guidelines.

Preventing and controlling outbreaks of epidemic livestock diseases

LEGS does not address the prevention or control of transboundary animal diseases because these are covered by other internationally accepted guidelines such as those produced by the Emergency Prevention System for Transboundary

Animal and Plant Pests and Diseases (FAO-EMPRES). These, and chapter 7.6 of the World Organisation for Animal Health's *Terrestrial Code* entitled 'Killing of Animals for Disease Control Purposes' (OIE, 2013) provide detailed information for dealing with disease outbreaks. See the *References* section at the end of the *Introduction*.

Companion animals

Given the humanitarian and livelihoods perspectives of LEGS, companion animals are not explicitly mentioned here although it is recognized that these animals provide important social benefits for their owners. Many of the LEGS Standard and Guidance notes apply to companion animals too, and specific guidance is available from the Animal Welfare Information Center at the United States Department of Agriculture (AWIC). See links in the *References* section at the end of the *Introduction*.

Animal welfare

Because LEGS is based on humanitarian principles and law, its starting point is the welfare of people. Although LEGS is not based on animal welfare objectives, many LEGS interventions lead to improved animal welfare, thus contributing to the 'five freedoms' commonly used as a framework for assessing animal welfare:

1. *freedom from hunger and thirst* – by providing ready access to fresh water and a diet to maintain full health and vigour
2. *freedom from discomfort* – by providing an appropriate environment, including shelter and a comfortable resting area
3. *freedom from pain, injury, or disease* – by preventing or rapidly diagnosing and treating the problem
4. *freedom to express normal behaviour* – by providing sufficient space, proper facilities, and company of the animal's own kind
5. *freedom from fear and distress* – by ensuring conditions and treatment that avoid mental suffering.[2]

Each of the technical chapters outlines how the LEGS interventions relate to animal welfare and the 'five freedoms'. Further guidelines for animal welfare, including issues such as the humane slaughter of livestock, are available in documents such as the *Terrestrial Animal Health Code* of the World Organisation for Animal Health (OIE). See *References* at the end of the *Introduction*.

How to use LEGS: Overview of the book

LEGS is primarily intended as a planning and decision-making tool to support appropriate emergency interventions. However, LEGS can also be used as a benchmark for reviewing and evaluating emergency response either in real time or after a project has ended. The LEGS Handbook covers two main areas:

Areas covered	Chapter
1. General principles, decision-making, and planning	
Overview of emergencies, livestock and livelihoods, and LEGS objectives	Chapter 1
The LEGS core standards	Chapter 2
Initial assessment and identifying responses	Chapter 3
2. Specific LEGS interventions	
Destocking	Chapter 4
Veterinary support	Chapter 5
Ensuring feed supplies	Chapter 6
Provision of water	Chapter 7
Livestock shelter and settlement	Chapter 8
Provision of livestock	Chapter 9

General principles, decision-making, and planning (Chapters 1–3)

Chapter 1: Livestock, livelihoods, and emergencies – overview of key issues

This chapter presents general guidance on questions such as:

- Why are livestock interventions an important aspect of humanitarian response?
- How does LEGS link with a rights-based approach?
- What are the LEGS livelihoods objectives?
- How do different types of emergency affect people who keep livestock?

Chapter 2: The LEGS core standards

This chapter describes the LEGS cross-cutting themes before going on to detail the standards common to all emergency livestock interventions that form a set of core principles and ways of working.

Chapter 3: Initial assessment and identifying responses

This chapter provides guidance on how to conduct an initial assessment for an emergency livestock project, and how to identify appropriate types of response. It allows users to answer questions such as *what information do I need to collect for decision-making?* and *what process should be followed to both gather and review the information with local stakeholders?* The chapter focuses on the use of the LEGS Participatory Response Identification Matrix (PRIM) to help identify the most appropriate technical interventions at each stage of an emergency.

Throughout the core standards (*Chapter 2, Core standards common to all livestock interventions*) and the specific LEGS interventions (*Chapters 4–9*), information is provided in the same format. This comprises the Standards, Key actions, and Guidance notes as follows:

> **Standard**
>
> Standards describe an essential part of an emergency response and are generally qualitative statements.

Key actions

- Key actions attached to each standard are key steps or actions that contribute to achieving the standard.

Guidance notes

1. Guidance notes, which should be read in conjunction with the Key actions, outline particular issues to consider when applying the Standards.

Specific LEGS interventions (Chapters 4–9)

The technical interventions covered by LEGS are the following: destocking (*Chapter 4*); veterinary support (*Chapter 5*); ensuring feed supplies (*Chapter 6*); provision of water (*Chapter 7*); livestock shelter and settlement (*Chapter 8*); and provision of livestock (*Chapter 9*). These chapters provide specific guidance and technical information, and include:

- an introduction that sets out important issues
- a decision-making tree to facilitate choices between different implementation options
- tables summarizing advantages and disadvantages, and timing
- Standards, Key actions, and Guidance notes (based on the same format as *Chapter 2, Core standards*)
- appendices containing case studies and additional technical information such as checklists for assessment, and key references. Many of these reference documents are available in the resources section of the LEGS website.

Case studies

Most chapters in the LEGS Handbook include case studies to illustrate experiences and approaches presented in the chapter. The case studies are of two main types:

- *Process case studies* describe project design and implementation, and can include descriptions of how activities were adapted to local conditions.
- *Impact case studies* focus more on the livelihoods impacts of livestock support during emergencies, and summarize the impacts on assets and human nutrition among other things.

References and further reading

CPWG (Child Protection Working Group) (2012) *Minimum Standards for Child Protection in Humanitarian Action*, CPWG, Geneva, <http://cpwg.net/minimum-standards> [accessed 14 May 2014].

FAO (Food and Agriculture Organization of the United Nations) (2015) *Technical Interventions for Livestock Emergencies: The How-to-do-it Guide*, Animal Production and Health Manuals Series, FAO, Rome.

FAWC (Farm Animal Welfare Council) (undated) *Five Freedoms* [web page], FAWC, London, <http://www.fawc.org.uk/freedoms.htm> [accessed 21 May 2014].

INEE (Inter-Agency Network for Education in Emergencies) (2010) *Minimum Standards for Education: Preparedness, Response, Recovery*, INEE, New York, <http://toolkit.ineesite.org/toolkit/Toolkit.php?PostID=1002> [accessed 15 May 2014].

LEGS (Livestock Emergency Guidelines and Standards) (2012) *LEGS and Resilience: Linking Livestock, Livelihoods and Drought Management in the*

Horn of Africa, Addis Ababa, <http://www.livestock-emergency.net/wp-content/uploads/2012/01/LEGS-and-Resilience-Discussion-Paper-final2.pdf> [accessed 19 May 2014].

NRC/CMP (Norwegian Refugee Council/Camp Management Project) (2008) *The Camp Management Toolkit*, NRC/CMP, Oslo, <http://www.nrc.no/camp> [accessed 24 June 2014].

OIE (World Organisation for Animal Health) (2013) 'Killing of Animals for Disease Control Purposes', in *Terrestrial Animal Health Code*, chapter 7.6, OIE, Paris, <http://www.oie.int/index.php?id=169&L=0&htmfile=chapitre_1.7.6.htm> [accessed 19 May 2014].

SEEP (Small Enterprise Education and Promotion) Network (2013) *Minimum Economic Recovery Standards* (MERS), SEEP Network, Washington, DC, Practical Action Publishing, Rugby. <http://www.seepnetwork.org/minimum-economic-recovery-standards-resources-174.php> [accessed 15 May 2014].

Sphere Project (2011) *Humanitarian Charter and Minimum Standards in Humanitarian Response* (the Sphere Handbook), The Sphere Project, Geneva, Practical Action Publishing, Rugby. <www.sphereproject.org/> [accessed 15 May 2014].

Websites

AWIC (Animal Welfare Information Center), United States Department of Agriculture National Agricultural Library, <http://awic.nal.usda.gov/companion-animals/emergencies-and-disaster-planning> [accessed 22 May 2014].

Cash Learning Partnership, Oxfam, Oxford, <www.cashlearning.org/> [accessed 19 May 2014].

FAO-EMPRES-AH (Food and Agriculture Organization of the United Nations Emergency Prevention System for Animal Health), Rome, <http://www.fao.org/ag/againfo/programmes/en/empres/home.asp> [accessed 21 May 2014].

Notes

1. In LEGS, the term 'camp' is used as defined in *The Camp Management Toolkit* (NRC/CMP, 2008) as 'a variety of camps or camp-like settings – temporary settlements including planned or self-settled camps, collective centres, and transit and return centres established for hosting displaced persons'. It also includes evacuation centres.

2 More information is available at <http://www.fawc.org.uk/freedoms.htm>.

CHAPTER 1

Livestock, livelihoods, and emergencies

Introduction

This chapter presents general guidance on questions such as:

- Why are livestock projects important to humanitarian response?
- How do different types of emergency affect people who keep livestock?
- How does LEGS link with a rights-based approach?
- What are the livelihoods objectives of LEGS?

Livelihoods and emergencies

Increasingly, it is recognized that humanitarian action must consider the livelihoods of affected populations – it is not just about *saving human lives* but *protecting and strengthening livelihoods*. This shift in focus helps the rapid recovery of those affected by an emergency and can also increase their long-term resilience and reduce their vulnerability to future shocks and disasters.

Taking a livelihoods approach also helps to harmonize relief and development initiatives, which historically have often been separate and at times contradictory (see *Box I.1* in the *Introduction to LEGS*). It is now acknowledged that some emergency responses may have saved lives in the short term but have failed to protect – and at times have even destroyed – local livelihood strategies. They have also undermined existing development initiatives and have negatively impacted on local service provision. While it may be true that development can sometimes have negative impacts and that maintaining a level of independence between emergency and development responses may be beneficial, it is nonetheless important that those responsible for relief efforts understand and take into account local development activities, particularly those that aim to strengthen local livelihoods. This is the premise on which LEGS is based.

Livestock and livelihoods

Animals play a significant role in the livelihoods of many people throughout the world. Livestock keepers range from pastoralists, whose livelihoods are largely dependent on livestock, and agro-pastoralists, who depend on a combination of herds and crops, to smallholder farmers, who depend largely on crops but whose cows, goats, pigs, or poultry provide an important supplementary source of protein or income. There are also a diverse range of service providers, such as mule or donkey cart owners, who depend on livestock for their income; then there are traders, shopkeepers, and other merchants whose businesses depend significantly on livestock. Animals also constitute a supplementary source of income or food for urban and peri-urban populations.

LEGS uses the term 'livestock' to refer to all species of animals that support livelihoods. LEGS also provides guidance on livestock kept by displaced people, including those living in camps.[1]

The Sustainable Livelihoods Framework (DFID, 1999) is a useful tool for understanding and analysing livelihoods in both emergency and development situations. Although different variations of the framework exist, all start with understanding the different 'assets' (see *Glossary*) that households use as the basis for their livelihood strategies. For humanitarian programming, assets are important because people with greater financial and social assets tend to be more resilient to crises. The ability of livestock keepers to use their assets to support their livelihoods is also affected by their vulnerability, by trends, and by external policies and institutions, all of which must be taken into account in any livelihoods analysis.

Livestock as financial and social assets

For many livestock keepers, animals are a critical financial asset, providing both food (milk, meat, blood, eggs) and income (through sale, barter, transport, draught power, and work hire). Livestock are also significant social assets for many livestock keepers, playing a key role in building and consolidating social relationships and networks within traditional social groups (clan members, in-laws, or friends, for instance), and they are commonly the currency of both gifts and fines.

Vulnerability

Vulnerability relates to people's ability to withstand shocks and trends. The Sphere Handbook defines vulnerable people as those 'who are especially susceptible to the effects of natural or manmade disasters or of conflict … due to a combination of physical, social, environmental and political factors' (Sphere, 2011: 54). For households and individuals that depend on livestock for their livelihoods, vulnerability is directly linked to livestock assets. The greater the value of livestock assets, the greater the resilience of households to cope with shocks.

Understanding the role of livestock in livelihoods and the impact of the emergency, as outlined in *Chapter 3, Initial assessment and identifying responses*, is essential for determining how appropriate a livestock-based response is. Non-livestock interventions such as food aid, cash grants, or cash/food-for-work can also complement livestock-based responses because they can remove some of the pressure on livestock assets in the short term, thus making recovery more feasible.

Trends

Trends are the long-term changes over time, such as demographic trends, climate change, and economic trends, that impact on livelihood strategies. Although often not considered when designing humanitarian response, attention to trends can be an important aspect of identifying appropriate livestock support. For example, for some people a livestock-based livelihood is so compromised before a crisis that rebuilding their livestock assets post-crisis is of questionable value, and other support, such as cash transfers, may be more useful.

Policies and institutions

In any emergency, both formal and informal policies and institutions influence the ability of people to use their livestock assets to support livelihoods. For example, veterinary service institutions and policies on taxation, marketing, and exports all have an impact on livestock-based livelihoods.

In general, livelihoods analysis can show how the protection and strengthening of livestock assets can be an important type of livelihood support during emergencies. This approach fits well with the Sphere Handbook, which emphasizes the importance of 'the protection and promotion of livelihood strategies', particularly 'preserving productive assets' (Sphere, 2011: 151 and 153).

Types of emergency and their impact on livestock keepers

As summarized in *Table 1.1*, humanitarian emergencies are categorized as slow onset, rapid onset, and complex. Examples are provided in *Box 1.1* following the table. Some emergencies may also be chronic, in that the stages of the crisis continue to repeat themselves – for example, a drought may move from Alert, to Alarm, to Emergency, and back to Alert, without returning to Normal.

Table 1.1 Types of emergencies and impacts

Type of emergency	Example of emergency	Impacts
Slow onset • Gradual, increasing stress on livelihoods over many months until an emergency is declared • Can be multi-year events • Specific geographical areas are known to be at risk, so there is some level of predictability • Drought has four main stages: alert, alarm, emergency, and recovery (see *Glossary*) • Early response is often inadequate even though early warning systems exist	Drought, *dzud* (in Mongolia)	• Livestock condition and production gradually worsen during alert and alarm phases, mainly because access to feed and water is reduced; livestock market values decline, and grain prices increase; human food security worsens • Livestock mortality is excessive and worsens during the emergency stage due to starvation or dehydration; human food security worsens • Rebuilding livestock herds is hindered if core breeding animals have died and/or if another drought occurs

Rapid onset
 • Occurs with little or no warning although specific geographical areas may have known risks
 • When an alarm is given, it tends to be with little notice
 • Most impact occurs immediately, or within hours or days
 • Following immediate aftermath (see *Glossary*), the following occurs:
   - first, an early recovery phase
   - second, the main recovery phase, which, depending on the type of emergency, could take days (e.g. receding floods), months, or years (e.g. earthquake)
	Flood, earthquake, typhoon, volcanic eruption, tsunami	• Human and/or livestock mortality is excessive and rapid during the initial event
		 • Infrastructure and services needed to support livestock are lost
		 • People and livestock are displaced, or people are separated from their animals
		 • Longer-term impacts are possible, especially if preventive livestock support is unavailable

Type of emergency	Example of emergency	Impacts
Complex • Associated with protracted political instability and/or internal or external conflict • Time frame is usually years or decades • Slow-onset or rapid-onset emergencies can also occur, worsening the impacts of the ongoing complex emergency	• Southern Somalia • Eastern DRC • Darfur, Sudan • Afghanistan	• People and livestock are killed or injured due to armed conflict • Armed groups steal livestock or 'asset-strip' • Services and markets are limited or completely lacking due to conflict • Infrastructure and communications are limited • Humans and livestock are displaced • Access to services, markets, grazing, or water is reduced due to conflict • There is protracted human food insecurity • All the above are exacerbated if additional emergencies occur

---

Box 1.1 Impact of slow-onset, rapid-onset, and complex emergencies – examples

Impacts of a slow-onset emergency

During the 1999–2001 drought in Kenya, it is estimated that over 2 million sheep and goats, 900,000 cattle, and 14,000 camels died. This represents losses of 30 per cent of small stock and cattle and 18 per cent of camel holdings among the affected pastoralists. Social impact was significant. Families separated, damaging the social networks that provide a safety net for pastoralists, and many people moved to settlements and food distribution centres. Without sufficient livestock to provide for their food needs, many pastoralists became dependent on food aid. Once the drought ended, the losses suffered by some pastoralists had effectively destroyed their livelihoods.

(*Source*: Aklilu and Wekesa, 2002)

Impacts of a rapid-onset emergency

The Indian Ocean tsunami in 2004 had a significant impact on the livestock of the affected people. This included the loss of domestic farm animals (poultry, sheep, goats, cattle, and water buffalo). In Indonesia, for example, over 78,000 cattle and 61,000 buffalo were killed, together with 52,000 goats, 16,000 sheep, and nearly 1.5 million chickens. Livelihoods were also affected by the destruction of livestock-related infrastructure, such as barns, stores, and processing facilities. Moreover, crop residues, straw, and inland pasture were destroyed.

(*Source*: FAO, 2005)

Impacts of a rapid-onset emergency following a drought

The 2001 earthquake in India's Gujarat State killed or injured nearly 9,000 cattle, buffalo, sheep, and goats. The earthquake occurred at 8 a.m., after most livestock had been taken out of the villages to graze; otherwise the losses caused by collapsing buildings would have been much greater. However, because initial relief efforts focused on the human population, livestock were generally left to wander in search of feed and water. Some died from their injuries and others from exposure. The impact of the earthquake on these livestock was magnified by a two-year drought. The lack of forage and pastures prior to the earthquake meant that many livestock were already in poor body condition. The earthquake also caused the collapse of many water tanks and veterinary buildings, which also negatively affected the provision of livestock services.

(*Source*: Goe, 2001)

Impacts of a complex emergency

The Darfur region of Sudan, where pastoralists and agro-pastoralists derive up to 50 per cent of their food and income from livestock, has suffered from chronic conflict and recurrent drought for several years. The combined effect of conflict and drought has caused significant livestock losses. Some villagers reported losses of 70–100 per cent due to looting. Overcrowding of livestock and the disruption of veterinary services (both the result of insecurity) added to livestock mortality rates. The closure of the Sudan–Libya border also severely affected livestock trade, significantly impacting on livelihoods. The natural resource base was depleted by the drought, and conflict restricted access to traditional migration routes and grazing lands. The surviving livestock were sold only as a last resort because prices were very low.

(*Sources*: ICRC, 2006; Hélène Berton, personal communication, 2008)

Principles and objectives of LEGS

Livestock and a rights-based approach

LEGS is influenced by a rights-based approach (see *Box 1.2*) and by two key international rights in particular: the right to food and the right to a standard of living.[2] Livestock keepers have a right to emergency support to protect and rebuild their livestock as a key asset that contributes significantly to their ability to produce food and maintain a standard of living that supports their families. International humanitarian law also highlights the importance of the protection of livestock as a key asset for survival during conflict or war.[3]

Box 1.2 ▶ Rights-based approach

A rights-based approach to development and emergency work includes the achievement of human rights as part of its objectives. In this context, human rights generally refers not only to the 1948 Universal Declaration on Human Rights but also to the various covenants and declarations that have been agreed since – in particular civil and political (CP) rights and economic, social, and cultural (ESC) rights, both agreed in 1966 – as well as additional covenants covering racial discrimination; discrimination against women; torture; the rights of the child and so on.

For each set of rights there are 'duty bearers' who have the responsibility to ensure that rights are protected and maintained. With regard to some rights (such as the right to food), nation states are required to work progressively towards achieving these rights.

A rights-based approach to development and emergency work draws on the range of human rights instruments and declarations in order to emphasize the responsibilities and duties of key stakeholders. This approach therefore encourages participation, empowerment, accountability, and non-discrimination in the delivery of development or emergency programmes. At the same time, specific rights – such as the right to food – can be highlighted. (*Source:* Aklilu and Wekesa, 2002)

Livelihoods objectives of LEGS

Underpinned by these rights and in recognition of the role of livestock in livelihoods, LEGS is based on three livelihoods-based objectives:

Objective 1:   to provide immediate benefits to crisis-affected communities using existing livestock resources;

Objective 2:   to protect the key livestock-related assets of crisis-affected communities;

Objective 3:   to rebuild key livestock-related assets among crisis-affected communities.

The intent of Objective 1 is to provide rapid assistance to people using livestock already present in the area – and by so doing, to provide immediate benefits such as food, income, or transport. One way to accomplish this is through a destocking project.

In contrast, Objective 2 focuses on asset protection (through the provision of feed, water, shelter, or veterinary support) with a view to maintaining critical livestock resources during an emergency so that production can resume after the emergency. The animals involved may or may not provide direct benefits to households during the emergency phase itself.

Objective 3 relates to situations where substantial livestock losses have occurred, i.e. where protection of key livestock (Objective 2) was not possible or supported. Traditionally, Objective 3 has focused on the provision of animals after an emergency, supported by the provision of feed, water, shelter, and/or veterinary support. However, alternative asset transfer approaches using cash might be preferable to livestock in some contexts, as discussed in *Chapter 9 (Provision of livestock)*.

Underlying all three LEGS objectives is support to existing local service providers, suppliers, and markets, wherever this is feasible and relevant. This is an important aspect of livelihoods-based programming in emergencies and applies to all types of emergency (see *Table 1.1*). LEGS aims to support these local systems to enable recovery and long-term development, rather than undermining them through emergency programmes.

References and further reading

Aklilu, Y. and Wekesa, M. (2002) *Drought, Livestock and Livelihoods: Lessons from the 1999–2001 Emergency Response in the Pastoral Sector in Kenya*, Humanitarian Practice Network Paper No. 40, Overseas Development Institute (ODI), London, <http://www.odihpn.org/documents/networkpaper040.pdf> [accessed 13 May 2014].

DFID (Department for International Development) (1999) 'Sustainable livelihoods guidance sheets'. Available from: <http://www.ennonline.net/resources/667> [accessed 20 May 2014].

FAO (Food and Agriculture Organization of the United Nations) (2005) 'Tsunami reconstruction' [web page] <http://www.fao.org/ag/tsunami/assessment/animal.html> [accessed 19 May 2014].

Goe, M.R. (2001) *Assessment of the Scope of Earthquake Damage to the Livestock Sector in Gujarat State, India*, Consultancy Mission Report, Food and Agriculture Organization (FAO) of the United Nations, Bangkok/Rome.

ICRC (International Committee of the Red Cross), Economic Security Unit (2006) *Food-Needs Assessment: Darfur*, ICRC, Nairobi.

OHCHR (Office of the High Commissioner for Human Rights) (1996–2014) 'International Human Rights Law' [web page] <http://www.ohchr.org/EN/ProfessionalInterest/Pages/InternationalLaw.aspx> [accessed 19 May 2014].

Sphere Project (2011) *Humanitarian Charter and Minimum Standards in Humanitarian Response* (the Sphere Handbook), The Sphere Project, Geneva, <www.sphereproject.org/> [accessed 15 May 2014].

Young, H., Taylor, A., Way, S.-A. and Leaning, J. (2004) 'Linking rights and standards: the process of developing "rights-based" minimum standards on food security, nutrition and food aid', *Disasters* 28(2): 142–159 <http://dx.doi.org/10.1111/j.0361-3666.2004.00249.x>.

Notes

1   As noted in the *Introduction to LEGS*, in LEGS the term 'camp' refers to the full range of temporary settlements in which displaced livestock keepers may find themselves.

2   International Covenant on Economic, Social and Cultural Rights, Article 11(2), and Universal Declaration of Human Rights, Article 25(1). For more information on human rights, see <http://www.ohchr.org/EN/ProfessionalInterest/Pages/InternationalLaw.aspx>.

3   Geneva Conventions of 1949: Additional Protocol on the Protection of Victims of International Armed Conflicts, Protocol I (Art. 54) 1977; Additional Protocol on the Protection of Victims of Non-International Armed Conflicts, Protocol II (Art. 14) 1977. For more information on international humanitarian law, see <http://www.icrc.org/eng/war-and-law/>.

CHAPTER 2

Core standards and cross-cutting themes common to all livestock interventions

Figure 2.1 LEGS core standards

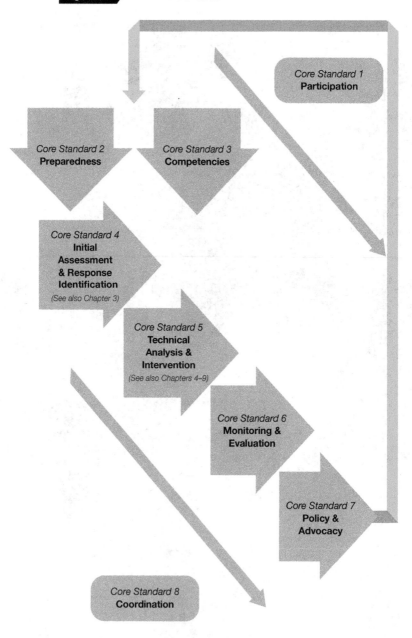

Core Standard 1
Participation

Core Standard 2
Preparedness

Core Standard 3
Competencies

Core Standard 4
**Initial
Assessment
& Response
Identification**
(See also Chapter 3)

Core Standard 5
**Technical
Analysis &
Intervention**
(See also Chapters 4–9)

Core Standard 6
**Monitoring &
Evaluation**

Core Standard 7
**Policy &
Advocacy**

Core Standard 8
Coordination

Introduction

The importance of the core standards

This chapter presents eight core standards common and integral to each of the livestock-related interventions described in later chapters. These are:

1. Participation

2. Preparedness

3. Competencies

4. Initial assessment and response identification

5. Technical analysis and intervention

6. Monitoring and evaluation and livelihoods impact

7. Policy and advocacy

8. Coordination

In a typical livestock project during an emergency, the core standards relate to each other as shown in *Figure 2.1*. The participation and coordination core standards are important throughout a project, whereas the other six core standards are associated with pre-project capacities or with specific stages of a project cycle (see *Annex E* for a summary of the *Stages of the LEGS response* based on a simple project cycle). By applying the core standards, agencies can support the achievement of the specific technical standards described in the later chapters.

The LEGS core standards draw on those of the Sphere Handbook (Sphere, 2011) but focus more specifically on livestock interventions. Readers should therefore refer to the Sphere Handbook for more general core standards for humanitarian response, and to the Humanitarian Accountability Partnership standard and benchmarks for accountability in humanitarian action (HAP, 2007).

This chapter also presents the four LEGS cross-cutting themes, which should be mainstreamed into any response.

Links to other chapters

As the core standards underpin all the individual technical interventions outlined in the LEGS Handbook, it is important to read this chapter first before turning to the technical chapters on specific types of livestock intervention.

Cross-cutting themes

The cross-cutting themes of LEGS are similar to those of Sphere (2011). The first three focus on vulnerability (gender and social equity, HIV/AIDS, and protection) while the final one addresses environmental and climate issues. As the Sphere Handbook notes: 'It is important to understand that to be young or old, a woman or a person with a disability, does not, of itself, make a person vulnerable or at increased risk. Rather, it is the interplay of factors that does so' (Sphere, 2011: 86).

At the same time, each beneficiary community has its own capacity for responding to an emergency. This includes their indigenous knowledge and skills, particularly as these relate to livestock production and natural resource management. Indigenous and local institutions can also play a substantial role in responding to emergencies, facilitating community involvement, and managing interventions.

The themes are presented here from the perspective of livestock projects in general, with further guidance provided in the specific technical chapters.

Gender and social equity

Differential impact. Emergencies affect different people in different ways. The rights-based foundations of Sphere and LEGS aim to support equitable emergency responses and to avoid reinforcing social inequality. This means giving special attention to potentially disadvantaged groups such as children and orphans, women, the elderly, the disabled, or groups marginalized because of religion, ethnic group, or caste. Gender is particularly important since, in any emergency, women and men have access to different resources and hence different coping strategies, which need to be understood and recognized by humanitarian agencies. In some cases women's coping strategies may increase their vulnerability (for example, exposing them to sexual abuse or exploitation).

Understanding roles, rights and responsibilities. For emergency livestock projects, issues of ownership and control of livestock as a livelihood asset become paramount. In many livestock-keeping societies, control over livestock may be considered more as a set of rights and responsibilities than a simple concept of 'ownership'. Emergency responses should therefore be based on a sound understanding of women's roles, rights, and responsibilities in livestock production. These include their daily and seasonal contributions and responsibilities as well as their access to and control of livestock assets (including rights of use and disposal). Another important consideration is the difference between the various livestock species and age categories – for example, women may be responsible for young stock but not adult stock. In some pastoralist communities, cultural norms prescribe that women control livestock products (such as milk, butter, hides, and skins) as part of their overall control of the food supply, while the men have disposal rights (sale, barter, or gift) over the animal itself. Emergencies often increase women's and girls' labour burden while simultaneously reducing their access to key assets and essential services such as education.[1]

Disaggregating data in analysis. As discussed in *Chapter 3 (Initial assessment and identifying responses)*, proper attention to gender and other vulnerability issues requires initial assessments to disaggregate information on the impact and extent of the emergency. The potential impact of any intervention on gender roles, especially on women's workload and control of livestock resources, needs to be clearly understood. Similarly, gender roles may change during an emergency. For example, women may take greater responsibility for livestock if men have migrated to look for work. Conversely, the women may be left in camps while the men remain with the livestock. Finally, cultural gender norms may need to be taken into account with regard to the gender of aid agency staff and the cultural accessibility of women. Methodologies for assessing this issue are discussed in *Appendix 3.2* (see also *References* at the end of this chapter, specifically IASC, 2006).

Understanding vulnerability and equity. Additionally, consideration needs to be given to the differing impacts of the emergency on other socially differentiated or vulnerable groups: how their access to and control of resources may be affected; and what potential impact any planned intervention may have on their workloads and roles. These groups may be based on age, ethnicity, or caste. Understanding gender and other social relationships that may increase vulnerability is important in order to ensure emergency interventions have positive outcomes and impacts.

HIV/AIDS

HIV/AIDS continues to be a major global human health problem. Sub-Saharan Africa is still the most affected region, and women are increasingly disproportionately infected. The pandemic has a significant impact on livestock keepers and their ability to meet their basic needs. Constraining factors such as livestock disease, drought, flood, conflict, poor infrastructure, and access to credit and markets are all exacerbated by the presence of HIV/AIDS. Specific issues to consider are the following:

- *Livestock and labour.* Because people living with HIV and AIDS (PLHIV) are less physically able to manage livestock, their livelihoods suffer from low animal production and related losses of food and income. Orphans and child- or elderly-headed households may have to take responsibility for livestock management. These challenges are aggravated during emergencies, and livestock support needs to be designed accordingly.

- *Livestock and nutrition.* PLHIV have particular nutritional needs that livestock products such as milk, milk products, and eggs can help to fulfil. Antiretroviral (ARV) drugs must be accompanied by good nutrition in order to be effective. Loss of livestock during emergencies has a negative impact on the diets of PLHIV.

- *Zoonotic diseases.* PLHIV are highly susceptible to certain other infections, including zoonoses – diseases that pass from livestock to people. Important zoonoses include forms of tuberculosis (TB), brucellosis, and toxoplasmosis. TB is particularly important, being a major killer of women of reproductive age and the leading cause of death in HIV-positive people (one-third of AIDS deaths worldwide). The disease threatens the poorest and most marginalized groups. TB enhances replication of HIV and may accelerate the progress to AIDS. The prevention of zoonoses is therefore important in reducing the vulnerability of PLHIV.

- *Knowledge and skills.* Know-how on livestock rearing is lost if parents die before they can pass information on to their children. Similarly, extension and veterinary services may lose capacity if staff are affected by HIV.

- *Social isolation or exclusion.* In addition to these issues, PLHIV face social isolation or exclusion. They may be prevented from accessing communal resources, such as water points for livestock, or can be forced to leave their home villages. When livestock are sold to cover medical and funeral expenses, family herds are depleted. During emergencies, PLHIV are therefore especially vulnerable as their fragile livelihoods are easily disrupted.

The impact of any emergency on PLHIV should therefore be noted, and their particular needs should be taken into account when planning interventions. Livestock-based interventions should build on current coping strategies being used by HIV/AIDS-affected households.

Protection

Sphere (2011) and the *Minimum Standards for Child Protection in Humanitarian Action* (CPWG, 2012) provide detailed guidance relating to the protection of people in humanitarian contexts that covers the safety, dignity, and integrity of people affected by crisis and draws on international humanitarian law and international human rights.[2] In emergencies, and particularly in those involving conflict, the protection of the affected population may be compromised, and communities and individuals may be victims of sexual violence, theft, looting, coercion, exploitation, attack, deprivation, misappropriation of land, and/or the destruction of services. Agencies responding to emergencies are therefore responsible for ensuring that their interventions do not increase risks to beneficiaries.

LEGS supports the four protection principles described in detail in the Sphere Handbook (Sphere, 2011: 25–47):

Protection principle 1: Avoid causing harm.

Protection principle 2: Ensure access to impartial assistance.

Protection principle 3: Protect people from violence.

Protection principle 4: Assist with rights claims, access to remedies, and recovery from abuse.

In many parts of the world livestock are valuable financial assets and a ready source of high-quality food. Livestock are also mobile. Therefore, in insecure environments livestock may be targeted by looters and armed groups. To ensure the protection of people involved in livestock-related emergency responses and to minimize risk, proper analysis of protection issues prior to intervention is needed. For example:

- The protection or distribution of livestock may increase individual household vulnerability to theft or looting as a deliberate tactic of war. The extent to which livestock are an asset rather than a liability depends on the particular security context.

- Livestock management may require women or girls to travel to remote areas to find feed or water for animals. This can place them at risk of violence, sexual abuse, or abduction.

- Displaced people in camps may be particularly vulnerable. Concentration of livestock may attract theft, and travelling through unfamiliar areas for water or grazing may increase vulnerability to attack.

- In times of natural resource scarcity, the movement of livestock to new areas can increase the potential for conflict between host and visiting communities.

Protection concerns of this nature show that livestock support must be considered against the backdrop of local conflict, and that the pros and cons of specific livestock inputs in terms of livelihood benefits versus protection risks must be weighed. This type of analysis should form part of the initial assessment (*Chapter 3, Initial assessment and identifying responses*), especially in conflict-related emergencies.

Environment and climate

Livestock keeping and environmental management. Sustainable environmental management is central to successful livestock-based livelihoods, since livestock usually depend on environmental resources such as pasture and water for survival and production. In the context of long-term development, environmental aspects of livestock development are complex and subject to much debate relating to wider food policies, commercialization, international trade, climate change, and other issues.

The more traditional livestock production systems in developing regions are very diverse and range from the extensive mobile systems of pastoralists across large areas of Africa and Asia to backyard production of poultry and pigs in towns and cities. Extensive production based on seasonal livestock movement has long been recognized as an efficient and sustainable land-use approach but is often threatened by restrictions on mobility. In intensive production systems, where animals are concentrated in one location (for example, feedlots, chicken houses), environmental concerns include the risk of soil and water pollution. Poor environmental hygiene and sanitary conditions can also contribute to livestock illness and death, lowering animal value and increasing management costs and the risk of human disease.

Conditions before or during an emergency can increase the risk of negative environmental impact from livestock. For example:

- Reduced pasture, fodder, and water due to drought can result in concentrations of livestock around declining water resources and localized overgrazing.
- Displaced persons may move to camps with their livestock, resulting in unusually high livestock populations in confined areas. Although the

provision of feed and water may sustain livestock in these situations, sanitary issues must be considered. Use of nearby grazing and water points already in use by local residents can lead to overuse and environmental damage.

- Displacement and restrictions on migration because of conflict or other factors limit the normal movement of animals and concentrate livestock, which may result in overgrazing and deterioration of animal health.

Further environmental considerations in some emergencies include the management of waste from livestock, the disposal of livestock offal following slaughter, and the disposal of livestock carcasses. Some emergencies, particularly those caused by flooding, can result in the death of tens of thousands of animals, presenting a considerable challenge if negative environmental (and human health) impacts are to be avoided.

Climate change. There is now an overwhelming consensus that the global climate is changing, driven by emissions of greenhouse gases, notably carbon dioxide, from human activity. Climate change will impact both directly and indirectly on livestock and their keepers in a range of interrelated ways. Direct impacts may include changes in temperature affecting animal performance, changes in water availability, changes in patterns of animal disease, and changes in the species composition of rangelands. Indirect impacts may include changes in the price and market availability of both animal feed and human food, and possible changes in land use towards the cultivation of biofuels as a response to climate change. Most importantly, from the point of view of LEGS, there are likely to be changes in the frequency and severity of extreme weather events, notably drought, but also floods and tropical storms. Some longer-term climate impacts may also increase the vulnerability of livestock keepers to disaster while decreasing the ease and speed with which they can recover.

Climate trends will play out differently in different parts of the world. For example, current projections suggest a drier southern Africa, considerable uncertainty about rainfall trends in West Africa, and a wetter East Africa (though increased average rainfall does not preclude the recurrence of drought).

Projections of extreme weather trends and the detection of recent and past trends are complex sciences, both of which are evolving rapidly. In general, scientific literature tends to ascribe less certainty to climate change than do some pronouncements by NGOs and the media. Recently, however, some scientific publications have expressed more readiness to attribute droughts, like the one in Somalia in 2011, to climate change. At present, climate science gives few specific pointers to the disaster risk reduction community on how to improve drought preparedness or to conduct interventions during droughts. As the science progresses, it is important for agencies involved in disaster risk reduction among livestock keepers to keep abreast of what is known about future trends and levels of certainty. It will also be important to take account of scientific views in public statements on the trends in and causes of droughts.

The core standards

Core standard 1: Participation

The affected population actively participates in the assessment, design, implementation, monitoring, and evaluation of the livestock programme.

Key actions

- Identify all specific subsets and vulnerable groups in a population, inform them that an assessment and possible intervention(s) will take place, and encourage them to participate (see *Guidance notes 1* and *2*). Monitor and evaluate the process (see *Guidance note 3*).
- Document and use key indigenous livestock production and health knowledge and practices, coping strategies, and pre-existing livestock services to ensure the sustainability of inputs (see *Guidance note 4*).
- Base interventions on an understanding of social and cultural norms (see *Guidance note 5*).
- Discuss planned programme inputs and implementation approaches with community representatives and/or community groups representing the range of population subsets and vulnerable groups (see *Guidance note 6*).

Guidance notes

1. **Representation of groups.** The effective identification, design, and implementation of livestock interventions requires the involvement of local people, particularly that of marginalized or vulnerable groups who keep livestock or who might benefit from access to livestock or livestock products (see *Case study 2.4* at the end of this chapter). This involvement should

encompass active participation in all stages of the initiative. Because the uses and ownership of livestock often vary within communities according to wealth, gender, or other factors, initial assessments should analyse these criteria to understand how interventions might be targeted at different groups with different potential impacts. While wealthier people might own larger animals such as cattle or camels and request assistance for these animals, it is possible that poorer groups would prefer assistance with sheep, goats, poultry, or donkeys. Agencies need to be sensitive to these differences. Barriers to the participation of women and vulnerable groups should be taken into account in both the assessment and implementation stages.

2. **Types of participation.** For LEGS, participation means that men and women in affected communities have the right to be involved in the programme and can make intellectual contributions that improve effectiveness and efficiency. Communities should also be able to exercise choice in terms of the type and design of emergency interventions in their area. The core standard of participation recognizes that local knowledge and skills are valuable resources for relief agencies and should be actively sourced. This core standard also recognizes that programmes based on active participation are more likely to result in sustained benefits or services. Community participation in targeting also provides an effective means of ensuring appropriate distribution of benefits (see *Core standard 5* below). While the challenges in achieving this level of participation are significant, especially in rapid-onset emergencies, participation remains a key goal of LEGS, reflecting the rights-based approach and the linkages with long-term sustainability of activities.

3. **Accountability and participation.** Attention to community participation in the monitoring and evaluation (M&E) of emergency interventions is an important way to improve the local accountability of humanitarian agencies and actors. See *Core standard 6: Monitoring, evaluation, and livelihoods impact*; see also the HAP standard (HAP, 2007).

4. **Sustainability.** Communities highly dependent on livestock often possess very detailed indigenous knowledge relating to livestock management and health, which can play a valuable role in livestock projects. Sustained services or inputs are most likely to emerge from emergency responses when these responses promote participation, recognize local knowledge and skills, build on sustainable indigenous coping strategies, and use and strengthen pre-existing services and systems. In the case of livestock

interventions, agencies need to be especially aware that when relief operations are implemented in isolation of local private service providers the local systems suffer.

5. **Social and cultural norms.** Social, cultural, and religious practices influence livestock ownership and the use of livestock products. Uses of certain types of animal or animal-derived feeds may seem appropriate and practical to outsiders but may be resisted because of local customs. Although people are not always averse to adopting new practices, this process often takes time and requires the support of agency staff with experience in the concerned communities. When rapid intervention is required, an understanding of social and cultural norms helps to ensure that interventions are appropriate.

6. **Community groups.** Customary or indigenous institutions can play a key role in emergency interventions. This may include identifying vulnerable beneficiaries, designing and managing interventions, and applying M&E. With regard to livestock, customary institutions often play a key role in the management of natural resources, including grazing land and water resources. Participation by these groups in livestock-based interventions is generally a necessary factor in ensuring the sustainability of the activities and a positive contribution to livelihoods.

Core standard 2: Preparedness

Emergency responses are based on the principles of disaster risk reduction (DRR), including preparedness, contingency planning, and early response.

Key actions

- Ensure that DRR forms part of agencies' emergency planning and implementation (see *Guidance note 1*).

- When developing long-term development programmes, conduct regular reviews of past emergencies in their operational area with regard to the type, frequency, severity, and lessons learned from emergency response (see *Guidance note 2*).

- Based on this information, develop contingency emergency plans with clearly defined triggers for action and the subsequent release of funds and other resources (see *Guidance note 2*).

- In developing contingency plans, take into account the agency's procurement and administrative procedures and any obstacles to future emergency responses (see *Guidance note 3*).

- Base contingency plans for drought on the principles of drought-cycle management and early response, with appropriate sequencing of interventions (see *Guidance note 4*).

- Encourage communities to prepare for future emergencies (both rapid and slow onset). External agencies should assist this preparedness through capacity building of local institutions, facilitation of social learning for improved adaptation, and, where appropriate, advocacy for policies that work over the long term to reduce vulnerability (see *Guidance note 5*).

- Ensure that all emergency intervention plans are accompanied by an exit strategy that links with post-emergency recovery and long-term support to livelihoods (see *Guidance note 6*).

- Where a long-term perspective is appropriate, base programming on the best available scientific information on climate trends, where possible localized to the particular area of operation (see *Guidance note 7*).

Guidance notes

1. **Disaster risk reduction.** Recognition of the need to mainstream DRR – and vulnerable communities' resilience to future emergencies – into long-term development planning and implementation is increasing. This may take the form of contingency planning by agencies and/or communities (setting aside funds and plans for scaling up activities in case of an emergency), or preparedness activities to reduce the impact of future emergencies. A good example is the preparation of feed reserves, or setting up supply chains for veterinary medicines.

2. **Contingency planning and action.** In areas affected by repeated crises, such as droughts or floods, contingency plans enable early and rapid response. Experience indicates that early response to drought is one of the key determinants of livelihoods impact. Even in rapid-onset emergencies like earthquakes or floods, some little warning can be given to enable prepared plans to be activated. Many of the most effective emergency livestock responses have been implemented by aid agencies with long-term development experience in a particular area, based on emergency response plans incorporated into development programmes. Such plans

CH 2 Core Standards

are informed by knowledge of past crises and the types of response that can be implemented within a given operational and funding context. It is important that contingency plans are developed with local partners and include specific, clearly defined, and pre-agreed triggers for prompting action and the release of contingency funds (see *Case study 2.3* at the end of this chapter). Linkages with early warning systems (EWS) are vital to support this process. Contingency planning may also need to include training of relevant staff and, where appropriate, community members so that pre-planned responses can be rolled out effectively.

3. **Procurement and administrative arrangements.** Agencies should review their administrative procedures in light of the need for flexibility and rapid decision-making during emergency response to ensure that potential interventions are administratively possible. Livelihoods-based emergency responses may require the rapid procurement of large quantities of animal feed. Contracts with private sector operators such as transport companies, feed suppliers, or veterinary workers may need to be drawn up. New cash or voucher mechanisms that require agency or donor approval may be needed.

4. **Drought-cycle management.** Drought-cycle management uses specific indicators to trigger different responses and enable combinations of interventions as appropriate for the different stages of a drought, not just the emergency phase (see *Glossary* for definitions of the drought-cycle management phases). The approach encourages early and timely response to drought so as to procure better cost–benefit ratios for livestock keepers than later interventions (for example, destocking compared to later feed or livestock provision).

5. **Community preparedness.** Agencies working long-term with communities should encourage community preparedness planning in preparation for future emergencies, whether slow or rapid onset. This may include, for example, earthquake-resistant livestock shelters (see *Chapter 8, Livestock shelter and settlement*); livestock feed banks (see *Chapter 6, Ensuring feed supplies*); preventive animal vaccination campaigns (see *Chapter 5, Veterinary support*); or developing livestock market opportunities (see *Chapter 4, Destocking*). Preparedness planning should build capacity in local organizations (existing community institutions or dedicated emergency management bodies) so that they learn more about the causes of vulnerability and how to reduce it. Lessons learned in this way should be

incorporated into the advocacy activity of these community organizations and external agencies as appropriate (see *Core standard 7*, below).

6. **Exit strategies.** All too often, emergency responses are planned and implemented without a clear strategy for either phasing out or linking with longer-term development initiatives. The sudden cessation of activities because emergency funding has ended (for example, when a crisis is believed to be over) can have significant negative consequences for beneficiary communities. From a livelihoods perspective, emergency responses in the recovery phase should be planned to converge with sustainable, long-term livelihood support activities implemented by the agency itself or by other stakeholders.

7. **Use of climate projections.** The long-term perspectives of available scientific projections of climate change (typically a minimum of 20 years ahead) are not always appropriate in preparedness planning, but agencies should consider making use of easily available resources such as the United Nations Development Programme Climate Change Country Profiles (UNDP, undated) or commissioning their own localized projections, for example through staff trained in the Hadley Centre PRECIS modelling system.

Core standard 3: Technical support and agency competencies

Staff possess appropriate qualifications, attitudes, and experience to effectively plan, implement, and assess livelihoods-based livestock programmes in emergency contexts.

Key actions

- Ensure staff possess relevant technical qualifications for livestock interventions as well as the knowledge and skills to conduct rapid participatory assessments, market assessments, and joint planning of interventions with all relevant population subsets and vulnerable groups (see *Guidance note 1*).

- Ensure staff are familiar with human rights and humanitarian principles and their relevance to livestock interventions (see *Guidance note 2*).

- Ensure staff are familiar with the principles of livelihoods-based programming (see *Guidance note 2*).

- Address staff security and safety issues (see *Guidance note 3*).

Guidance notes

1. **Technical skills and qualifications.** The professionalism and effectiveness of livestock workers depend on an appropriate combination of technical knowledge, experience, attitude, and communication skills. In general, programme managers or country directors may know a great deal about emergency response but relatively little about livestock. This contrasts with livestock professionals, such as veterinary surgeons or animal scientists, who have technical knowledge of livestock but may not necessarily be equipped with skills in participatory assessment, project design, or livelihoods-based programming. Practical field experience with vulnerable communities is a key determinant of a person's ability to work with communities and design relevant interventions. Training in participatory approaches for programme design, implementation, and M&E should be standard for professional livestock aid workers.

2. **Rights-based and livelihoods-based approaches.** Livestock interventions are relevant to human rights (see *Chapter 1, Livestock, livelihoods, and emergencies).* Livestock aid workers therefore need to be aware of rights-based approaches to humanitarian intervention. In addition, workers need to be familiar with livelihoods-based programming and, where appropriate, basic market analysis. All of these knowledge requirements can be addressed by short training courses before emergencies occur.

3. **Staff safety.** The physical safety of agency staff and their ability to access and operate in affected areas are the responsibility of the intervening agency. Insecurity can lead to high implementation costs due to the need for good communications systems, extra vehicles, armed escorts, and so on. Consequent delays in implementation may lead to inappropriate timing of interventions and/or last-minute changes that may affect the quality and impact of the response. More information and support on security for agency staff can be found in the People in Aid Code of Good Practice (People in Aid, 2003).

Core standard 4: Initial assessment and response identification

Initial assessment provides an understanding of the role of livestock in livelihoods, an analysis of the nature and extent of the emergency, and an appraisal of the operational and policy context. It also feeds into a participatory process to identify the most appropriate, timely, and feasible interventions.

Key actions

- Ensure the assessment covers the key topics outlined in *Chapter 3 (Initial assessment and identifying responses)*, using systematic, participatory inquiry conducted by trained workers; findings should be triangulated with pre-existing technical data when available (see *Guidance note 1*).

- Disaggregate findings according to the population subsets and vulnerable groups in the affected community.

- Ensure the assessment reviews the capacity of relevant authorities to protect populations in the territory under their control, and includes an analysis of the operational environment and the implications of different livestock interventions (see *Guidance note 2*).

- Ensure the assessment clearly describes existing local service providers and markets, explains if and how the interventions will work with these actors and systems, and defines an exit strategy intended to maximize the sustained use of local services and markets (see *Guidance note 3*).

- Check that the assessment includes a rapid analysis of policies and regulations that affect livelihoods or that may prevent certain interventions, and that it reviews the capacity of local regulatory bodies to enforce official rules and regulations (see *Guidance note 4*).

- Identify responses through a participatory process involving all key stakeholders, including community representatives, as presented in *Chapter 3 (Initial assessment and identifying responses)*, (see *Guidance note 5*).

- Select responses that are appropriate, timely, and feasible, and that respond to at least one of the LEGS livelihoods objectives (see *Guidance note 6*).

Guidance notes

1. **Assessment topics and methods.** *Chapter 3 (Initial assessment and identifying responses)*, outlines the key topics for assessment, covering the role of livestock in livelihoods, the nature and extent of the emergency, and a situational analysis. Checklists for assessment, and sources of additional information are available in *Chapter 3*.

2. **Protection.** Livestock assets are valuable, and the ownership or management of livestock may place people at greater risk of violence, abduction, or abuse (see the *Protection* cross-cutting theme above).

Analysis of the local security environment in relation to livestock ownership patterns, recent history of looting or raiding, husbandry practices, and the need to access livestock services or markets should indicate high-risk practices and activities. These include moving livestock to insecure grazing areas or water points, using grazing areas that have been mined or that have unexploded ordnance, containing livestock in unprotected areas at night, or keeping types or species of livestock that may be targeted by armed groups. The assessment should analyse the trade-offs between the potential livelihood benefits of greater livestock ownership or access to livestock products and the protection risks. In some cases, traditional livestock management practice may be modified to enhance protection. Particularly vulnerable groups should be targeted in this assessment process in order to ensure that their protection needs are identified. For general information on protection in emergencies, see the Protection Principles in the Sphere Handbook (Sphere, 2011), and the *Minimum Standards for Child Protection in Humanitarian Action* (CPWG, 2012).

3. **Local services and markets.** Livestock interventions that support local services and markets are an important aspect of livelihoods-based programming. Local service providers include livestock feed suppliers, water suppliers, veterinary and paraprofessional workers, livestock traders, and livestock transporters. As part of the situation analysis (see *Chapter 3, Initial assessment and identifying responses)*, the assessment should describe these actors, their current and potential capacity, and the impact of the crisis on market systems (for additional information on market analysis see SEEP Network, 2010; Albu, 2010; and Barrett et al., 2009). In some countries and following incomplete privatization of livestock services, competition between public and private sector workers may lead government partners to downplay the role of the private sector.

4. **Policy and regulations.** National policies or regulations may hinder or support certain types of livestock intervention. In some countries, community-based animal health workers are not officially recognized or can only handle a very limited range of veterinary medicines. In other situations, local taxation, customs duties, or bureaucracy may hinder rapid market-based responses. The situation analysis should assess policy and regulations, but it also needs to determine the likely enforcement of such regulations in an emergency setting, since to some extent the testing of new approaches in an emergency context can provide evidence to inform

policy change. In some emergencies, particularly when they are conflict-related, policies are instigated by governments or other actors expressly to impact negatively on the livelihoods of civilians. Examples include restrictions on cross-border movement, closure of markets, or deliberate asset-stripping of communities. An initial analysis of such policies can help agencies identify policy activities (see also *Core standard 7: Policy and advocacy*).

5. **Response identification.** *Chapter 3 (Initial assessment and identifying responses)* contains detailed guidance and a participatory tool – the Participatory Response Identification Matrix (PRIM) – to support a consultative process for identifying livestock-based emergency responses using the findings of the initial assessments. This process should include local actors (particularly those who have been operational in the area for some time), local authorities, and community representatives (including both host and displaced communities where appropriate, women as well as men, and representatives of key vulnerable groups).

6. **Livelihoods objectives.** Livestock interventions in emergencies should be designed to meet at least one of the livelihoods objectives (see *Chapter 1, Livestock, livelihoods, and emergencies*); that is, to provide immediate benefits, to protect assets, or to rebuild assets.

> **Core standard 5: Technical analysis and intervention**
>
> Livestock interventions are based on sound technical analysis and are implemented fairly, based on transparent and participatory targeting.

Key actions

- Analyse the appropriateness and feasibility of prioritized technical interventions and options using a range of participatory tools before implementation (see *Guidance note 1*).

- Base targeting criteria on an understanding of the actual or potential uses of livestock by vulnerable groups, and ensure the criteria are clearly defined and widely disseminated (see *Guidance note 2*).

- Agree targeting methods and the actual selection of beneficiaries with communities, including representatives of vulnerable groups (see *Guidance note 3*).

Guidance notes

1. **Technical analysis.** Each technical chapter of LEGS contains a number
   of key tools for analysing the suitability and feasibility of the selected
   intervention(s) and options. These include specific technical assessment
   checklists, tables showing both advantages and disadvantages, decision-
   making trees, timing tables, and discussion of cross-cutting themes and
   other issues, as well as the Standards, Key actions, and Guidance notes.
   These tools support the design and implementation of appropriate and
   timely livestock-based interventions. *Annex E* at the end of the LEGS
   Handbook summarizes the five steps for designing a response programme
   using these tools.

2. **Targeting criteria.** Targeting criteria should be developed with community
   representatives and should be informed by prior knowledge of vulnerable
   groups obtained during the initial assessment. In communities that rely
   heavily on livestock, indigenous social support systems often exist to
   support vulnerable individuals or groups according to the local criteria of
   wealth, gender, or social relationship. Where appropriate and feasible, local
   community groups can help develop a targeting system based on these
   indigenous approaches. Targeting criteria may also vary depending on
   the context (urban/rural) and whether cash is one of the mechanisms for
   intervention.

3. **Targeting methods.** To ensure transparency and impartiality during
   the selection of beneficiaries, targeting methods should be agreed with
   representatives of the wider community and/or specific vulnerable groups.
   Where possible, public meetings should be held to increase transparency
   and accountability. At these meetings, the targeting criteria are explained
   and the actual selection takes place. However, in some communities, such
   public selection may be inappropriate for social or cultural reasons. Targeting
   methods may include blanket targeting covering the whole community,
   targeting of a specific category (gender, age, geographical focus), self-
   selection, and others. Whichever methods are used, the targeting process
   should be clearly explained and remain as far as possible in the control of
   beneficiary communities to avoid concerns about inequitable distribution
   of benefits and to help ensure accountability and transparency. Targeting
   should be checked during the implementation of the project to ensure that
   vulnerable groups continue to be targeted as planned.

Core standard 6: Monitoring, evaluation, and livelihoods impact

Monitoring, evaluation, and livelihoods impact analysis is conducted to check and refine implementation as necessary, as well as to draw lessons for future programming.

Key actions

- Establish an M&E system as soon as possible during planning (see *Guidance note 1*).

- As much as is feasible and appropriate, base the M&E system on participation by the beneficiary communities (see *Guidance note 2*).

- Conduct monitoring with sufficient frequency to enable rapid detection of required changes and modification of implementation (see *Guidance note 3*).

- Ensure M&E systems take into account the market impact of interventions (whether inputs are cash-based or in kind) (see *Guidance note 3*).

- Ensure the monitoring system combines both technical progress indicators and impact indicators identified by beneficiaries; ensure impact indicators are measured by beneficiaries working with agency staff (see *Guidance note 4*).

- Conduct an evaluation with reference to the stated objectives of the project and ensure that it combines measurement of technical indicators and community-defined indicators (see *Guidance note 4*).

- Assess impact according to changes in the livelihoods of the affected communities (see *Guidance note 5*).

- When multiple agencies are involved in livestock interventions, standardize M&E systems to allow programme-wide progress and impact to be measured. Share M&E reports with all relevant actors, including community groups and coordination bodies (see *Guidance note 6*).

- Ensure M&E systems facilitate learning by all stakeholders (see *Guidance note 7*).

Guidance notes

1. **Monitoring and evaluation as a priority.** To date, relatively little is known about the impact on people's livelihoods of the many livestock interventions conducted as part of a humanitarian response over the last few decades. One reason for this is that M&E of livestock relief projects is not fully considered

during project design, is poorly implemented, or is improperly funded. Although rapid-onset emergencies may hinder attention to M&E during the design stage of an intervention, many livestock interventions are associated with slow-onset crises or complex emergencies. In these situations, there is usually enough time to conduct proper M&E of interventions. Baselines for M&E may be available from existing documentation (such as vulnerability assessments) or may otherwise be created through retrospective analysis using participatory inquiry tools. M&E checklists are included in the appendices to each technical chapter of LEGS.

2. **Participatory monitoring and evaluation.** Following the core standard of participation, the M&E of livestock interventions should be as participatory as possible. While fully participatory monitoring systems may not be feasible in an emergency context, participation in evaluation and impact assessment is vital to promote accountability and ensure the collection of quality data, since livestock users are well placed to observe the impact of the interventions over time.

3. **Monitoring.** Monitoring is an important management tool during emergency livestock interventions although it is often one of the weakest aspects. It allows agencies to track their implementation and expenditure against objectives and work plans while ensuring the timely identification of changes in needs or operating context in order to improve practice. For example, in destocking operations (whether commercial or slaughter destocking) livestock prices should be monitored to ensure that destocking does not increase vulnerability. In monitoring veterinary support, commonly accepted human health indices – accessibility, availability, affordability, acceptance, and quality – may also be usefully applied to livestock health. Such monitoring systems should also include information on the incidence of livestock disease and hence contribute to disease surveillance. Interventions involving the provision of livestock require detailed baselines and monitoring systems to assess livestock growth and herd development in order to analyse impact. Because most interventions have an impact on local markets, regardless of whether inputs are cash-based or in kind, monitoring should take into account price fluctuations of key goods and services. Compiled monitoring data are necessary for accountability upwards to donors and governments as well as downwards to beneficiary communities and institutions. They are also useful for evaluation.

4. **Local monitoring and evaluation indicators.** Participatory approaches to M&E can use local people's own indicators of the benefits derived from

livestock. When combined with monitoring data on project activities, an accurate picture of project impact can be developed.

5. **Livelihoods impact.** When evaluations of emergency livestock interventions are conducted, they tend to measure only the implementation of activities and progress towards objectives, while ignoring the impact on livestock assets, and consequently on livelihoods. If stated project objectives do not include changes to people's livelihoods, evaluations may overlook the impact of the project. Such impacts can include consumption of livestock-derived foods by vulnerable groups, uses of income derived from the sale of livestock or livestock products, benefits derived from access to pack animals, or social benefits such as livestock gifts or loans. Impact assessments should aim to understand the role of projects in increasing or decreasing these benefits. Participatory methodologies for impact assessment can help ensure quality results as well as increase beneficiary knowledge and involvement in future project design.

6. **Coordinated approaches.** For programmes involving multiple agencies, standardized and coordinated approaches to M&E allow programme-wide lessons to be generated. Standardized approaches can be based on a set of core objectives, issues, or questions common to all agencies, while also allowing for the flexible use of community-defined indicators in different locations.

7. **Learning.** Experience has shown that mistakes are often repeated and that lessons are not learned by implementing agencies in emergencies (see, for example, ProVention, 2007). A commitment of time and effort on the part of all stakeholders to carrying out effective M&E of emergency interventions and to sharing the lessons learned should help to address this issue. M&E systems should be designed to facilitate this learning process through the sharing of documentation as well as through the use of methodologies that support learning and response (real-time evaluation, for example). M&E information may also be a useful source of data in support of advocacy initiatives to address policy issues constraining effective livelihoods-based emergency responses (see *Core standard 7* below).

Core standard 7: Policy and advocacy

Where possible, policy obstacles to the effective implementation of emergency response and support to the livelihoods of affected communities are identified and addressed.

Key actions

- Identify policy constraints affecting the protection, use, or rebuilding of livestock assets (see *Guidance note 1*).

- In coordination with other stakeholders, address policy constraints through advocacy or other activities at the relevant (local, national, regional, or international) level (see *Guidance note 2*).

- Examine the underlying causes of vulnerability through policy analysis and action (see *Guidance note 3*).

- Ensure M&E systems provide evidence that contributes directly to policy dialogue and advocacy (see *Guidance note 4*).

- In advocacy on livestock-based interventions, ensure that references to climate and environmental change make use of the best available scientific knowledge (see *Guidance note 5*).

Guidance notes

1. **Analysis of policy constraints.** Policy constraints have the potential to impede the implementation of livelihoods-based emergency responses or restrict their effectiveness and impact. It is important that these constraints are assessed during the initial stages of emergency response: first, to ensure that the planned interventions are realistic and feasible; and second, to identify issues that have the potential to be addressed by relevant agencies and stakeholders. The LEGS situation analysis checklist in *Chapter 3 (Initial assessment and identifying responses)* includes questions on the policy context that could affect the implementation of livestock-based emergency response. Examples include restrictions on livestock movements or export bans, slaughter laws, licensing regulations, taxation policy, poor coordination of aid agencies, cross-border movement of people or stock, national disaster management policies, and organizational policies of key stakeholders.

2. **Advocacy on policy issues.** Interest in advocacy as an appropriate emergency response is increasing, largely because a growing number of agencies have adopted a rights-based approach to emergency and development work. However, their ability to address these issues on behalf of or in partnership with affected communities depends on the context in which they are operating. Policy change is a long-term process and there may be a limit to what can be achieved in an emergency context (see *Guidance note 3*). In some conflict-based emergencies, policy constraints

may result from a deliberate strategy by governments or governing bodies to put pressure on communities, rebel groups, or those they see as opposition. In such cases, advocacy with governments may be ineffective and even dangerous for its proponents. In cases where advocacy is undertaken, coordination among different stakeholders (donors, national and international implementing agencies, civil society) is vital.

3. **Underlying causes.** Advocacy to support the livelihoods of livestock keepers is not solely an emergency activity but needs to address the longer-term political and institutional factors that cause or increase vulnerability to disaster. This creates the links between emergency response and long-term development and policy initiatives that are necessary for effective emergency management and livelihood support.

4. **M&E evidence.** One of the uses of M&E information can be to inform advocacy and policy activities in support of livelihoods-based emergency responses. M&E systems should therefore be designed with this potential use in mind.

5. **Transparency in advocacy on climate change.** The perceptions of livestock keepers on climate change have significant value but may be subject to bias in recall, as well as a limited ability to distinguish global climate change from climate variability, regional trends, or changes in well-being from sources other than climate. Agencies should triangulate livestock-keeper perceptions of climate change with scientific knowledge, wherever possible, and be transparent about the basis for their observations concerning the impacts of climate change.

Core standard 8: Coordination

Different livestock interventions are harmonized and are complementary to humanitarian interventions intended to save lives and livelihoods; they do not interfere with immediate activities to save human lives.

Key actions

- Coordinate livestock interventions to ensure that approaches between agencies are in harmony, and that they comply with agreed implementation strategies (see *Guidance note 1*).

- When an agency cannot conduct a livestock assessment or respond to livestock needs, make these deficits known to other agencies that may have the capacity for livestock responses (see *Guidance note 2*).

- Where people's lives are at risk, ensure livestock interventions do not hinder life-saving humanitarian responses (see *Guidance note 3*).

- Where possible, integrate livestock interventions with other types of humanitarian assistance to maximize impact and ensure efficient use of shared resources (see *Guidance note 4*).

- Ensure livestock interventions at the very least do not harm livelihoods, nor increase the vulnerability of beneficiaries (see *Guidance note 5*).

- Ensure all stakeholders prioritize coordination, including the harmonization of donor and government approaches, for both emergency response and longer-term development initiatives (see *Guidance note 6*).

Guidance notes

1. **Coordination.** Given the range of emergency livestock interventions and the need to tailor them to specific sub-populations or vulnerable groups, coordination of response is critical. If different agencies are providing different types of support, coordination is needed to avoid duplication and to ensure that an important type of support is not overlooked. This is crucial if a combined feed–water–health response is needed because failure to provide one type of support risks the effectiveness of the others. For example, animals may be fed and watered but then succumb to disease. When different agencies provide similar support, coordination should ensure harmonized approaches and consistent programming. For example, if agencies covering adjacent areas set different purchase prices for destocked livestock, or employ different distribution policies for restocking (free, loan, subsidized, etc.), the initiatives may undermine each other. In veterinary support, differing policies on cost recovery can weaken interventions and cause confusion among beneficiaries. In slow-onset emergencies such as drought, one aspect of the coordination effort should also be to promote appropriate sequencing of interventions according to the stage of the drought (see the timing tables in each technical chapter below).

2. **Capacity and expertise.** Livelihoods-based livestock assessment and response is a specialized area, and not all agencies have the necessary in-house expertise. Agencies without sufficient expertise working in situations where action is called for should seek assistance from other agencies.

3. **Humanitarian priorities.** In an emergency, the most urgent need may be to provide life-saving assistance to affected human populations. Such assistance should not be compromised or adversely affected by the provision of livestock assistance. In practice, this means that when emergency transportation, communication, or other resources are limited, livestock teams and inputs should follow the food, shelter, water, and health inputs required to assist people in need. For example, water delivery programmes should either cater simultaneously to the needs of people and their livestock, or make use of different quality water for the two groups.

4. **Integrated responses and resource sharing.** In most humanitarian crises, various interventions take place simultaneously. Good coordination can lead to effective joint programming and sharing of resources and facilities with other sectors (see *Case studies 2.1* and *2.2* at the end of this chapter). Where possible, livestock interventions should be integrated with other sectors to maximize use of resources. For example, trucks delivering aid supplies could be backloaded with livestock as part of a destocking programme; refrigerators might store both human and animal medicines; discarded or damaged items for human shelter could be used for animal shelter.

5. **Do no harm.** Livelihoods-based interventions in emergencies, like life-saving activities, should at the very least do no harm. They should therefore ensure that they do not have any negative impacts on livelihoods, markets, or services, and that they avoid increasing risks to the protection of the beneficiaries or exacerbating social inequities.

6. **Prioritization of coordination.** Experience has shown that coordination between implementing agencies, donors, and governments is vital for effective humanitarian response, but that this coordination requires a commitment of time and staff from all partners. Donors and governments have a responsibility to understand the implications of the emergency responses they support and the linkages with livelihoods. At the broader level, the UN cluster system or similar national coordination bodies may take the lead in coordinating emergency response. More specifically, the creation of working groups for particular regions or for particular types of emergency may help to harmonize approaches, agree roles and responsibilities, and create linkages with livelihoods and ongoing development initiatives (see, for example, *Case study 2.1*). Donors may also be well placed to encourage or even demand harmonization of approaches by implementing agencies.

Core standards case studies

2.1 Process case study: Coordination in a slaughter destocking project in Kenya

In Turkana, Kenya, in early 2005, Vétérinaires sans Frontières (VSF) Belgium implemented a destocking project to create markets for livestock sales and improve the nutritional status of target groups. The project was designed and implemented by VSF in collaboration with a number of stakeholders, in particular the government's District Steering Group and the Livestock Service Providers Forum. These bodies provided an effective coordination forum for the operation.

Goats were purchased from Turkana pastoralists by private traders at an agreed price and distributed to schools and health centres throughout the district. The pastoralists were reimbursed by project funds, with an additional 20 per cent of the purchase price as their profit. The project succeeded in destocking over 6,000 goats from 2,500–3,000 pastoralists through more than 300 traders and distributing them to nearly 100 health centres and schools. The project faced several key challenges. These included:

- fixing an appropriate price and ensuring that all traders adhered to it
- concerns from the traders about low profit margins, high bank charges, and feeding costs
- accessibility to the markets for vulnerable or remote pastoralists
- capacity of the institutions to handle the influx of goats (which were supposed to be slaughtered on the day of arrival)
- the tendency of the institutions to use the meat to substitute for other protein, rather than to supplement the existing diet.

While challenges remained with regard to involving the pastoralists more in this process, the reported success of the project was largely attributed to the positive collaboration and coordination between implementing agencies (*Source:* Watson and van Binsbergen, 2008).

2.2 Impact case study: Long-term participation and coordination in a complex emergency, South Sudan

Between 1993 and 2000, a large-scale livestock programme was coordinated by Tufts University and UNICEF in South Sudan, where protracted conflict and a long-standing complex emergency existed. Covering an area of over 600,000 square kilometres and aiming to include more than 10 million livestock, the programme was based on partnerships with up to 12 NGOs as well as the Sudan People's Liberation Movement. Collectively, these partners developed implementation approaches for a community-based animal health system and formulated guidelines for project design, implementation, and monitoring in different areas. Community participation was central to the approach, with NGOs working with communities to prioritize local livestock diseases, select and train people as community-based animal health workers (CAHWs), and conduct participatory evaluations of programme activities. Local veterinary coordination committees were established to oversee livestock activities, CAHWs, and other veterinary workers. Over time, the programme expanded to include 1,500 CAHWs, supported by 150 local veterinary supervisors and coordinators, and 40 NGO field veterinary surgeons and livestock officers.

One of the main outcomes of the strong coordination of the livestock programme and the commitment to community participation was the eradication of rinderpest from South Sudan. Before the participatory approach was introduced in 1993, around 140,000 cattle were vaccinated against rinderpest each year. After 1993, there was a 10.6-fold increase in vaccination coverage, reaching 1.48 million in 1993 and 1.78 million in 1994. Since 1998, no confirmed outbreaks of rinderpest have been reported in South Sudan (*Sources:* Leyland, 1996; Jones et al., 2003).

2.3 Process case study: Coordination and contingency planning in southern Ethiopia

In southern Ethiopia, the Catholic Organization for Relief and Development Aid (Cordaid) had been supporting a local NGO, the Ethiopian Pastoralist Research and Development Association (EPaRDA), to implement the South Omo Risk Management Project. Given the history of the area, the project assumed that either slow-onset emergencies such as drought or rapid-onset emergencies such as floods would occur during the project. Therefore, the project included a contingency planning and budgeting system to allow for effective and timely emergency response. In August 2006 the Omo River in southern Ethiopia burst its banks and flooded 14 villages in the Dassenetch and Nyangatom districts. The flood took communities and local government by surprise and resulted in the loss of 363 people and 3,200 cattle. Over 21,000 people lost their homes, while many lost their crops and stored grain.

The contingency plans enabled EPaRDA to work with other organizations to mount a relief operation in response to the crisis. Cordaid, EPaRDA, and Farm

Africa began livestock interventions alongside a human food and shelter response, focusing on veterinary inputs and logistical support. The district administration established a range of emergency committees, including veterinary, human health, logistics, and relief distribution ones. These committees reported to a general steering committee chaired by the district administrator. Cordaid and partners were coordinated by the veterinary emergency committee, which reported daily to the general committee, enabling the coordination of all livestock emergency responses, including the mobilization of veterinary professionals and CAHWs as well as the organization of mass treatment and vaccination. This coordination process brought together all relevant stakeholders and helped to avoid duplication of effort (*Source:* Cordaid, 2006).

2.4 Impact case study: Donkeys, participation, and livelihoods among Eritrean returnees

Following the resolution of the Eritrea–Ethiopia conflict in 1991, it was estimated that 500,000 Eritrean refugees were living in eastern Sudan. To begin the organized repatriation of refugees, the Eritrean government worked with UN agencies to design the Programme for Refugee Reintegration and Rehabilitation of Resettlement Areas in Eritrea (PROFERI). The pilot stage of PROFERI aimed to repatriate 4,500 refugee families (about 25,000 people) and offered assistance in the form of shelter, rations, water supplies, clinics, schools, improved roads, and provision of seeds, tools, and livestock.

A livestock package comprising different species of animals, and valued at approximately US$420 per household, was provided as a gift to every household. The numbers of animals in the package, by species, are shown in *Table 2.1*. However, during the design of the PROFERI project, contact with Eritrean refugees in Sudan had been minimal, so very little was known about people's preferences for different types of livestock. The lack of returnee participation in the project prompted a reassessment of the livestock inputs, using interviews with returnee households to understand their livestock needs better. This process resulted in marked changes to the livestock package, most notably a substantial increase in the number of donkeys and small ruminants. Few large stock were requested, but the number of donkeys asked for increased more than sixfold.

These interviews and later project monitoring showed that donkeys were highly valued owing to their use as pack animals and for transport. People needed them to move goods to and from markets, to carry water and firewood, and for personal transport. These were the most frequently mentioned benefits of livestock among returnees, with 80 per cent of households reporting these benefits. Donkeys were also relatively inexpensive and easily managed and tended to suffer from fewer health problems than other types of livestock (*Sources*: Catley and Blakeway, 2004; Hamid, 2004). This experience indicated the importance of involving beneficiaries in the design of livestock provision and illustrates why participation is a LEGS core standard.

Table 2.1 Numbers of animals requested by Eritrean refugees in the PROFERI project

Source of information	Number of livestock proposed per 500 households					
	Camels	Donkeys	Cows	Oxen	Sheep	Goats
PROFERI project plan	50	50	100	150	1000	1000
Interviews with beneficiary households (n=2090)	38	313	79	12	2060	1724

References and further reading

Albu, M. (2010) *Emergency Market Mapping and Analysis Toolkit*, Practical Action Publishing, Rugby.

ALNAP (Active Learning Network for Accountability and Performance in Humanitarian Action) (2003) *ALNAP Annual Review 2003, Humanitarian Action: Improving Monitoring to Enhance Accountability and Learning*, ALNAP, London, <http://www.alnap.org/resource/5198.aspx> [accessed 20 May 2014].

ALNAP (2006) *Review of Humanitarian Action in 2005, Evaluation Utilisation, Global Welfare: A Realistic Expectation for the International Humanitarian System?* ALNAP, London, <http://www.alnap.org/resource/5223> [accessed 19 May 2014].

Barrett, C.B., Bell, R., Lentz, E.C. and Maxwell, D.G. (2009) 'Market information and food insecurity response analysis', *Food Security* 1: 151–168 <http://dx.doi.org/10.1007/s12571-009-0021-3>.

Benson, C. and Twigg, J. with Rossetto, T. (2007) *Tools for Mainstreaming Disaster Risk Reduction: Guidance Notes for Development Organisations*, ProVention Consortium, Geneva, <http://www.preventionweb.net/english/professional/publications/v.php?id=1066> [accessed 14 May 2014].

Catley, A. and Blakeway, S. (2004) 'Donkeys and the provision of livestock to returnees: lessons from Eritrea', in P. Starkey and D. Fielding (eds), *Donkeys, People and Development: A Resource Book of the Animal Traction Network for Eastern and Southern Africa* (ATNESA), pp. 86–92, Technical Centre for Agricultural and Rural Cooperation, Wageningen, The Netherlands, <http://

www.atnesa.org/donkeys/donkeys-catley-returnees-ER.pdf> [accessed 14 May 2014].

Catley, A., Leyland, T. and Bishop, S. (2008) 'Policies, practice and participation in protracted crises: the case of livestock interventions in South Sudan', in L. Alinovi, G. Hemrich and L. Russo (eds), *Beyond Relief: Food Security in Protracted Crises*, pp. 65–93, Practical Action Publishing, Rugby.

Cordaid (2006) *Ethiopian Partners Emergency Report*, Cordaid, Addis Ababa.

CPWG (Child Protection Working Group) (2012) *Minimum Standards for Child Protection in Humanitarian Action,* CPWG, Geneva, <http://cpwg.net/minimum-standards> [accessed 14 May 2014].

Emergency Capacity Building Project (2007) *Impact Measurement and Accountability in Emergencies: The Good Enough Guide*, Oxfam, Oxford.

FAO/WFP (Food and Agriculture Organization of the United Nations/World Food Programme) (undated) *Passport to Mainstreaming a Gender Perspective in Emergency Situations: Key Analytical Questions for Designing Gender-Sensitive Humanitarian Interventions*, Socio-Economic and Gender Analysis Programme (SEAGA), FAO/WFP, Rome, <http://www.livestock-emergency.net/userfiles/file/assessment-review/FAO-WFP.pdf>[accessed 14 May 2014].

Goe, M.R. (2005) *Livestock Production and HIV/AIDS in East and Southern Africa*, [Working Paper], FAO, Rome, <http://www.livestock-emergency.net/userfiles/file/assessment-review/Goe-2005.pdf> [accessed 15 May 2014].

Gosling, L. and Edwards, M. (2003) *Toolkits: A Practical Guide to Planning, Monitoring, Evaluation and Impact Assessment*, Save the Children, London.

Hallam, A. (1998) *Evaluating Humanitarian Assistance Programmes in Complex Emergencies*, Good Practice Review No. 7, Humanitarian Practice Network, Overseas Development Institute (ODI), London, <http://www.odihpn.org/documents/gpr7.pdf> [accessed 15 May 2014].

Hamid, E. (2004) 'The importance of donkeys in a restocking programme in Eritrea', in P. Starkey and D. Fielding (eds), *Donkeys, People and Development: A Resource Book of the Animal Traction Network for Eastern and Southern Africa* (ATNESA), pp. 84–85, Technical Centre for Agricultural and Rural Cooperation, Wageningen, The Netherlands, <http://www.atnesa.org/donkeys/donkeys-ezedeen-restocking-ER.pdf> [accessed 14 May 2014].

HAP (Humanitarian Accountability Partnership), Editorial Steering Committee (2007) *Standard in Humanitarian Accountability and Quality Management,* HAP-International, Geneva, <www.hapinternational.org/> [accessed 25 June 2014].

Harvey, P. (2004) *HIV/AIDS and Humanitarian Action*, Humanitarian Policy Group (HPG) Report 16, ODI, London, <http://www.odi.org.uk/sites/odi.org.uk/files/odi-assets/publications-opinion-files/283.pdf> [accessed 19 May 2014].

Herson, M. and Mitchell, J. (2005) 'Real-time evaluation: where does its value lie?', in *Humanitarian Exchange Magazine*, Issue 32, December 2005, Humanitarian Practice Network, ODI, London, <http://www.odihpn.org/humanitarian-exchange-magazine/issue-32/real-time-evaluation-where-does-its-value-lie> [accessed 15 May 2014].

IASC (Inter-Agency Standing Committee) (2006) *Women, Girls, Boys and Men: Different Needs – Equal Opportunities*, Gender Handbook in Humanitarian Action, IASC, Geneva, <http://www.humanitarianinfo.org/iasc/documents/subsidi/tf_gender/IASC%20Gender%20Handbook%20(Feb%202007).pdf> [accessed 15 May 2014].

ICRC (International Committee of the Red Cross) (2013) *Professional Standards for Protection Work*, ICRC, Geneva, <http://www.icrc.org/eng/assets/files/other/icrc-002-0999.pdf> [accessed 15 May 2014].

INEE (Inter-Agency Network for Education in Emergencies) (2010) *Minimum Standards for Education: Preparedness, Response, Recovery*, INEE, New York, <http://toolkit.ineesite.org/toolkit/Toolkit.php?PostID=1002> [accessed 15 May 2014].

Jones, B., Araba, A., Koskei, P. and Letereuwa, S. (2003) 'Experiences with community-based and participatory methods for rinderpest surveillance in parts of southern Sudan', in K. Sones and A. Catley (eds), *Primary Animal Health Care in the 21st Century: Shaping the Rules, Policies and Institutions*, proceedings of an international conference, Mombasa, 15–18 October 2002, African Union Interafrican Bureau for Animal Resources, Nairobi, <http://sites.tufts.edu/capeipst/files/2011/03/Jones-et-al-Mombasa.pdf> [accessed 15 May 2014].

Leyland, T. (1996) 'The case for a community-based approach with reference to southern Sudan', in *The World Without Rinderpest*, pp. 109–120, FAO Animal Production and Health paper 129, FAO, Rome. Available from: <http://www.fao.org/docrep/003/w3246e/w3246e00.htm#TOC> [accessed 28 May 2014].

ODI (Overseas Development Institute) (1999) *What Can We Do with a Rights-based Approach to Development?* ODI Briefing Paper 3, ODI, London. Available from: <http://www.livestock-emergency.net/resources/assessment-and-response/> [accessed 15 May 2014].

OHCHR (Office of the High Commissioner for Human Rights) (2006) *Frequently Asked Questions on a Human Rights-Based Approach to Development Cooperation*, OHCHR, New York and Geneva, <http://www.ohchr.org/Documents/Publications/FAQen.pdf> [accessed 15 May 2014].

Pasteur, K. (2002) *Gender Analysis for Sustainable Livelihoods Frameworks: Tools and Links to Other Sources*, draft. Available from: <http://www.livestock-emergency.net/resources/assessment-and-response/> [accessed 15 May 2014].

People in Aid (2003) *Code of Good Practice in the Management and Support of Aid Personnel,* People in Aid, London, <http://www.peopleinaid.org/code/> [accessed 15 May 2014].

ProVention Consortium (2007) *M&E Sourcebook*, ProVention Consortium, Geneva.

Roche, C. (1999) *Impact Assessment for Development Agencies: Learning to Value Change*, Oxfam, Oxford, <http://policy-practice.oxfam.org.uk/publications/impact-assessment-for-development-agencies-learning-to-value-change-122808> [accessed 15 May 2014].

Sandison, P. (2003) *Desk Review of Real-Time Evaluation Experience*, Evaluation Working Paper, UNICEF, New York, <http://www.unicef.org/evaldatabase/files/FINAL_Desk_Review_RTE.pdf> [accessed 15 May 2014].

SEEP (Small Enterprise Education and Promotion) Network (2010) *Minimum Economic Recovery Standards* (MERS), SEEP Network, Washington, DC, <http://www.seepnetwork.org/minimum-economic-recovery-standards-resources-174.php> [accessed 15 May 2014].

Slim, H. and Bonwick, A. (2005) *Protection: An ALNAP Guide for Humanitarian Agencies*, ODI, London.

Sphere Project (2011) *Humanitarian Charter and Minimum Standards in Humanitarian Response* (the Sphere Handbook), The Sphere Project, Geneva, <www.sphereproject.org/> [accessed 15 May 2014]. See chapter on 'Protection principles' (pp. 25–47).

UNDP (United Nations Development Programme) *Climate Change Country Profiles* [online] <http://www.geog.ox.ac.uk/research/climate/projects/undp-cp/> [accessed 19 May 2014].

Vavra, J. (2005) *Best Practices: Gender and Conflict in Africa*, Management Systems International and US Agency for International Development, Washington, DC. Available from: <http://www.livestock-emergency.net/resources/assessment-and-response/> [accessed 15 May 2014].

Watson, D.J. and van Binsbergen, J. (2008) *Review of VSF-Belgium's 'Turkana Emergency Livestock Off-Take' Intervention* 2005, Research Report 4, International Livestock Research Institute (ILRI), Nairobi, Kenya, <http://cgspace.cgiar.org/bitstream/handle/10568/234/RR4_LivestockOfftakeIntervention.pdf?sequence=1> [accessed 19 May 2014].

Wood, A., Apthorpe, R. and Borton, J. (eds) (2001) *Evaluating International Humanitarian Action: Reflections from Practitioners*, Zed Books/ALNAP, London.

World Vision (2012) *Minimum Inter-Agency Standards for Protection Mainstreaming*, World Vision UK and World Vision Australia, London and Sydney, <https://www.humanitarianresponse.info/topics/procap/document/world-vision-minimum-inter-agency-standards-protection-mainstreaming-march> [accessed 15 May 2014].

Notes

1. For further information on education in emergencies, see *Minimum Standards for Education: Preparation, Response, Recovery* (INEE, 2010).

2. See also World Vision (2012) *Minimum Inter-Agency Standards for Protection Mainstreaming*, and ICRC (2013) *Professional Standards for Protection Work*.

CHAPTER 3

Initial assessment and identifying responses

Introduction

This chapter provides guidance on the initial assessment that should be carried out to decide if livestock support is appropriate for a given humanitarian crisis. Assuming that livestock support is appropriate, the chapter then describes the Participatory Response Identification Matrix (PRIM), a tool designed to help users decide which types of livestock assistance are required.

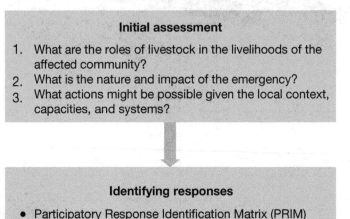

Initial assessment

1. What are the roles of livestock in the livelihoods of the affected community?
2. What is the nature and impact of the emergency?
3. What actions might be possible given the local context, capacities, and systems?

Identifying responses

- Participatory Response Identification Matrix (PRIM)

Specific technical assessment checklists and decision-making trees are provided in each of the relevant technical chapters (4–9).

Initial assessment

Prior to any form of emergency response, an initial assessment is required to ascertain whether livelihoods-based livestock interventions are appropriate and feasible in the specific context, according to the type, phase, and severity of the emergency, or indeed whether a response is necessary at all. This initial assessment is not an end in itself, but the first step to enable decisions to be made about which technical interventions to explore. The initial assessment also generates useful background information to assist more detailed assessments in specific technical areas (*Chapters 4–9*).

The initial assessment comprises three sets of key questions, which can be answered rapidly using appropriate approaches and methods. The areas covered by the key questions can all be considered at the same time.

Assessment questions

1 The role of livestock in livelihoods

Livestock support is most likely to be needed if livestock are important in the livelihoods of the people affected by the emergency. The following is a set of questions that can be asked to determine the significance of livestock in local livelihoods and the role they play. The answers to these questions will help users of this manual decide whether a livestock-related response is appropriate. It is important to understand how livestock are managed, and how the benefits, ownership, and care of livestock are affected by factors such as gender, wealth, or vulnerable group. The key questions are not fixed, and can be adapted to suit a particular context.

Key questions

1.1 What are the main livelihood strategies in the affected area in usual times?

1.2 What are the key uses of livestock (food, income, social, draught, transport)?

1.3 What percentage of food is derived from livestock in usual times?

1.4 What percentage of income is derived from livestock in usual times, and how is it managed?

1.5. What roles do different household members play with regard to livestock care and management, including use and disposal rights, with particular reference to gender and age? Take note of different livestock species and ages as well as seasonal variations.

1.6 What customary institutions and leaders are involved in livestock production and natural resource management and what are their roles?

1.7 What are the key social relations and power dynamics that affect livestock care and management?

1.8 What are the main coping strategies and indicators for difficult times (for example, famine foods, high livestock slaughter or sales, migration, dispersal of household members, sale of other assets)? Do these strategies have negative implications for future livelihood security?

Conclusion/Exit point

Do livestock play a significant role in the livelihoods of the affected people and is a livestock-related response therefore appropriate?

2 The nature and impact of the emergency

The initial assessment should provide an understanding of the impact of the emergency on the affected populations; determine whether an emergency response is necessary; and identify what further information is needed.

Key questions

2.1 What type of emergency is it: rapid onset, slow onset, or complex?

2.2 What is the cause of the emergency (drought, flood, war, etc.)?

2.3 What is the history of this type of emergency in this context?

2.4 Which stage has the emergency reached (alert, alarm, emergency, recovery/immediate aftermath, early recovery, recovery)?

2.5 What human and livestock populations are affected?

2.6 What has been the impact of the emergency on the affected population? Specifically:

- What is the nutritional status of the affected population?
- What is the prevalence of disease?
- What is the mortality rate?
- What has been the impact on vulnerable groups – women, children, PLHIV, ethnic groups? (See references on vulnerability analysis at the end of this chapter.)
- Are there signs that the coping strategies and 'difficult times' indicators from question 1.8 above are being implemented?
- Has there been significant migration or displacement of (parts of) the affected populations? If so, who is affected and have they taken their livestock with them?
- What is the impact on the host community?

2.7 What has been the impact of the emergency on livestock management strategies? Specifically:

- What is the impact on access to grazing and/or feed?

- What is the impact on access to water resources for livestock?
- What is the impact on daily and seasonal movements?
- What is the impact on livestock traders and key livestock input and output markets (sales, prices, terms of trade between livestock and cereals, feed and drug suppliers)?
- What is the impact on livestock services (veterinary services, extension services, pharmacies)?
- What has been the impact on natural resources?
- What has been the impact on the gender division of labour?
- What future plans do the affected people have for their livestock?

2.8 What has been the impact of the emergency on livestock? (Differentiate by species if necessary.) Specifically:

- How has livestock condition deteriorated?
- What is the impact on livestock welfare?
- Has livestock productivity fallen (offtake of milk, blood, eggs, etc.)?
- Has livestock morbidity increased?
- Has livestock slaughter for home consumption increased?
- How significant are the livestock losses?
- Has there been any impact on livestock shelter/enclosures?
- What is the scale of these impacts?

2.9 How has the environment been impacted by the emergency? The environmental impact of the emergency, and of any planned interventions, should be carefully assessed. A number of methodologies have been developed for this purpose; see, for example, the Rapid Environmental Assessment tool devised by the Benfield UCL Hazard Research Centre and CARE International, as well as the FRAME assessment tool (Kelly, 2005; UNHCR, 2009).

2.10 What are the forecast and trends (where relevant) for the forthcoming season (anticipated snow, rains, heat, dry season, increasing insecurity, access to food, etc.)?

Conclusion/Exit point

Is an emergency intervention necessary?

3 Situation analysis

The key questions under the situation analysis ensure an understanding of the operating environment, potential logistical constraints, and overlap or potential complementarity with other stakeholders.

Key questions

3.1 Who are the key actors in the affected area and what are they doing?

3.2 Is any stakeholder playing a coordination role?

3.3 What services and facilities (government administration, markets, private sector animal production and health services) are usually available, and what has been the impact of the emergency on them?

3.4 What resources are available (in particular indigenous coping strategies)?

3.5 What is the history of emergency response in the affected area – both positive and negative – and what are the lessons learned from it?

3.6 What is the current context? Further detailed assessments with regard to these issues may need to be conducted depending on the technical options selected (see *Chapters 4–9*). These questions become especially significant – and in some cases identify 'killer assumptions' – in conflict situations:

- How are communications functioning?
- What is the security situation?
- What are the implications for livestock movement and migration (rights of access, potential conflict)?
- What are the key protection issues facing livestock keepers?
- What is the current infrastructure, such as roads and transport?
- What is the context for potential cash- or voucher-based interventions (for example, in terms of security, financial transfer mechanisms, and delivery options)?
- Are there any cross-border issues?
- In situations of conflict what are the causes, and the implications for programming?
- What are the policy and/or legal constraints affecting livestock-related interventions? Examples include livestock movement or export bans,

slaughter laws, taxation policy, licensing regulations, coordination of aid agencies, national emergency management policies, and organizational policies of key stakeholders.

- Have recent changes in policy affected vulnerability?

Conclusion/Exit point

Do answers to any of the above constitute 'killer assumptions' that prevent any form of intervention in the area? For example, does the security situation hinder any kind of movement at present? Are other actors already providing sufficient support to affected populations?

Assessment approaches and methods

Reviewing existing information

Ideally, some of the assessment information should have been collected before the onset of the emergency as part of preparedness planning (see *Chapter 2, Core standards common to all livestock interventions, Core standard 2*). Even in rapid-onset emergencies, some form of preparedness information collection should be possible for areas that are known to be disaster-prone. Agencies already working in the area on longer-term development initiatives are therefore often best placed to develop this preparedness capacity both internally and together with communities. In these circumstances, knowledge and understanding of livelihood strategies, production systems, social and cultural norms, and key actors and institutions are already available, thus significantly increasing the accuracy of the rapid initial assessments.

Secondary data should be compiled from government reports, health and veterinary statistics, NGO reports, and other available documentation. Other agencies operating in the area may also have conducted preliminary or detailed emergency assessments, including vulnerability assessments, which are a useful source of secondary data. Stakeholders themselves may be additional sources of key information, both quantitative and qualitative (see below). Spatial data from satellite photographs and geographic information systems (GIS) may also be useful for mapping water points and other natural resources.

Early warning systems have been developed in different regions to anticipate emergencies and allow time for preparation and mitigation before disaster strikes. These systems generally focus on food security and human nutrition data, although some incorporate livelihood indicators such as the condition of livestock. The number of classification systems to assist in the interpretation of early warning and emergency assessment data is also growing (*Appendix 3.1*).

Early warning and classification system results can be extremely useful in the analysis of an emergency, and help to inform emergency response. However, the need for sound analysis and accurate classification of an emergency should not draw attention from the need to respond quickly and effectively. Early and timely response is particularly important in slow-onset emergencies such as drought, where the benefit-to-cost ratio of interventions may decrease with time.

Participatory approaches

The assessments described in this chapter are designed to be part of a participatory planning process involving key stakeholders and including representatives of the beneficiary communities (see *Chapter 2, Core standards common to all livestock interventions, Core standard 1: Participation*). In the context of emergencies, particularly rapid-onset crises, the need for speed and an urgent response may be considered to limit the opportunities for participatory approaches. However, the approach taken for the assessments is as important as the methodologies selected, if not more so, as it has the potential to lay a sound footing for a response based on collaboration and participation – local participation improves the quality of the data. The assessment team should therefore include community representatives and involve local institutions as partners. With regard to vulnerability and the LEGS cross-cutting theme of gender and social equity, it is important to ensure that the team is gender-balanced, and that marginalized groups are represented. What is more, local information gathering should ensure proper coverage of vulnerable groups. The assessment team should also include generalists and livestock specialists with local knowledge.

The three sets of assessment questions can be addressed simultaneously, either during community discussions in consultation with local officials, or from secondary data. Compared with human emergency assessments, livestock-based assessments may be more qualitative because they are based on the judgement of expert opinion. In any case, quantitative data collection and analysis is rarely feasible. For example, there is at present no livestock-based equivalent to rapid human nutritional assessment and no standard methodology for measuring livestock mortality. Moreover, livestock keepers are sometimes reluctant to reveal livestock numbers. The role of livestock in livelihoods is a key aspect of the assessment and will vary by community and region.

Participatory methods

A range of well-tested participatory methods are available for rapid assessment of livestock issues, problems, and solutions. These methods fall into the following three main groups:

- *Informal interview methods*
    - key informant interviews: local NGO and government staff; traditional and community leaders; religious leaders; women's groups; and other civil society organizations (CSOs)
    - focus group discussions (separately with men and women, and repeated with different wealth groups)
    - semi-structured interviews as a stand-alone method to support visualization and scoring methods (see below).
- *Visualization methods*
    - participatory mapping of local resources, services, markets, grazing areas, water points, veterinary services, and other information, such as insecure areas and livestock movement
    - seasonal calendars
    - Venn diagrams.
- *Ranking and scoring methods*
    - simple ranking of livestock problems
    - matrix scoring of different potential livestock interventions
    - proportional piling of livestock disease impacts.

Additional issues relating to the use of participatory methods for rapid livestock assessments include the following:

- *Training.* The value of information produced by participatory methods and analysis depends heavily on the skills and experience of team members, and whether they have been trained in participatory rural appraisal (PRA), participatory epidemiology, or similar subjects.
- *Cross-checking.* Information derived from participatory methods can be cross-checked (triangulated) using both pre-existing information collated before the community-level assessment and local government or other reports (such as livestock and cereal prices in local markets). Direct

observation is also important for checking the condition of livestock, natural resources, and infrastructure.

- *Sampling.* Given the time constraints, participatory methods are used with samples of informants judged by the assessment team and stakeholders to be critical both for answering the three main sets of questions and for ensuring that all vulnerable groups are involved. This judgemental (purposive) approach involves the selection of representative individuals and groups based on agreed characteristics. Examples of useful informant groups are poor livestock keepers affected by drought, women livestock keepers, or inhabitants of a flood-affected village. Using this sampling approach, the information gathered is automatically structured by vulnerable group.[1]

- *Baselines.* When conducted well, participatory assessments produce information that often includes important baseline data. For example, proportional piling might be used to estimate livestock mortality by species and age group. These data are useful for the assessment and immediate decision-making and could also form a useful baseline indicator for a supplementary feed project (see *Chapter 6 , Ensuring feed supplies*) or a veterinary project (see *Chapter 5, Veterinary support*).

- *Numerical data.* Scoring and ranking methods produce numerical data. Repetition of these methods can produce datasets that can be summarized using conventional statistical tests.

Appendix 3.2 shows how participatory methods can be used to answer the three sets of initial assessment questions listed above.

See *References* at the end of this chapter for further information on assessment approaches and methods.

Identifying livestock-related emergency responses

Linking the LEGS objectives with the LEGS technical options

To achieve one or more of the three LEGS livelihoods objectives, different technical options can be used, either alone or in combination. LEGS presents six key areas of intervention: destocking; veterinary support; feed; water; shelter; and the provision of livestock/restocking. The relationship between livelihoods objectives and these technical interventions is shown in *Table 3.1*, together with some key implications to consider for each technical option. These implications are considered in more detail in each of the technical chapters (4–9).

Table 3.1 LEGS livelihoods objectives and technical options

Livelihoods objective	Technical interventions (and options)	Implications and issues
1. Provide immediate benefits to crisis-affected communities through existing livestock resources	**Destocking** (commercial destocking)	• May be appropriate in early stages of slow-onset emergency • Allows longer-term protection of remaining livestock assets • Provides cash support to livestock keepers • Potential also in some rapid-onset emergencies to provide cash to households that may lack feed, shelter, or labour to care for their livestock • Requires infrastructure, interested traders, and a conducive policy environment
	Destocking (slaughter destocking)	• May be appropriate when emergency too far advanced for commercial destocking • Provides cash or food • Requires slaughter infrastructure, skills, and distribution mechanisms • May require greater input from external agencies
2. Protect the key livestock assets of crisis-affected communities	**Veterinary support** (clinical veterinary services; support to public sector veterinary functions)	• Potential for positive impact on protecting and rebuilding assets at all stages of an emergency • Can include preparedness measures such as vaccination and preventive treatment • Can be conducted in conjunction with other activities (e.g. feed, water, provision of livestock) to increase asset protection • Requires operational or potential service sector (government, private and/or community-based) and veterinary supplies
	Ensuring feed supplies (emergency feeding in situ; feed camps)	• Important for protecting remaining livestock assets during and after an emergency • Requires available feed, transport, and/or storage facilities • In drought, can complement water provision • Can be very expensive and logistically demanding
	Provision of water (water points; water trucking)	• Important for protecting remaining livestock assets • Requires available water sources of sufficient quality and quantity, or potential to establish new sources • Requires effective local water management systems • May be very capital-intensive (particularly if new water points are established) or expensive (water trucking)

Livelihoods objective	Technical interventions (and options)	Implications and issues
	Livestock shelter and settlement (livestock and settlement interventions; temporary and longer-lasting livestock shelter)	• Responds to a range of livestock needs: protection against cold or hot climates; security; prevention of wandering; provision of healthy environment for livestock and humans; and convenience of management • Generally (though not exclusively) more appropriate to rapid-onset emergencies in harsh climates than to slow-onset emergencies such as drought • Can involve preventive measures (e.g. earthquake-resistant livestock shelters) as well as those designed to protect livestock assets after an emergency • Addresses wider settlement issues (such as land rights, environmental implications, and access to feed and water)
3. Rebuild key livestock assets among crisis-affected communities	**Provision of livestock** (replacing livestock assets; building livestock assets)	• Can include helping livestock keepers to rebuild herds after an emergency, or the replacement of smaller numbers of animals (e.g. draught or transport animals, poultry), which contribute to livelihoods • Appropriate in the recovery phase once immediate aftermath is over and asset loss can be assessed • Potentially very expensive and challenging to manage effectively • Requires supply of appropriate livestock either locally or within feasible transporting distance • Requires sufficient natural resources to support distributed livestock • Success is highly dependent on: appropriate targeting of beneficiaries; selection of appropriate livestock; beneficiary capacity for livestock care and management; and availability of livestock support services • Complementary animal health interventions, including training, can increase survival rates • Herd replacement may require additional short-term food and non-food support for beneficiaries
	Veterinary support; water; feed; shelter and settlement	• See above • Continued intervention in the recovery phase can help to rebuild and strengthen livestock assets and reduce vulnerability to future emergencies

The LEGS Participatory Response Identification Matrix (PRIM)

The PRIM is a tool that uses the findings of the initial assessment to facilitate discussions with local stakeholders in order to decide which livestock interventions are most appropriate and feasible for achieving LEGS objectives (see *PRIM case studies* below). A PRIM should be completed by a group of stakeholders (including both male and female community representatives) using the initial assessment findings.

In the light of the assessment findings, the PRIM considers the three LEGS livelihoods objectives of 1) providing immediate livestock-based benefits; 2) protecting assets; and 3) rebuilding assets against the range of possible technical interventions (destocking; veterinary support; feed; water; shelter; and provision of livestock). The PRIM also emphasizes the importance of all three objectives in order to support livelihoods in an emergency context, and it addresses how the different interventions can fit and overlap within the phasing of an emergency.

The right-hand side of the matrix can help agencies plan the timing of their interventions and allow sufficient time for preparation and lead-in for later activities.

The emergency phases vary for rapid-onset and slow-onset emergencies. Broad definitions of these phases are given in the *Glossary*, but PRIM participants should agree on their own definitions specific to the context in which they are working. For complex emergencies that include either a slow- or rapid-onset emergency, the relevant PRIM may be used (see, for example, *Case study C* below). For chronic and/or complex emergencies that do not include a slow- or rapid-onset crisis, only the left-hand side of the PRIM (i.e. the livelihoods objectives) may be appropriate.

The PRIM, which can be completed in a workshop setting with local stakeholders, is a rapid, visual, and participatory way to summarize the LEGS technical options against LEGS objectives and the phases of the emergency in question.

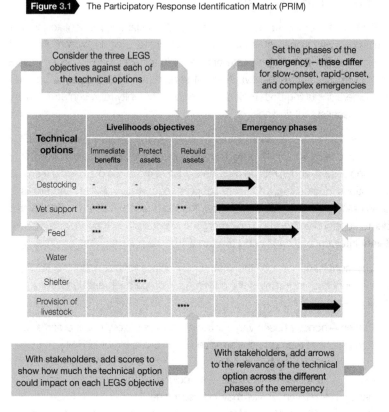

Figure 3.1 The Participatory Response Identification Matrix (PRIM)

Consider the three LEGS objectives against each of the technical options

Set the phases of the emergency – these differ for slow-onset, rapid-onset, and complex emergencies

Technical options	Livelihoods objectives			Emergency phases		
	Immediate benefits	Protect assets	Rebuild assets			
Destocking	-	-	-			
Vet support	*****	***	***			
Feed	***					
Water						
Shelter		****				
Provision of livestock			****			

With stakeholders, add scores to show how much the technical option could impact on each LEGS objective

With stakeholders, add arrows to the relevance of the technical option across the different phases of the emergency

Examples of completed PRIMs are given in the case studies below, while blank matrix tables for both rapid-onset and slow-onset emergencies are presented in *Appendix 3.3* and can also be downloaded from the LEGS website. Note that none of the LEGS technical options are exclusive. In order to protect and strengthen livelihoods, an integrated response involving more than one technical option at a time may be appropriate, as well as different interventions implemented sequentially over the course of the emergency. The specific technical interventions, including detailed assessment checklists and guidance on selecting sub-options within them, are outlined in *Chapters 4–9*.

The findings of the initial assessment and the outcome of participatory planning discussions based on the PRIM, together with an analysis of the capacity and mandate of the intervening agency, should enable the selection of technical interventions that are *appropriate*, *feasible*, and *timely* to support and protect livestock-based livelihoods in an emergency.

PRIM case studies

The following case studies show how the PRIM can be used for different emergency types. In each case study, a PRIM matrix is followed by an explanation of the results.

Note that the PRIM is a tool designed to help in the planning process, based on the findings of assessments and the judgement of the participants. It should *not* be used to dictate action, and these examples are for illustration only. Participants should also be aware of potential biases based on individuals' personal interests or expertise when completing the matrix. It is also important to note that there is no universally correct PRIM for a given emergency; each PRIM is developed by participants based on their specific location and needs.

Case study A: Rapid-onset emergency – an earthquake in Asia

Table 3.2 ▶ PRIM of Case study A

Technical interventions	Livelihoods objectives			Emergency phases		
	Immediate benefits	Protect assets	Rebuild assets	Immediate aftermath	Early recovery	Recovery
Destocking	n/a	n/a	n/a			
Vet support	**	*****	*****	⟶		
Feed	**	*****	*****	⟶		
Water	*	*	*	⟶		
Shelter	***	***	***	⟶		
Provision of livestock	n/a	n/a	*****			⟶

Scoring against LEGS livelihoods objectives:

*****	Very positive impact on objective	**	Small impact on objective
*****	Good impact on objective	*	Very little impact on objective
***	Some impact on objective	n/a	Not appropriate

Emergency phases:
⟶ appropriate timing for the intervention

Notes on Case study A

- Commercial destocking cannot provide rapid assistance to crisis-affected households since, in this particular case, the normal market system is not operating. Slaughter destocking is most appropriate in cases where the livestock might otherwise die from lack of water or feed and are therefore less likely to bring significant benefits to affected households.

- Veterinary interventions could both provide some rapid assistance, by helping to keep surviving animals alive in the immediate aftermath, and make a significant contribution to protecting and rebuilding livestock assets in the early recovery and recovery phases.

- The provision of feed may contribute to protecting and rebuilding these livestock assets although it may not be of much rapid assistance. If there is advance warning of the earthquake, some measures may be taken to stockpile feed and water.

- The provision of water may provide some small benefit, depending on the effect of the earthquake on existing supplies.

- Shelter-related interventions may contribute both to immediate benefits and to protecting and rebuilding assets, depending on the types of livestock kept and their shelter needs. If sufficient warning is given, shelter provisions for livestock may help save their lives in an alarm phase by moving them out of and away from buildings that may collapse. In the immediate aftermath and early recovery phases, the provision of warm and/or dry shelter for affected animals is a significant contribution to the protecting and rebuilding of assets.

- In terms of rebuilding assets, provision of livestock may contribute significantly by helping those who have lost their stock to begin to recover some livestock assets. However, this can only take place in the recovery phase.

Case study B: Slow-onset emergency – a drought in Africa

Table 3.3 PRIM of Case study B

Technical interventions	Livelihoods objectives			Emergency phases			
	Immediate benefits	Protect assets	Rebuild assets	Alert	Alarm	Emergency	Recovery
Destocking	*****	***	**	→→→ •••►			
Vet support	*	*****	****	→→→→→→→→→→			
Feed	*	***	****	→→→→→→			
Water	*	***	****	→→→→→			
Shelter	n/a	n/a	n/a				
Provision of livestock	n/a	n/a	*****				→

Scoring against LEGS livelihoods objectives:

*****	Very positive impact on objective	**	Small impact on objective
****	Good impact on objective	*	Very little impact on objective
***	Some impact on objective	n/a	Not appropriate

Emergency phases:
➡ appropriate timing for the intervention

Notes on Case study B

- A slow-onset drought in Africa shows a very different pattern of interventions and timing compared with the Asian earthquake in *Case study A*. In the alert and alarm phases, commercial destocking can contribute significantly to providing immediate benefits to affected families through the provision of cash that can be used to support them. It can also contribute to a certain extent to protecting assets (the remaining livestock have less competition for scarce resources and also some of the cash may be used to support these remaining animals). If the timing of the intervention is delayed until the emergency phase, then commercial destocking may no longer be possible because the animals' condition will be too poor. In this case, slaughter destocking (shown by the dotted arrow) can provide some immediate benefits to affected households.

- In this example, because the drought is in the early stages (alert/alarm), the preference would be for commercial destocking rather than slaughter destocking, as the former places cash in the hands of the livestock keepers and encourages market processes.

- Animal health interventions, which may be carried out during all phases of a drought, can have a significant impact on protecting and rebuilding livestock assets through preventing death and disease in the herd and strengthening livestock resistance to drought.
- The provision of feed and water during the alarm and emergency phases of a drought can help to protect the remaining livestock assets and rebuild the herd for the future.
- In this particular example, the provision of shelter is not appropriate.
- In the recovery phase, the provision of livestock ('restocking') can make a significant contribution to rebuilding livestock assets.

The final case study shows how the combination of conflict and a slow-onset emergency can affect the appropriateness and feasibility of some of the options.

Case study C: Complex emergency – protracted conflict in Africa, worsened by drought

Table 3.4 PRIM of Case study C

Technical interventions	Livelihoods objectives			Emergency phases			
	Immediate benefits	Protect assets	Rebuild assets	Alert	Alarm	Emergency	Recovery
Destocking	***	*	*			···▶	
Vet support	*	*****	****	————————————————————▶			
Feed	*	*****	*****	——————————▶			
Water	*	**	**	——————————▶			
Shelter	***	***	***	————————————————————▶			
Provision of livestock	n/a	n/a	*****				———▶

Scoring against LEGS livelihoods objectives:

*****	Very positive impact on objective		**	Small impact on objective
****	Good impact on objective		*	Very little impact on objective
***	Some impact on objective		n/a	Not appropriate

Emergency phases:
➡ appropriate timing for the intervention

Notes on Case study C

- Comparing this PRIM with *Case study B*, most of the possible interventions (such as veterinary support, feed, water, and provision of livestock) remain appropriate and have the potential to deliver significant benefits to the affected communities.

- However, commercial destocking is not appropriate in this conflict situation since market systems and infrastructure are severely disrupted. Slaughter destocking (shown by the dotted arrow) could be possible, depending on the operational constraints under which agencies are working.

- The provision of feed has the potential to help protect and rebuild livestock assets, particularly for communities confined to camps and unable to take their stock to pasture. Similarly, the provision of water for livestock that cannot be taken to the usual water sources because of insecurity may help to protect and rebuild livestock assets.

- Shelter or enclosures for livestock, though irrelevant in *Case study B*, may become an important issue here because of displacement and insecurity (looting, for example).

- All these interventions depend on the ability of the agencies to operate within the conflict situation.

Indirect ways to achieve LEGS objectives: Cash transfers and vouchers

With the increasing use of cash transfers in humanitarian programmes, the use of cash-based responses constitutes an option for achieving the LEGS objectives. *Table 3.5* summarizes the most common types of cash transfer and provides examples of how they can be used. Detailed guides on market assessment and cash response mechanisms are listed in the *References* at the end of this chapter.

Table 3.5	Cash transfer definitions and examples of use

Cash transfer mechanisms	Definition
Unconditional cash transfers	*Money disbursed as a direct grant without conditions or work requirements* These can be grants provided in emergency or development settings (for example, as part of social protection programmes) to meet basic needs and/or to protect or recover livelihoods. Unconditional cash transfers are provided soon after an emergency once basic needs have been identified through assessments. Where markets are still functioning, they are an appropriate response because they allow households to prioritize their own needs.
Conditional cash transfers	*Money disbursed with the condition that recipients do something in return (such as attend school, plant seeds, or demobilize)* These transfers are often given in instalments and monitored to ensure that the money is being used appropriately before additional instalments can be received. Conditional transfers are sometimes used as a development response to encourage households to access certain services, such as keeping children in school, bringing children for vaccination, etc. Conditional transfers should not be provided unless the intended service is readily available and functioning to an acceptable standard.
Indirect cash transfers to reduce expenditure (and thus release income)	*Grants or waivers to reduce the cost of basic services, such as waivers for health-care user fees or grants to schools to cover education fees* These are mainly used in development settings, but a few examples exist for emergencies. Indirect transfers in livestock projects could include waivers of slaughterhouse fees, movement permit fees, market fees, veterinary fees, or else subsidized trucking costs, provision of fuel to water users' associations, or government subsidy/price caps on feed supplements.

Cash transfer mechanisms	Definition
Cash for work, employment, public works	*Payments using cash (or vouchers) for taking part in rehabilitation or construction of community assets* These can be part of emergency recovery programmes or social protection. Cash-for-work (CFW) projects can be implemented when there is a large amount of available labour and adequate micro-projects can be identified. The purpose of CFW is to ensure that beneficiaries earn enough income to meet basic needs and/or other essential long-term or short-term needs.
Vouchers	*A printed piece of paper, document or token that the recipient can exchange for a set quantity or value of goods* Vouchers can either specify a cash amount (exchangeable for any goods with any vendor) or specific commodities or services. Both cash and commodity vouchers are commonly designed to be exchanged in preselected shops with specified traders/service providers.

Source: Vetwork, 2011, based on Jaspars et al., 2007; Harvey, 2007; and Horn Relief, 2010

Some of these mechanisms may be appropriate for delivering livestock interventions in emergencies, as shown in *Table 3.6*. Further information is given in each technical chapter.

Table 3.6	Options for using cash transfer mechanisms to deliver LEGS technical interventions

Technical interventions and options	Types of cash transfer				
	Unconditional cash grant	Conditional cash grant	Cash for work (CFW)	Indirect grants	Vouchers
Destocking Commercial destocking Slaughter destocking	* *			√	√ √
Veterinary support Clinical vet services Support to public sector functions	√	√		√	√
Feed Emergency feeding in situ Feed camps	√	√ √			√ √
Water Water points Water trucking	√	√	√		√
Shelter Temporary livestock shelter Longer-lasting livestock shelter	√	√ √	√ √		√ √
Provision of livestock Replacing livestock assets Building livestock assets	√	√ √			√ √

NB: * *Both commercial and slaughter destocking may be considered as a type of unconditional cash transfer, in that households receive a cash payment in return for their livestock assets.*
Source: Vetwork, 2011

Appendix 3.1: Selected emergency warning and classification systems

- *Coping Strategies Index.* Designed by CARE, this is a rapid assessment methodology of household food security based on four key categories of change: dietary change; increasing short-term food access; decreasing numbers of people to feed; and rationing. Weighted scores result in an index giving current and anticipated relative food security status.

- *Famine Early Warning Systems Network (FEWS-NET).* This initiative is funded by the United States Agency for International Development (USAID) to provide early warning information on food security threats, create information networks, and build local capacity for provision and sharing of information.

- *Global Information and Early Warning System (GIEWS).* This is a Food and Agriculture Organization (FAO) service providing reports on the world food situation and early warning of potential food crises in individual countries. GIEWS also conducts food supply assessment missions with the World Food Programme (WFP) to provide information to governments and international agencies.

- *Household Economy Approach (HEA).* Developed by Save the Children UK, HEA uses the sustainable livelihoods framework as a baseline to ascertain livelihood zones, and then analyses the impact of an emergency on the disruption of livelihoods, enabling the quantification of food needs.

- *Integrated Food Security and Humanitarian Phase Classification (IPC).* Designed by the FAO-managed Food Security and Nutrition Analysis Unit for Somalia (FSNAU) to respond to the need for consistent classification of food security situations across locations and emergencies, IPC uses a reference table of human welfare and livelihood indicators linked to strategic response and early warning. It also includes cartographic protocols for communicating visually complex information, analysis templates for documenting evidence, and population tables.

- *Standardized Monitoring and Assessment of Relief and Transitions (SMART) Protocol.* This is an inter-agency initiative that provides reliable and consistent data on mortality, nutritional status, and food security. It also facilitates decision-making. SMART has developed a survey manual and an analytical software program; it has also developed a database on complex emergencies called CE-DAT.

- *Vulnerability Assessment Committees (VACs).* Established by the Southern Africa Development Community (SADC) countries to coordinate vulnerability and emergency needs assessment in member countries, the VACs combine analyses of existing secondary data with primary livelihoods data.

References to Appendix 3.1

FEWS-NET (Famine and Early Warning Systems Network) [online] <www.fews.net/> [accessed 15 May 2014].

FSNAU (Food Security and Nutrition Analysis Unit for Somalia) (2006) *Integrated Food Security and Humanitarian Phase Classification: Technical Manual, Version 1*, FAO/FSNAU, Nairobi, <http://www.fao.org/docrep/009/a0748e/a0748e00.htm> [accessed 15 May 2014].

See also the Integrated Food Security Phase Classification (IPC) website: <www.ipcinfo.org/> [accessed 15 May 2014].

GIEWS (Global Information and Early Warning System) [online] <http://www.fao.org/GIEWS/english/index.htm> [accessed 19 May 2014].

LEGS (Livestock Emergency Guidelines and Standards) (2014), *Livestock Emergency Guidelines and Standards, 2nd Edition*, Practical Action Publishing: Rugby.

Save the Children UK (2005) *The Household Economy Approach: What is It and What can It be Used For?* Save the Children UK, London. Available from: <http://www.livestock-emergency.net/resources/assessment-and-response/> [accessed 15 May 2014].

Save the Children UK (2008) *The Household Economy Approach: A Guide for Programme Planners and Policy Makers*, Save the Children UK, London, <http://www.savethechildren.org.uk/resources/online-library/household-economy-approach-guide-programme-planners-and-policy-makers> [accessed 15 May 2014].

SMART (Standardized Monitoring and Assessment of Relief Transitions) (2005) *Measuring Mortality, Nutritional Status and Food Security in Crisis Situations: The SMART Protocol, Version 1*, SMART, Tulane University, New Orleans, <www.smartindicators.org/> [accessed 15 May 2014].

Appendix 3.2: Participatory methods

Method	Assessment checklist*	Topic
Daily/seasonal calendar	1.5	Gender/age roles and seasonality
Gender analysis – access to resources tool (see Pasteur, 2002)	1.5 1.7	Gender control and access to resources Gender relations and power analysis
Mapping	2.5 2.6 2.7 2.7 2.9 2.10	Extent of affected area Vulnerable groups affected 'Usual' and emergency services and facilities Natural-resource mapping (before and after): grazing; water; movements Impact on environment Seasonal changes
Timeline/time trend	2.4 2.7 2.7 2.7 2.8	Stages of the emergency Livestock sales trends Livestock price trends Livestock productivity trends Livestock disease trends
Proportional piling	1.3, 1.4 2.6 2.6 2.7, 2.8	Sources of income/food Changes in nutritional status Changes in human disease Livestock sales, price, productivity changes
Ranking/scoring	1.3, 1.4 2.8 3.5	Sources of income/food Livestock condition, morbidity, diseases History and effectiveness of previous response
Wealth ranking	2.6	Affected population (to inform targeting)
Venn diagrams	1.6 3.1, 3.2	Customary institutions' roles and relationships Key actors and coordination

Numbers refer to the key questions at the beginning of the chapter.

Further information on participatory rural appraisal (PRA) methodologies is listed in the *References* to this chapter.

Appendix 3.3: LEGS Participatory Response Identification Matrix

Table 3.7	Rapid-onset emergency PRIM

Technical interventions	Livelihoods objectives			Emergency phases		
	Immediate benefits	Protect assets	Rebuild assets	Immediate aftermath	Early recovery	Recovery
Destocking						
Vet support						
Feed						
Water						
Shelter						
Provision of livestock						

Table 3.8	Slow-onset emergency PRIM

Technical interventions	Livelihoods objectives			Emergency phases			
	Immediate benefits	Protect assets	Rebuild assets	Alert	Alarm	Emergency	Recovery
Destocking							
Vet support							
Feed							
Water							
Shelter							
Provision of livestock							

Scoring against LEGS livelihoods objectives:

*****	Very positive impact on objective	**	Small impact on objective
****	Good impact on objective	*	Very little impact on objective
***	Some impact on objective	n/a	Not appropriate

Emergency phases:
➡ appropriate timing for the intervention

References and further reading

ActionAid International (undated) *Participatory Vulnerability Analysis: A Step-by-Step Guide for Field Staff*, ActionAid International, London. Available from: <http://www.livestock-emergency.net/resources/assessment-and-response/> [accessed 17 May 2014].

Albu, M. (2010) *Emergency Market Mapping and Analysis Toolkit (EMMA),* Practical Action Publishing, Rugby.

Barrett, C.B., Bell, R., Lentz, E.C. and Maxwell, D.G. (2009) 'Market information and food insecurity response analysis', *Food Security* 1: 151–168 <http://dx.doi.org/10.1007/s12571-009-0021-3>.

Catley, A. (2005) *Participatory Epidemiology: A Guide for Trainers*, African Union/Interafrican Bureau for Animal Resources, Nairobi, <http://www.participatoryepidemiology.info/userfiles/PE-Guide-electronic-copy.pdf> [accessed 17 May 2014].

Catley, A., Alders, R.G, and Wood, J.L.N. (2012) 'Participatory epidemiology: approaches, methods, experiences', *The Veterinary Journal* 191: 151–160. <http://dx.doi.org/10.1016/j.tvjl.2011.03.010>.

Currion, P. (2014) 'Sphere for Assessments', The Sphere Project and ACAPS, Geneva.

FAO (undated) *Gateway to Farm Animal Welfare* [website], FAO, Rome, <http://www.fao.org/ag/againfo/themes/animal-welfare/en/> [accessed 17 May 2014].

FAO and ILO (Food and Agriculture Organization of the United Nations and International Labour Organization) (2009) *The Livelihood Assessment Toolkit: Analysing and Responding to the Impact of Disasters on the Livelihoods of People*, FAO and ILO, Rome and Geneva, <http://www.fao.org/fileadmin/user_upload/emergencies/docs/LAT_Brochure_LoRes.pdf> [accessed 17 May 2014].

FAWC (Farm Animal Welfare Council) (2012) *Opinion on Contingency Planning for Farm Animal Welfare in Disasters and Emergencies,* FAWC, London. Available from: <http://www.defra.gov.uk/fawc/> [accessed 23 May 2014].

FAWC (undated) *Five Freedoms* [web page], Farm Animal Welfare Council, London, <http://www.fawc.org.uk/freedoms.htm> [accessed 19 May 2014].

Harvey, P. (2007) *Cash-Based Responses in Emergencies*, Humanitarian Policy Group (HPG), Overseas Development Institute (ODI), London, <http://www.odi.org.uk/sites/odi.org.uk/files/odi-assets/publications-opinion-files/265.pdf> [accessed 29 May 2014].

Harvey, P. and Bailey, S. (2011) *Cash Transfer Programming in Emergencies*, Humanitarian Practice Network, Good Practice Review No. 11, ODI, London.

Heath, S.E. (1999) *Animal Management in Disasters: A Handbook for Emergency Responders and Animal Owners*, Mosby, Maryland Heights, Missouri.

Hermon-Duc, S. (2012) *MPESA Project Analysis: Exploring the Use of Cash Transfers Using Cell Phones in Pastoral Areas*, Télécoms Sans Frontières and Vétérinaires Sans Frontières, Germany and Nairobi.

Holland, J. (ed.) (2013) *Who Counts? The Power of Participatory Statistics*, Practical Action Publishing, Rugby.

Horn Relief (2010) *Guidelines for Cash Interventions in Somalia*, Horn Relief, Nairobi.

ICRC and IFRC (International Committee for the Red Cross and International Federation of Red Cross and Red Crescent Societies) (2007) *Guidelines for Cash Transfer Programming*, ICRC and IFRC, Geneva.

IDS (Institute of Development Studies) (2005) *Desk Review: Identification of Factors that Trigger Emergency Needs Assessments in Slow-Onset Crises*, Strengthening Emergency Needs Assessment Capacity (SENAC) Project, Emergency Needs Assessment Branch (ODAN), World Food Programme, Brighton, <http://www.ids.ac.uk/files/FinalTriggeringFactorsFeb06.pdf> [accessed 17 May 2014].

IIED (International Institute for Environment and Development) (1995) *RRA Notes 20: Livestock* [online], IIED, London, <http://pubs.iied.org/6089IIED.html?k=PLA Notes&r=p> [accessed 17 May 2014].

IIED (2002) *PLA Notes 45: Community-Based Animal Healthcare*, IIED, London, <http://pubs.iied.org/9218IIED.html?k=PLA Notes&r=p> [accessed 17 May 2014].

Jaspars, S., Harvey, P., Hudspeth, C. and Rumble, L. (2007) *A Review of UNICEF's Role in Cash Transfers to Emergency-Affected Populations,* Working Paper, United Nation's Children's Fund (UNICEF) Office of Emergency Programmes (EMOPS), Geneva.

Kelly, C. (2005) *Guidelines for Rapid Environmental Impact Assessment in Disasters*, [Rapid Environmental Assessment Tool], Benfield Hazard Research Centre, UCL, London and CARE International. Available from: <http://www.proactnetwork.org/proactwebsite/resources/tools-for-environmental-assessment> [accessed 26 June 2014].

Mattinen, H. and Ogden, K. (2006) 'Cash-based interventions: lessons from southern Somalia', *Disasters* 30(3): 297–315 <http://dx.doi.org/10.1111/j.0361-3666.2005.00322.x>.

OIE (World Organisation for Animal Health) (2012b) *Terrestrial Animal Health Code*, 22nd edn, vol. 1, OIE, Paris, <http://www.oie.int/international-standard-setting/terrestrial-code> [accessed 17 May 2014].

Oxfam (2007) *Programme Guidelines on Animal Welfare*, Oxfam, Oxford.

Oxfam (2008) *Situation Analysis Knowledge Map*. Interactive program available on request from Oxfam. Contact: <EFSLteam@Oxfam.org.uk>.

Pasteur, K. (2002) 'Gender analysis for sustainable livelihoods frameworks: tools and links to other sources', draft. Available from: <http://www.livestock-emergency.net/resources/assessment-and-response/> [accessed 17 May 2014].

Pretty, J.N., Guijt, I., Thompson, J. and Scoones, I. (1995) *Participatory Learning and Action: A Trainer's Guide*, IIED, London, <http://pubs.iied.org/6021IIED.html?c=part&r=p> [accessed 17 May 2014].

ProVention Consortium (2007) *Community Risk Assessment Toolkit*, ProVention Consortium, Geneva, <http://www.eldis.org/go/topics/resource-guides/climate-change/key-issues/disaster-risk-reduction/disaster-risk-reduction-thematic-areas&id=31537&type=Document#.U3pe1rkU_Vh> [accessed 17 May 2014].

SEEP (Small Enterprise Education and Promotion) Network (2010) *Minimum Economic Recovery Standards,* SEEP Network, Washington, DC, <http://www.seepnetwork.org/minimum-economic-recovery-standards-resources-174.php> [accessed 15 May 2014].

Sphere Project (2011) *Humanitarian Charter and Minimum Standards in Humanitarian Response* (the Sphere Handbook), The Sphere Project, Geneva. See Core Standard 3: Assessment (pp. 61–65). <www.sphereproject.org/> [accessed 15 May 2014].

Trench, P., Rowley, J., Diarra, M., Sano, F. and Keita, B. (2007) *Beyond any Drought: Root Causes of Chronic Vulnerability in the Sahel*, The Sahel Working Group, IIED, London, <http://pubs.iied.org/pdfs/G02317.pdf> [accessed 17 May 2014].

UNHCR and CARE (United Nations High Commissioner for Refugees and Cooperative for Assistance and Relief Everywhere) (2009) *Framework for Assessing, Monitoring and Evaluating the Environment in Refugee-Related Operations* (FRAME Toolkit), joint UNHCR and CARE project, <http://www.unhcr.org/4a97d1039.html> [accessed 15 May 2014].

UNICEF (United Nations Children's Fund) (2005) *Emergency Field Handbook: A Guide for UNICEF Staff*, UNICEF, New York, <http://www.unicef.org/publications/files/UNICEF_EFH_2005.pdf> [accessed 17 May 2014].

Vetwork (2011) *The Use of Cash Transfers in Livestock Emergencies and their Incorporation into the Livestock Emergency Guidelines and Standards (LEGS)*, Animal Production and Health Working Paper No. 1, FAO, Rome. Available from: <http://www.livestock-emergency.net/resources/general-resources-legs-specific/>.

Young, H. and Jaspars, S. (2006) *Food-Security Assessments in Emergencies: A Livelihoods Approach*. Humanitarian Practice Network Paper 36, ODI, London. <http://www.odihpn.org/documents/networkpaper036.pdf> [accessed 17 May 2014].

Zicherman, N. with Khan, A., Street, A., Heyer, H. and Chevreau, O. (2011) *Applying Conflict Sensitivity in Emergency Response: Current Practice and Ways Forward*, Humanitarian Practice Network Paper No. 70, ODI, London.

Notes

1. Participatory inquiry is the systematic (and if necessary rapid) analysis of problems, opportunities, and solutions in participation with local people. When conducted well, participatory inquiry seeks to understand the perceptions of vulnerable and marginalized groups and therefore information is automatically presented by each of the groups in question.

Technical standards
for destocking

Destocking

Standard 1
Standard 1
Assessment and planning

Standard 2	Standard 3
Standard 2	**Standard 3**
Commercial destocking	Slaughter destocking

Introduction

During slow-onset emergencies such as drought, the condition of animals deteriorates as feed and water become scarce. Destocking is the removal of affected animals before they become emaciated, lose their value, die, or pose a risk to public health. Destocking releases the value tied up in these animals and provides much needed cash (or meat) to vulnerable communities.

This chapter discusses the importance of destocking in emergency response. It presents the options for destocking interventions together with tools to determine their appropriateness. The Standards, Key actions, and Guidance notes follow each option. Case studies are found at the end of the chapter. They are followed by appendices containing checklists for assessment and monitoring and evaluation. Key references are listed at the end.

Links to the LEGS livelihoods objectives

Destocking can provide immediate assistance to affected families, protecting their remaining livestock and relating directly to the first and second LEGS livelihoods objectives. It can:

- provide immediate benefits to crisis-affected communities using existing livestock resources, by providing cash from the sale of surplus or unmarketable animals
- protect key livestock assets, by ensuring the survival of remaining animals.

The importance of destocking in emergency response

Destocking is a common response to drought when animals would otherwise deteriorate and die. It allows potential livestock losses to be converted into cash or meat. Removing animals relieves pressure on scarce feed, grazing, and water supplies to the benefit of the remaining stock. Meat from slaughtered animals can supplement the diets of vulnerable families. However, destocking is not usually applicable in rapid-onset emergencies like earthquakes and floods since livestock are either killed or they survive. However, when natural disasters such as cyclones or fires destroy available feed supplies, the removal of animals may be an appropriate response.

Destocking also contributes to two of the animal welfare 'five freedoms', as described in the Introduction: *freedom from hunger and thirst* and *freedom from discomfort*. Removing animals to a more favourable location may allow them to resume their normal behaviour. Where necessary, slaughter destocking will relieve animals from the pain and distress associated with starvation and thirst. As destocking involves handling, transporting, and slaughtering animals, special attention is needed to ensure they do not suffer pain, fear, or distress.

➡ Options for destocking

The two most common destocking interventions are commercial destocking and slaughter destocking.

Option 1: Commercial destocking

Commercial destocking supports livestock traders when the livestock market begins to fail. Market failure can result from the following: weak demand; a poor supply of animals; the inaccessibility of animals; animals in poor condition; and unwillingness of livestock keepers to sell. The result is usually a collapse in livestock prices and traders withdrawing from the market.

The aim of commercial destocking is to assist the marketing of livestock before they deteriorate in condition and value and become impossible to sell. There are several benefits:

- It provides cash for the affected communities.
- It promotes a longer-term relationship between traders and livestock keepers.
- It can have an impact on larger numbers of livestock and their owners.
- It is one of the more cost-effective drought interventions since it does not involve agencies purchasing animals directly.

To succeed, commercial destocking requires an active private trade in livestock and an accessible domestic or export demand for meat or live animals. Animals do not always go directly to an abattoir but may be sent elsewhere to regain condition. They can then be slaughtered or resold at a later date.

Typical support to livestock traders includes assistance in bringing together buyers and sellers of animals and facilitating short-term credit, subsidies, and tax exemptions. Bringing the livestock owners and traders together is the simplest and most effective intervention.

Some aid agencies and governments have intervened directly to purchase animals in emergencies rather than work with the livestock traders. Despite good intentions, caution is required to ensure that such activities do not undermine the longer-term sustainability of the private market.

Option 2: Slaughter destocking

Unlike commercial destocking, slaughter destocking is initiated by external agencies rather than private traders. It is appropriate when the local market for livestock has failed and traders have withdrawn. Invariably animals are in a poor condition and prices have collapsed. In these cases, the agency purchases animals and arranges for their humane slaughter. Fresh meat is then distributed to the affected communities. Because fresh meat is perishable, immediate action must be taken to preserve it by salting, boiling, or drying if it cannot be distributed straight away.

Slaughter destocking is a more costly option than commercial destocking as it involves the direct purchase of animals. The cost is partly offset by the additional benefits from meat distribution, including employment opportunities and the processing of hides and skins. There are also animal welfare and public health benefits associated with improved slaughter and meat processing. Beneficiaries include:

- those eligible to sell animals for slaughter, especially female-headed households and those from marginalized communities
- those eligible to receive meat, especially large families, single-parent and orphan households, the elderly, and other vulnerable groups; (if there are sufficient quantities, it may be simpler to distribute the meat equally to the whole community to avoid potential resentment – often the meat is given to another relief agency for distribution as part of a broader food relief programme, which may include schools, hospitals, and prisons)
- those who may be employed in the slaughter and processing of animals, thus providing income, and skills for the future.

Additional option 3: Slaughter for disposal

When animals are so emaciated or diseased that they are unfit for human consumption, the decision is made by the relevant veterinary or public health authorities based on ante- and post-mortem inspections. In such cases, the carcasses must be disposed of to minimize risk to public health. Considerations for carcass disposal are discussed in *Chapter 5, Veterinary support*.

The advantages, disadvantages, and key requirements of the different options are summarized in *Table 4.1*.

Table 4.1 Advantages, disadvantages, and key requirements of destocking options

Option	Advantages	Disadvantages	Key requirements
1. Commercial destocking	• Provides cash for immediate needs and/or reinvestment in livestock • Builds on existing coping strategies • Relieves pressure on scarce feed/grazing and water supplies • Can handle large numbers of animals • Is relatively low in cost (majority of costs borne by traders) • Promotes longer-term relationships between buyers and sellers • Has potential animal welfare benefits	• Has to be carried out before stock deteriorate significantly • Targeting vulnerable groups is difficult • Carries potential risks to animal welfare through inappropriate handling and transport • Remaining animals may be insufficient to rebuild stock numbers later	• Interested traders • Willing sellers • Accessible domestic or export markets • Infrastructure: roads; holding grounds; feed and water; security • Conducive attitude within agencies to livestock trade and credit provision • Conducive attitude within agencies to engage with the private sector
2. Slaughter destocking for consumption	• Provides cash for immediate needs and/ or reinvestment • Relieves pressure on scarce feed/grazing and water supplies • Provides supplementary food relief • Surplus fresh meat can be preserved • Provides employment opportunities within local community	• Operationally more complex • Higher administration costs • More expensive, as it includes the purchase of animals • Less long-term sustainability[1] • Less conducive to handling larger number of animals • Remaining animals may be insufficient to rebuild stock numbers later	• Local institutions able to organize, manage, and help target beneficiaries • Coordination between implementing agencies to agree methodologies and, in particular, pricing strategies • Food relief operations willing to accept meat • Implementing agency with organizational capacity to manage the programme • Slaughter infrastructure available or potential to construct • Conducive public health policy • Agency-managed slaughter and distribution appropriate to cultural norms
3. Slaughter for disposal	• Relieves animal suffering • Livestock keepers get something back from a worthless asset	• No food relief or longer-term benefits	• Livestock in terminally poor condition without market or food value • Capacity to undertake ante- and post-mortem inspections

Timing of interventions

The stage of the emergency usually determines the type of destocking undertaken. Removal of marketable animals (commercial destocking) is most effective in the alert and alarm phases of a slow-onset emergency (see *Glossary*). Slaughter destocking invariably takes place in the late alarm, emergency, or early recovery phases when livestock are in such poor condition that they are unmarketable (*Table 4.2*).

Livestock keepers rarely value their animals solely in financial terms. They take into account many factors, including the chance of their animals surviving – in whatever condition. At the height of a drought, they may be willing to sell animals at almost any price, but at the first signs of rain they may change their minds. Flexibility is needed to respond quickly to changing circumstances and to switch resources into alternative interventions.

Table 4.2 Possible timing of destocking interventions

Options	Rapid onset			Slow onset			
	Immediate aftermath	Early recovery	Recovery	Alert	Alarm	Emergency	Recovery
1. Commercial destocking	Generally not applicable			⟶			
2. Slaughter destocking – consumption	Generally not applicable				⟶		
3. Slaughter for disposal	⟶					⟶	

Links to Sphere and other LEGS chapters

An important aim of destocking is to improve the survival chances of the remaining livestock, especially the core breeding animals. Destocking is therefore often undertaken with other LEGS interventions as part of an integrated approach. Typically, these include the provision of veterinary support, feed, and water (see *Chapters 5–7*). The LEGS Participatory Response Identification Matrix (PRIM) described in *Chapter 3* is a valuable tool in making these assessments. *Chapter 5, Veterinary support* contains further information on the disposal of carcasses.

After a drought, rebuilding stock numbers to levels that can sustain a household can take years. In pastoralist and agro-pastoralist communities, livestock interventions alone may not be enough. Additional humanitarian assistance such as food aid may be required. The Sphere Handbook provides detailed guidance on this.

Cross-cutting themes and other issues to consider

Gender

In many societies, women and men have different roles in owning and managing the various species of livestock. Understanding gender implications is important when choosing destocking options and selecting beneficiaries. For example, meat distribution will help women feed their families. However, cash from selling animals may increase male spending power, over which the women may have little control. Extra attention is needed to ensure that widows and female-headed households are not excluded as beneficiaries.

HIV/AIDS

HIV/AIDS is responsible for creating vulnerable households, many of which are headed by single parents or orphans. People living with HIV/AIDS (PLHIV) may be subjected to discrimination within their communities and excluded from beneficiary groups. Those taking antiretroviral drugs (ARVs) have additional nutritional requirements to optimize their therapy, which can be supplied by relatively small quantities of meat in their diets.

Protection

Both livestock and herders can be at risk from rustling and ethnic conflict. Destocking activities can exacerbate the risk if they involve carrying large amounts of cash or bringing large numbers of animals together in one location. Increasingly, agencies are using vouchers instead of cash where security is a risk.

Environment and climate

There are environmental implications, both positive and negative, associated with destocking, some of which remain contentious. Issues to be aware of include:

- Slaughter of animals generates local waste (including condemned carcasses) that needs to be disposed of safely to avoid pollution. Tanning of hides and skins has similar issues.
- Removal of large numbers of livestock can relieve the localized pressure on natural resources during a time of scarcity, such as a drought.

- Concentration of animals around camps and markets may have a short-term detrimental effect on the immediate environment.
- Where indigenous breeds are under threat, care should be taken not to exacerbate any loss of local biodiversity.

Targeting

Community participation is essential in order to ensure the fair selection of beneficiaries, and this should be based on agreed criteria and recent vulnerability assessments. Private traders aim to maximize profit and may exclude communities with poor access, poor security, or inadequate facilities. Any assistance given to livestock traders should therefore be conditional so as to ensure that the vulnerable are not excluded.

Coping strategies and indigenous knowledge

Livestock-owning communities traditionally have their own coping strategies for responding to emergencies. Their husbandry skills and knowledge of the local animals are invaluable in selecting which animals to keep and which to destock. Invariably, they also have expertise in slaughtering as well as meat preparation and preservation.

Camp settings

Special attention may be required in camps that contain displaced livestock keepers. Large concentrations of animals make them an attractive target for thieves, so additional security measures may be required. Slaughtering animals, distributing meat, or disposing of carcasses in camps also increases public health risks, including poor hygiene and contamination.

The Standards

Destocking enables livestock keepers to salvage some value from animals that, without intervention, may have little or no value. *Figure 4.1* presents a decision-making tree of the key questions to ask in planning a destocking initiative. Commercial destocking is only feasible before animals lose condition and market prices collapse. Beyond this point, slaughter destocking may be the only alternative. Preparedness and early analysis of the situation are essential in order to decide whether destocking is a feasible and appropriate response.

Figure 4.1 Decision-making tree for destocking options

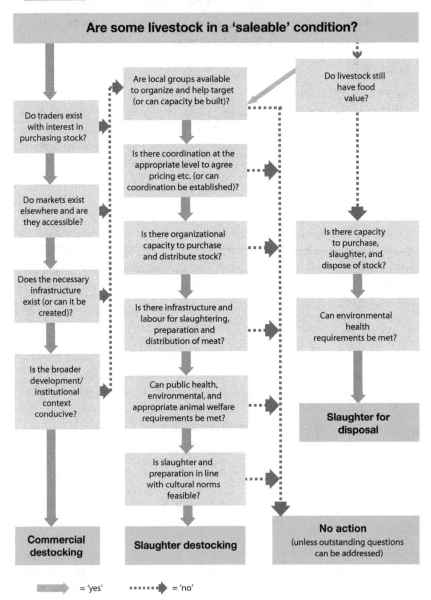

Are some livestock in a 'saleable' condition?

Are local groups available to organize and help target (or can capacity be built)?

Do livestock still have food value?

Do traders exist with interest in purchasing stock?

Is there coordination at the appropriate level to agree pricing etc. (or can coordination be established)?

Do markets exist elsewhere and are they accessible?

Is there organizational capacity to purchase and distribute stock?

Is there capacity to purchase, slaughter, and dispose of stock?

Does the necessary infrastructure exist (or can it be created)?

Is there infrastructure and labour for slaughtering, preparation and distribution of meat?

Can environmental health requirements be met?

Is the broader development/ institutional context conducive?

Can public health, environmental, and appropriate animal welfare requirements be met?

Slaughter for disposal

Is slaughter and preparation in line with cultural norms feasible?

Commercial destocking

Slaughter destocking

No action
(unless outstanding questions can be addressed)

➡ = 'yes'   ┅┅➡ = 'no'

Note
The result 'No action (unless outstanding questions can be addressed)' does not necessarily mean that no intervention should take place, but rather that further training or capacity building may be required in order to be able to answer 'yes' to the key questions.

The type of destocking activity selected is appropriate to market conditions and the state of the livestock.

Key actions

- Assess and act upon relevant early warning data and emergency preparedness plans (see *Guidance notes 1* and *2*).
- Monitor the livestock market closely (see *Guidance note 3*).
- Monitor livestock condition and welfare closely (see *Guidance note 4*).
- Consider commercial destocking only when traders are willing to buy, and animals are in a suitable condition (see *Guidance notes 3* and *4*).
- Ensure destocking involves appropriate species, age, and type of animal, depending on local circumstances, knowledge, and practices (see *Guidance note 5*).
- Ensure assessments take into account the broader development and institutional context of the emergency (see *Guidance note 6*).
- Ensure the affected communities are fully involved in planning and assessing activities (see *Guidance note 7*).
- Assess the security situation to ensure the safety of livestock, their keepers, and agency staff (see *Guidance note 8*).
- Prepare exit strategies in advance (see *Guidance note 9*).

Guidance notes

1. **Early warning and emergency preparedness.** Most drought-affected areas have some form of early warning scheme and/or emergency preparedness plan that can alert agencies to consider destocking.

2. **Timing.** Destocking activities must be relevant to the phase of the emergency (*Table 4.2*).

3. **Monitoring livestock markets.** Increased numbers of animals for sale without a corresponding increase in demand, or falling livestock prices may indicate 'distress sales', where livestock keepers try to salvage some value from their animals through the normal market. A 25 per cent drop in livestock prices or a 25 per cent increase in the cereal–livestock price ratio

is commonly regarded as a trigger point for initiating destocking. See also the destocking assessment checklist in *Appendix 4.1*.

4. **Monitoring livestock condition.** Deteriorating livestock condition may be an indicator of impending crisis with important animal welfare considerations. Local knowledge can determine if the condition of animals is worse than usual for the time of year.

5. **Which animals to destock.** Removing cattle has the greatest impact on the immediate environment and injects the most cash into the local economy. However, with cattle there are equity and gender issues, as vulnerable groups, including women, may be excluded. The inclusion of sheep and goats will allow more vulnerable groups to benefit. As a general principle, young breeding female stock should be excluded, as they are required for rebuilding the herds/flocks of the future.

6. **Development and institutional context.** The broader context of the emergency needs to be understood to ensure that the risks and opportunities associated with destocking are identified (see *Core standard 7: Policy and advocacy*). Pertinent information may include:

   - restrictions on cross-border trade and the internal movement of livestock; licensing/tax regimes; access to credit and money transfer; public health and veterinary regulations; and infrastructure
   - assistance provided by other agencies to ensure activities are coordinated and do not compete with each other
   - policies of the implementing agency, which may regulate their involvement with the private sector or with credit provision as well as how they can acquire animals or local services.

7. **Community involvement.** Arrangements (usually a coordination group) for community involvement should be established – key partners, beneficiaries (including women), representatives of the local authorities, and other agencies operating similar schemes should all be included.

8. **Security.** The extent to which destocking may aggravate existing security problems needs to be assessed. Agencies have a responsibility to protect and ensure the safety of their staff and contractors. Alternatives to carrying cash, such as vouchers, should be explored.

9. **Exit strategies.** To ensure destocking has no long-term adverse consequences, it is important to plan how and when operations will finish.

Flexibility is needed to accommodate sudden changes in circumstances (market prices, condition of animals, onset of rain, etc.) that could affect the willingness of livestock keepers to sell animals or traders to participate in the market.

Destocking standard 2: Commercial destocking

Support is provided for selling marketable animals.

Key actions

- Involve the affected communities (see *Guidance note 1*).
- Assess demand for meat and animals, and identify weaknesses in value/supply chain (see *Guidance note 2*).
- Identify key partnerships (see *Guidance note 3*).
- Select areas for intervention, taking account of available animals, infrastructure, and security (see *Guidance note 4*).
- Agree and publicize criteria for selecting animals and setting pricing guidelines (see *Guidance note 5*).
- Assess transaction costs (see *Guidance note 6*).
- Identify and assess support essential for the success of the intervention (see *Guidance note 7*).
- Provide and monitor essential ongoing support (see *Guidance notes 8* and *9*).

Guidance notes

1. **Consultations and coordination.** The aim of a coordination group (see *Destocking standard 1, Guidance note 7*) is to oversee and evaluate activities and to ensure that the most vulnerable people are not excluded. The group should also act to pre-empt and resolve disputes. Participation of trader representatives is essential.

2. **Livestock market and value/supply chains assessed.** There must be a demand to absorb the extra animals entering the market as a result of a destocking initiative. This may be a terminal (domestic or export) market or an intermediate market for holding or fattening weakened animals. Information on prices, number of animals sold, supply and demand patterns, market facilities, and trade networks may be available from government or

parastatal departments (Ministry of Agriculture, Ministry of Trade, Statistics Office, etc.).

3. **Partnerships.** Successful commercial destocking is dependent on partnerships between the implementing agency and the private traders in livestock. Trade associations may assist in identifying suitable partners. Where possible, a core group of committed partners should be identified who have the interest and capacity to lead the initiative (see *Case study 4.1*).

4. **Intervention areas.** Selection of appropriate locations for commercial destocking should be based on assessments of:

   - the prevailing security situation as it affects traders, livestock keepers, and agency staff
   - a sufficient supply of animals for sale
   - livestock traders willing to buy
   - suitable infrastructure: roads, temporary markets, holding grounds, etc.
   - veterinary restrictions on moving animals.

5. **Livestock selection and pricing.** Commercial destocking aims to facilitate the normal market in difficult circumstances. Ideally, it also establishes new and continuing relationships between livestock keepers and traders. The species and types of animals purchased should be similar to those marketed under normal conditions – generally surplus males. The prices paid for livestock supported by commercial destocking should be agreed within the coordination group (see *Guidance note 1* above) to ensure transparency and fairness.

6. **Transaction costs.** Fees for markets, movement permits, abattoirs, and meat inspection are transaction costs usually borne by the trader. If these costs are too high, they may restrict trade in the more remote markets or of animals in poorer condition. These fees are also important sources of income for often cash-strapped local institutions. Paying such fees directly may be preferable to temporary suspensions.

7. **Key support.** It is important to understand the critical constraints and weaknesses when markets are under stress so as to identify the appropriate support required. In order not to disrupt the normal market,

support should be the minimum required to facilitate and overcome the immediate constraints. Support may include:

- bringing interested traders and livestock keepers together by organizing and publicizing temporary markets and by providing holding facilities, additional security arrangements, on-site feed and water, arbitration services, etc.

- providing credit (or facilitating access to credit) for traders to purchase animals

- supporting transport costs to remote areas – fuel subsidies may be necessary to encourage traders to enter these markets; opportunities may exist to make use of empty trucks returning from carrying relief supplies into the affected areas

- compensating local authorities for temporary reductions/suspensions of local fees and levies.

8. **Ensuring ongoing support.** Having identified the support required, it is important that the agency ensures it has the necessary resources for the duration of the activity. Support should be flexible enough to respond to changing circumstances, such as when the condition of the animals deteriorates to a level where there is no viable market for them.

9. **Monitoring.** It is important that qualitative and quantitative records of the operation are kept for evaluation, impact assessment, and documentation of best practices. See the destocking monitoring and evaluation indicators in *Appendix 4.2*.

Destocking standard 3: Slaughter destocking

Value is salvaged from crisis-affected livestock to provide cash, meat, and employment to affected communities.

Key actions

- Involve the affected communities (see *Guidance note 1*).
- Determine purchase sites and market dates and publicize them through community participation (see *Guidance note 2*).
- Agree on purchase prices and payment methods for each species and class of animal (see *Guidance notes 3, 4,* and *5*).

- Agree on criteria for selecting beneficiaries and in-kind contributions, and identify beneficiaries (see *Guidance notes 6, 7,* and *8*).
- Agree on criteria for selecting animals for slaughter (see *Guidance note 9*).
- Agree on criteria for distributing fresh or dry meat (see *Guidance note 10*).
- Follow local customs concerning slaughter, butchering, and preservation methods, and observe animal welfare standards (see *Guidance note 11*).
- Assess and act upon public health risks associated with animal slaughter (see *Guidance note 12*).
- Assess and agree on opportunities for processing hides and skins (see *Guidance note 6*).
- Safely dispose of carcasses unfit for human consumption (see *Guidance note 13*).

Guidance notes

1. **Community involvement.** Coordination arrangements from earlier destocking interventions may be resurrected or new groups established (see *Destocking standard 1, Guidance note 7*; and *Destocking standard 2, Guidance note 1*) to assist in planning and implementation. Details to be determined will include:
   - selection criteria for different groups of beneficiaries
   - selection criteria for animals to be purchased for slaughter
   - sites and dates of temporary markets
   - whether vouchers should be used instead of cash
   - suitable slaughter sites
   - criteria for when to distribute fresh or dried meat.

2. **Purchase sites and dates.** Temporary markets should be as close as possible to the affected communities to avoid excessive trekking of already weakened animals. Market days should be fixed in advance and well publicized. They should also be scheduled so as to allow adequate time for agency staff to rotate between the sites. The availability of basic infrastructure (holding areas, water, feed, etc.) and services (veterinary inspectors, agency staff, etc.) should be ensured.

3. **Purchase price.** The purchase price for the different species and types of animals needs to be agreed with and publicized in the affected communities. Coordination with other agencies operating similar schemes in adjacent areas is essential to avoid competition and confusion (see also *Core standard 8: Coordination*). Actual market prices, if available, should be monitored and the intervention price (what the agency pays) reviewed and, if necessary, adjusted accordingly. The intervention price may be higher than the actual market price, which may be too low to benefit prospective sellers. However, if the intervention price is set too high, it may destabilize an already fragile market.

4. **Vouchers.** Consideration should be given to using vouchers as an alternative to carrying cash in high-risk areas. Vouchers can be redeemed for cash at a later date and in a safer environment (see *Case study 4.5*). It is important to explain how the voucher system works.

5. **Procurement.** Agencies may purchase animals directly or contract out to local groups or individuals. Contracting out, where possible, is preferable because it is simpler, less costly, and supports local institutions. Both the price the agency pays the contractor and the price the contractor pays the producer must be transparent and agreed (see *Case study 4.3*).

6. **Selection of beneficiaries.** Slaughter destocking involves different groups of beneficiaries, who need to be identified and selected (see *Targeting* above). Agreement over who owns and benefits from the hides and skins also needs to be agreed (see *Case studies 4.3* and *4.5*).

7. **Meat distribution.** Meat recipients can be individual households, local institutions (schools, hospitals, prisons), or camps for displaced people. Meat distributions may be organized through the coordination group or in conjunction with an ongoing food relief operation, which would have its own selection criteria and distribution networks (see *Case study 4.3*).

8. **In-kind contributions.** Most communities benefiting from a destocking intervention are expected to make some kind of in-kind contribution. These contributions need to be negotiated and agreed, and could include taking responsibility for security arrangements and/or contributing labour or materials.

9. **Selection of animals for slaughter.** As with commercial destocking, priority should be given to older, non-reproductive stock, mainly surplus males. Young breeding stock should be excluded if possible.

10. **Fresh versus dried meat.** Fresh meat is generally considered preferable by many communities and is the simplest option. Because fresh meat is perishable, the logistics of distribution limit the number of animals that can be slaughtered at any one time. Drying meat has the advantage of allowing more animals to be slaughtered and the surplus meat preserved for later use. Preservation also allows for a more staggered and widespread distribution than is possible with fresh meat, assuming dried meat is culturally acceptable. It has the additional advantage of providing extra employment and the opportunity to acquire new skills. However, drying meat safely requires additional preparation, hygienic facilities, clean water, and suitable storage facilities.

11. **Slaughter methods.** Killing and butchering animals should be based on local customs and expertise, provided that basic animal welfare criteria are not compromised. To ensure animals are dispatched humanely and safely will require basic equipment (ropes, pulleys, captive-bolt stun guns, knives and saws, buckets/plastic crates etc.) and simple slaughter slabs with access to water, fly protection, and the means to collect and dispose of blood and waste material. Sufficient labour must be available to carry out the work and, if required, training and supervision provided.

12. **Public health risks.** Certain diseases (zoonoses), such as anthrax and Rift Valley fever, and parasites (*Echinococcus*, hydatid cysts) are transmissible to humans, particularly people already stressed by hunger and malnutrition. An assessment of the potential risks to public health should be conducted before proposing slaughter interventions (see also *Chapter 5, Veterinary support*). Ante- and post-mortem inspection by qualified personnel of all animals and carcasses is essential. Any animal or carcass that is unfit for human consumption should be safely disposed of (see *Guidance note 13*). Rotating slaughter sites can help minimize the risk of spreading disease. Meat is highly perishable, and good hygiene is essential to reduce the risk of food-borne disease. Slaughter and butchering in camp settings may require careful planning and the construction of temporary facilities to ensure public health and avoid the spread of disease.

13. **Disposal of condemned carcasses and slaughter waste.** Condemned carcasses and waste water, stomach contents, etc. need to be safely disposed of. This usually involves burying (preferably with lime), burning, or quarantining the carcasses. Waste water and body contents must not contaminate sources of drinking water. See also *Veterinary public health standard 3: Disposal of dead animals*.

Destocking case studies

4.1 Impact case study: Commercial destocking in Ethiopia

This case study presents the results of an impact assessment of a commercial destocking intervention in Moyale, southern Ethiopia, in 2006. Two private livestock traders were linked with pastoralists to facilitate the offtake of cattle and were provided with loans of US$25,000 each from Save the Children USA. The intervention led to the purchase of cattle far exceeding the value of these loans, as the traders then invested substantial sums of their own funds. Overall, an estimated 20,000 cattle, valued at $1.01 million, were purchased. Approximately 5,405 households sold cattle and, on average, each household received $186 from cattle sales. The estimated benefit–cost ratio of the commercial destocking intervention in terms of aid costs was 41:1.

During the drought, income from destocking accounted for 54 per cent of household income and was used to buy food, care for livestock, meet various domestic expenses, support relatives, and either pay off debts or add to savings. Seventy-nine per cent of the income derived from destocking was used to buy goods or services locally. An estimated 37 per cent of the derived income was spent on the remaining animals and included trucking of livestock to better grazing areas. The buoyant export trade in live cattle and chilled meat in Ethiopia was considered an important driver for commercial destocking, demonstrating a positive linkage between livestock and meat exports and pastoral vulnerability during drought (*Source:* Abebe et al., 2008).

4.2 Process case study: Transport subsidy for commercial destocking in Kenya

In 2001, VSF-Belgium assisted drought-affected communities in Turkana, northern Kenya, using various interventions.

➡ *Transport subsidies*

To increase offtake, VSF-Belgium provided a 40 per cent transport subsidy to itinerant traders who were buying livestock from Turkana pastoralists and reselling to markets within the district and to large-scale traders. Subsidies were also given to large-scale traders who were exporting to markets outside Turkana. Verification procedures included:

- a form signed by the control officer at the district's terminal point, including photographs of the vehicles involved
- transport receipts and letters from the local chief and veterinary officer detailing the origin, type, and number of livestock together with the purchase location and date of departure
- receipts from the local authorities where the livestock were offloaded.

In total, 1,175 cattle and 3,584 sheep and goats, valued at $117,070, were transported to markets in Nairobi, and a further 20,688 sheep and goats were moved within the district, either for fattening or for slaughter. In all, the subsidies came to $52,790, which was $3,340 over budget. One of the strengths of the intervention was its accounting and administration. Nevertheless, fraud proved difficult to control and the budget was rapidly exhausted. Although collaboration with chiefs, marketing associations, and local government officials was vital to the project's success, this left it vulnerable to corruption (*Source:* Aklilu and Wekesa, 2002).

➡ *Employment opportunities*

VSF-Belgium also distributed dried meat and employed community members for the processing operation. It paid women members $4 for each kilogram of dried meat that they processed. In addition, it paid $0.15 per kg for slaughtering, and a total of $1.15 per kg of dried meat for watchmen, storage, and meat inspection services (*Source:* Aklilu and Wekesa, 2002).

4.3 Process case study: Contract purchase for slaughter destocking in Kenya

Arid Lands Development Focus (ALDEF), a local NGO operating in northern Kenya, implemented a destocking operation in 2000.

ALDEF requested the community to identify trustworthy contractors from among themselves to supply livestock to the programme. Those selected included members of the 200 plus women's groups which ALDEF was already supporting with a microcredit programme. These groups supplied the bulk of the sheep/goats. Individual contractors, mostly women, also supplied cattle and camels to schools and hospitals. The purchasing price was fixed at $15 per sheep or goat, and at $66 per head of cattle or per camel. This was later raised to $17.50 per sheep or goat, $73 per camel, and $80 per head of cattle. The contractors sold the livestock to ALDEF at these prices, retaining the profit for themselves. Contractors were instructed on the number and type of animals to buy, i.e. old and barren animals. Purchased animals were handed over to community committees and delivery notes issued to effect payment.

A total of 950 cattle or camels and 7,500 sheep or goats were supplied by the contractors. The project covered seven peri-urban and seven rural areas. Slaughtering took place twice a week at the sites. Fresh meat was then distributed regularly to beneficiaries based on two sheep or goats between eight families per week. Institutions also received weekly meat from the scheme: two bulls/camels per school; three to four bulls/camels per high school; six goats to a hospital; three goats to a TB centre; and an unspecified number of goats plus one bull to each of six orphanages.

ALDEF involved community members in the committees that were formed to select beneficiaries for its slaughtering programme. Vulnerable households were targeted, and the list was read out in public. People unhappy with the list were given the right to appeal, and disputes were referred back to the committee for a decision. In addition to selecting beneficiaries, the committees were entrusted with receiving livestock from contractors, distributing it to eligible families, witnessing the slaughtering and meat distribution, collecting skins and hides, managing disputes, and liaising with ALDEF. A high level of community involvement meant that project activities were completed on time (*Source:* Aklilu and Wekesa, 2002).

4.4 Impact case study: Slaughter destocking and dried meat distribution in Ethiopia

CARE Ethiopia implemented a destocking operation during a drought in southern Ethiopia in early 2006. The aim was to promote the offtake of animals that would otherwise have died, and to provide meat to the drought-affected communities. Purchased animals were slaughtered and the meat was dried and distributed.

A total of 2,411 animals of different species were slaughtered, and a total of 2,814 kg of dried meat was packed and distributed. The packs varied in weight from 0.5 kg to 0.75 kg. On average, each household received 2.16 kg of dried meat. A fixed price was set for cattle at $33, camels at $66, and sheep and goats at $7.50. Purchasing was organized through the local cooperative for an agreed profit margin plus the hides and skins. In total, 1,121 households sold livestock and received $25,590 in return – $23 per household.

An impact assessment of the project indicated that income derived from livestock sales under the destocking project accounted for 38 per cent of household income during the drought (n=61 households). About 45 per cent of this income was used to buy food for the household, but around 18 per cent was spent on veterinary care, and another 6 per cent was used for other types of livestock costs (*Source:* Demeke, 2007).

The nutritional impact of the dried meat was also estimated. Assuming that the main nutritional value of the dried meat was as a protein supplement, it was possible to calculate the number of days for which 2.16 kg of dried meat would meet the recommended dietary allowance (RDA) for different individuals by age and gender. For example:

- for a child between 1 and 3 years, 2.16 kg of dried meat could supply the RDA of protein for 92 days
- for pregnant women between 19 and 30 years, 2.16 kg of dried meat could supply the RDA of protein for 17 days (*Source:* Catley, 2007).

4.5 Process case study: Voucher and meat distribution in Kenya

CARE implemented a destocking programme in Kenya in 2000. However, operating in the Garissa District was difficult, and access required military escorts because of security problems. Rather than using cash, payments were made using vouchers that could be cashed at CARE's office in Garissa. Beneficiaries could either give their vouchers to a trusted person to collect their cash, or they could take them to local, authorized traders and exchange them for cash there. Under the voucher system, 850 head of cattle and 250 sheep and goats were purchased.

CARE Kenya also supplemented its food distribution programme with meat supplied from its destocking operations. Thirty-nine food beneficiary centres were allocated either 25 head of cattle or 50 sheep/goats. CARE staff witnessed the slaughtering of the animals, but distribution of the fresh meat to beneficiaries was left to the local relief committees. The relief committees were also entrusted with giving the hides and skins to women's groups (*Source:* Aklilu and Wekesa, 2002).

4.6 Process case study: Meat relief committees in Kenya

In 2000, the Northern Relief Development Agency (NORDA) implemented a destocking operation in 20 centres in northern Kenya. Sheep, goats, and cattle were purchased for fixed prices from temporary markets agreed with the communities.

Beneficiary families were asked to organize themselves into groups – four families per sheep/goat or 30 families per cow – and each group then slaughtered, flayed, and distributed the fresh meat among themselves. Meat was distributed only once in any one area. A total of 13 tonnes of fresh meat was distributed to 6,000 beneficiaries (*Source:* Aklilu and Wekesa, 2002).

4.7 Process case study: Complementary feed provision and destocking in Niger

In Niger in late 2004, pasture growth was poor, rainfall low, and a crisis appeared imminent. Jeunesse en Mission Entraide et Développement (JEMED) supported an assessment of pasture throughout central Niger by community teams. It then established a scheme to help interested families market their animals. JEMED provided transport so that representatives of beneficiaries could take animals (one or two cattle or several small ruminants per family) to the border with Nigeria for sale since a reasonable price could still be obtained there. The scheme was linked to a supplementary feeding initiative, whereby beneficiaries agreed to purchase grain or fodder to support their remaining livestock.

By the time the programme was completed, a total of 4,849 small stock and 462 large ruminants had been sold, while 317,199 kg of grain had been purchased as well as wheat bran and sorghum stalks (*Source:* Jeff Woodke, personal communication, 2008).

Appendix 4.1: Assessment checklist for destocking

For destocking in general

- What phase has the emergency reached?
- What is the condition of the livestock being brought to market?
- Is the number of livestock being brought to market increasing?
- What is happening to the price of livestock?
- What stakeholders are operating in the area?
- Which are the most vulnerable communities, households, and individuals affected by the emergency?
- Who could benefit from destocking?
- Can a coordination group be established?
- Have animal welfare criteria been taken into account?
- Is the area secure for the movement of stock and cash?
- What indigenous and local institutions exist that can facilitate destocking? What roles do they play?

For commercial destocking

- Are traders already operating in the area?
- Is the infrastructure in place to enable livestock offtake?
- Do (temporary) holding grounds exist?
- Is there access for trucks?
- Are feed and water available?
- Are there animal welfare issues regarding trucking livestock?
- Are there any key policy constraints to livestock movement and trade?
- What constraints would hamper access to markets by the most vulnerable?

For slaughter for human consumption

- What slaughter facilities exist?
- What are local religious and cultural requirements with regard to livestock slaughter? Do they compromise accepted animal welfare criteria?
- What are local gender roles with regard to slaughter, meat preparation, tanning, etc.?

- Which are the most vulnerable communities, households, and individuals affected by the emergency who could benefit from the slaughter of animals?
- Should temporary market sites be established to reach remote villages?
- Which vulnerable groups should be targeted to receive the meat from destocking operations?
- Which individuals could benefit from the employment opportunities that destocking could provide?
- Can acceptable ante- and post-mortem inspections be undertaken?
- Can a system be established to process hides and skins?

For slaughter for disposal

- Can the hides and skins of condemned carcasses be processed?
- What provisions exist for disposal of carcasses?

Appendix 4.2: Examples of monitoring and evaluation indicators for destocking

Commercial destocking

	Process indicators (measure things happening)	Impact indicators (measure the result of things happening)
Designing the system	• Number of meetings held with government and traders; range and type of stakeholders participating in meetings • Number of community-level meetings; number and type of people participating in meetings	• Meeting minutes with action plan and clear description of roles and responsibilities of different actors • Trader preferences for types of livestock for purchase documented against market demands • Holding areas clearly defined as needed • Taxes and other administrative issues agreed with government • Community-level action plans developed, with agreed prices for livestock, payment mechanisms, and system and schedule for local collection and purchase of livestock.
Implementation: livestock purchases	• Number of traders involved • Number and type of livestock purchased by household and area[2]	• Income derived from livestock sales by household • Uses of income derived from livestock sales (e.g. buy food; buy livestock feed; relocate animals; buy medicines) • Herd size in recovery phase relative to non-destocked households (by wealth group) • Herd growth after drought relative to non-destocked households (by wealth group) • Influence on policy

Slaughter destocking

	Process indicators (measure things happening)	Impact indicators (measure the result of things happening)

Designing the system	• Number of community-level meetings; number and type of people participating in meetings
	• Formation of community-level destocking committee in each target location
		• Meeting minutes with clear description of roles and responsibilities of different actors
		• Terms of reference for destocking committee agreed
		• Action plans developed with agreement on:
		  - selection criteria for beneficiaries
		  - types of livestock for purchase together with prices and payment mechanisms
		  - amount of meat to be distributed
		  - system for local collection and purchase of livestock, with timing
		  - hire and payment of community members involved in slaughter, meat preparation, handling skins, etc.

	Process indicators (measure things happening)	Impact indicators (measure the result of things happening)
Implementation: slaughter and meat distribution	• Number of beneficiary households and people • Number and type of livestock purchased by household and area[3] • Amount of meat distributed per household • Number of local people hired for temporary work	• People selling livestock – income derived from livestock sales by household and uses of income • People receiving meat – meat consumption and nutritional value to women and children • People hired for temporary work – income received and uses of income

See also the LEGS Evaluation Tool available on the LEGS website:
<http://www.livestock-emergency.net/resources/general-resources-legs-specific/>.

References and further reading

Abebe, D., Cullis, A., Catley, A., Aklilu, Y., Mekonnen, G. and Ghebrechirstos, Y. (2008) 'Impact of a commercial de-stocking relief intervention in Moyale district, southern Ethiopia', *Disasters* 32(2): 167–186, <http://dx.doi.org/10.1111 /j.1467-7717.2007.01034.x>.

Aklilu, Y. and Wekesa, M. (2002) *Drought, Livestock and Livelihoods: Lessons from the 1999–2001 Emergency Response in the Pastoral Sector in Kenya*, Humanitarian Practice Network Paper 40, Overseas Development Institute (ODI), London.

Barton, D. and Morton, J. (1999) 'Livestock marketing and drought mitigation in northern Kenya', unpublished paper, Natural Resources Institute (NRI), London.

Catley, A. (ed.) (2007) *Impact Assessment of Livelihoods-Based Drought Interventions in Moyale and Dire Woredas, Ethiopia*, Pastoralists Livelihoods Initiative, Feinstein International Center, Tufts University, Medford, MA, together with CARE, Save the Children USA, and USAID-Ethiopia, <https://wikis.uit.tufts.edu/confluence/ download/attachments/14553622/IMPACT~1.PDF?version=1> [accessed 17 May 2014].

Catley, A. and Cullis, A. (2012) 'Money to burn? Comparing the costs and benefits of drought responses in pastoralist areas of Ethiopia', *Journal of Humanitarian Assistance*, 24 April 2012, <http://sites.tufts.edu/jha/archives/1548> [accessed 17 May 2014].

Demeke, F. (2007) 'Impact assessment of the PLI/ENABLE emergency livestock interventions in Dire Woreda, Borana Zone', in A. Catley (ed.), *Impact Assessment of Livelihoods-Based Drought Interventions in Moyale and Dire Woredas*, briefing paper, pp. 22–42, Pastoralists Livelihoods Initiative, Feinstein International Center, Tufts University, Medford, MA, <https://wikis.uit.tufts.edu/ confluence/download/attachments/14553622/IMPACT~1.PDF?version=1> [accessed 17 May 2014].

Gill, R. and Pinchak, W. (1999) *Destocking Strategies during Drought*, Texas A&M University, College Station, Texas, <http://varietytesting.tamu.edu/forages/

drought/Destocking%20Strategies%20During%20Drought.pdf> [accessed 17 May 2014].

LEGS (Livestock Emergency Guidelines and Standards) (2014), *Livestock Emergency Guidelines and Standards, 2nd Edition*, Practical Action Publishing: Rugby.

Morton, J. and Barton D. (2002) 'Destocking as a drought-mitigation strategy: clarifying rationales and answering critiques', *Disasters* 26(3): 213–228 <http://dx.doi.org/10.1111/1467-7717.00201>.

Toulmin, C. (1994) 'Tracking through drought: options for destocking and restocking', in I. Scoones (ed.), *Living with Uncertainty: New Directions in Pastoral Development in Africa,* pp. 95–115, Intermediate Technology Publications, London.

Turner, M.D. and Williams, T.O. (2002) 'Livestock market dynamics and local vulnerabilities in the Sahel', *World Development* 30(4): 683–705 <http://dx.doi.org/10.1016/S0305-750X(01)00133-4>.

Notes

1. However, involvement in the preparation of dried and fresh meat as well as hides and skins does have the potential to provide short-term employment and also to help develop skills.

2 Household figures can be summated to provide total figures by area and project.

3 Household figures can be summated to provide total figures by area and project.

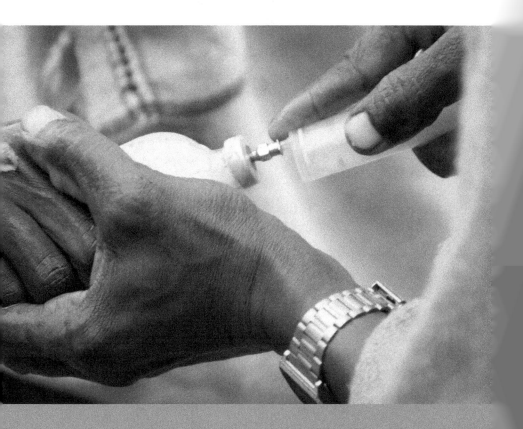

CHAPTER 5

Technical standards for veterinary support

Veterinary support

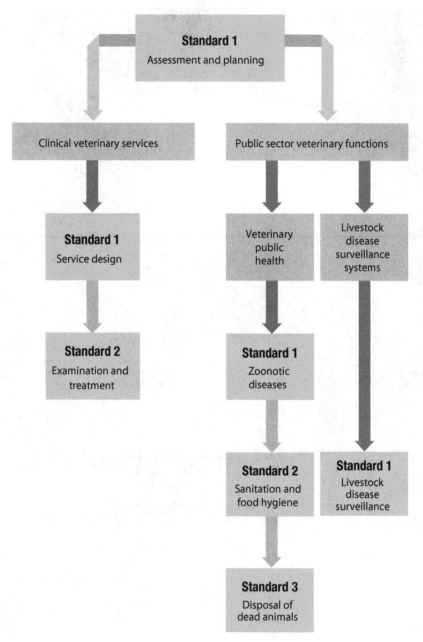

Standard 1
Assessment and planning

Clinical veterinary services

Public sector veterinary functions

Standard 1
Service design

Veterinary public health

Livestock disease surveillance systems

Standard 2
Examination and treatment

Standard 1
Zoonotic diseases

Standard 2
Sanitation and food hygiene

Standard 1
Livestock disease surveillance

Standard 3
Disposal of dead animals

Introduction

This chapter discusses the importance of veterinary support in emergency response. It presents the options for veterinary interventions and introduces tools to determine their appropriateness. The Standards, Key actions, and Guidance notes follow each option. Case studies are found at the end of the chapter. They are followed by appendices containing checklists for assessment and monitoring and evaluation. Key references are listed at the end.

Links to the LEGS livelihoods objectives

Providing veterinary support in an emergency helps achieve two LEGS livelihoods objectives:

- to protect the key livestock assets of crisis-affected communities
- to rebuild key livestock assets among crisis-affected communities.

The importance of veterinary support in emergency response

Emergencies can increase disease risk and animal vulnerability. Different kinds of emergency impact on animal health. For example:

- Droughts, floods, and harsh winters reduce access to grazing, resulting in weaker animals with lower disease resistance.
- Flooding displaces topsoil, creating favourable conditions for anthrax.
- Disasters such as earthquakes can injure animals.
- The risk of disease transmission increases when livestock are brought together from different areas.
- Where people and livestock are displaced, animals are moved to places with diseases to which they may not be immune.
- Risk of zoonotic disease transmission between animals and people increases in crowded camp conditions.

Veterinary support can protect and strengthen animals, thus protecting livestock assets. Through improved animal health, the supply of livestock products can be maintained during emergencies. In general, veterinary vaccines and medicines are inexpensive items relative to the value of livestock. Veterinary care, such as vaccination or early diagnosis and treatment, can help to prevent sudden, large-scale livestock losses resulting from infectious diseases that cause high mortality. LEGS does not cover the prevention and control of major, internationally recognized epidemic livestock diseases because specific guidelines are available from the World Organisation for Animal Health (OIE) and the Food and Agriculture Organization of the United Nations (FAO), as indicated in the *Introduction*.

Besides controlling epidemics, veterinary care can limit the impact of chronic diseases. This care can increase benefits derived from animals, whether from milk production, fertility, or use as pack animals. Where high livestock mortality has occurred, it can take years for communities to recover. Veterinary care can help rebuild valuable livestock assets, whether these consist of pastoralists' herds, a single donkey, a pair of draught oxen, or just a few chickens.

As part of emergency response, veterinary support also contributes to one of the animal welfare 'five freedoms' described in the *Introduction*; namely, *freedom from pain, injury, or disease*. It does this in several ways, including:

- preventing disease, for example, by vaccination
- enabling rapid diagnosis and treatment
- improving herd health by treatment for parasites or by providing vitamins and minerals to malnourished animals
- enabling rapid response to disease as a consequence of enhanced surveillance and disease reporting.

➡ Options for veterinary support

The options for veterinary support in emergency response presented in this chapter are divided into two areas: *clinical veterinary services* and *public sector veterinary functions*. The options for veterinary support are not exclusive: more than one option or sub-option may be selected and implemented. Their selection depends on local conditions and follows on from appropriate assessment and planning (see *Veterinary support standard 1*).

Option 1: Clinical veterinary services

Clinical veterinary services, comprising treatments and vaccinations, are usually the priority during an emergency. Support to clinical work can be extended to beneficiaries either through the government or through a private veterinary system, with or without veterinary paraprofessional workers such as community-based animal health workers (CAHWs). In many developing countries, clinical veterinary services are in transition from public to private sector delivery. The growing private veterinary sector may therefore be the main source of quality veterinary care. However, most veterinary professionals are likely to be based in major urban centres or near the most developed farms. In remote areas, veterinary paraprofessionals may be the main service providers.

Community-based animal health-care (CBAH) approaches are often very appropriate during the response to emergencies. CAHWs can have important roles in both clinical and public sector veterinary support. Particularly in protracted crises, studies show that CBAH systems have resulted in reduced livestock mortality and improved service accessibility, availability, affordability, and acceptance. When designed using participatory approaches, and when they include both male and female veterinary paraprofessionals, these systems respond well to livestock keepers' priority animal health problems. In some countries, however, CAHWs have no legal basis to work, and other animal health service delivery mechanisms are more appropriate.

In humanitarian crises, preventive and curative clinical veterinary interventions fall into two broad categories that can be implemented simultaneously through stationary or mobile services. These are:

1.1   *examination and treatment of individual animals or herds*
1.2   *mass vaccination or medication programmes.*

1.1 Examination and treatment of individual animals or herds. This option allows for animals or herds to receive treatment specific to the diseases present at the time of the treatment. The option assumes that animals in different households or herds may have different diseases, and therefore allows for flexibility in the clinical care provided. In some countries, this approach is increasingly supported by veterinary voucher systems that are developed jointly by community, private sector, and government partners (see *Case studies 5.1* and *5.2* at the end of this chapter). Similarly, responses that provide cash, directly or indirectly, to households can enable people to pay for veterinary care from private workers. In addition to providing case-by-case clinical care, these approaches aim to avoid situations in which the free provision of medicines undermines existing private veterinary services.

1.2 Mass vaccination or medication programmes. These programmes are widely used with the aim of preventing diseases in livestock populations during emergencies. Most commonly, emergency mass medication or vaccination programmes are one-off events and are implemented at no cost to livestock keepers. Care must be taken to ensure that the financial viability of existing veterinary services is not undermined.

- Mass medication programmes often use anti-parasite medicines, especially for worms and ectoparasite infestations such as ticks or lice. Practitioners and beneficiaries of these widely used programmes have reported positive impacts. However, because some systematic reviews have indicated limited impact or cost-effectiveness (see *Case study 5.4* on mass deworming during drought), LEGS does not yet include a standard on mass medication. Should agencies choose the mass medication option, LEGS recommends proper evaluation (see *Core standard 6: Monitoring, evaluation, and livelihoods impact*) to better document the impacts of mass medication and understand when and how it should be used. It is recognized that a particular challenge with evaluating mass deworming programmes is that some impacts may only be observed after the emergency, so this is something that needs to be factored into the timing and design of evaluations.

- Mass vaccination programmes usually cover infectious diseases such as anthrax, clostridial diseases, forms of pasteurellosis, and Newcastle disease. Although widely used, evidence of the livelihoods impact of mass vaccination during rapid-onset and slow-onset emergencies is very limited (see *Case study 5.3*). Therefore, LEGS does not include a standard on mass vaccination. If agencies choose to support mass vaccination, LEGS recommends proper evaluation (see *Core standard 6: Monitoring, evaluation, and livelihoods impact*).

Option 2: Public sector veterinary functions

Support to public sector veterinary functions is most applicable during protracted emergencies or the recovery phase of either rapid- or slow-onset emergencies. Support may supplement weakened government capacity, or intervene where no officially recognized government authority is present. It includes two key areas:

2.1   veterinary public health
2.2   livestock disease surveillance systems.

2.1 Veterinary public health. Veterinary public health, defined by the World Health Organization (WHO), FAO, and OIE as 'the contributions to the physical, mental and social well-being of humans through an understanding and application of veterinary science', relates to the understanding, prevention, and control of zoonotic diseases as well as to food safety issues. It plays an important role in the protection of consumers against zoonotic diseases, particularly those that can be transmitted through food products like meat and milk. Veterinary public health involves not only veterinary surgeons in the public and private sectors but also other health and agriculture professionals, communication specialists, and paraprofessionals.

Zoonotic diseases are transmissible to humans either through animal-derived food, such as meat or milk, or by contact with animals. Control of these diseases is a key public sector function. Zoonotic diseases include anthrax, salmonellosis, tuberculosis, brucellosis, rabies, mange, Rift Valley fever, and highly pathogenic avian influenza ('bird flu'). Specific guidelines for prevention and control of these diseases are available from FAO and OIE (including animal welfare considerations), as mentioned in the *Introduction*.

Veterinary public health also includes the food safety of animal-derived foods like meat or milk. A specific concern is that some veterinary medicines leave residues in food, leading to possible consumption of these residues by people. In the context of humanitarian crises, the trade-offs between human food security and human food safety are not well understood. However, emergencies can occur in areas characterized by severe food insecurity where there are high levels of child malnutrition. In some cases, malnutrition levels exceed WHO cut-off for emergencies even in normal periods. For people in this situation, the risk of continuing or worsening food insecurity seems far to outweigh the risk of ill health due to the consumption of meat or milk that is contaminated with drug residues.[1]

2.2 Livestock disease surveillance systems. These systems are concerned with searching, reporting, and mapping diseases. CAHWs may have a valuable role in reporting suspicious cases and outbreaks. In some regions, such as parts of the Horn of Africa, international trade in livestock or livestock products is very important to livestock keeper livelihoods. Trade is affected by international animal health standards, disease information, and the risk of exporting/importing livestock diseases. Government surveillance systems are one major source of information. All disease surveillance activities in emergencies therefore need to be designed in collaboration with government authorities, where these are able to function.

Examples of disease surveillance and investigation activities during humanitarian crises include:

- raising public awareness in order to stimulate disease reporting
- training veterinary paraprofessional workers to report disease outbreaks

- supporting government surveillance systems by linking veterinary paraprofessional workers' disease-reporting systems to official structures
- facilitating timely disease outbreak investigation and response
- providing regular feedback in the form of disease surveillance summaries to the workers who report.

The advantages and disadvantages of the veterinary support options and sub-options are summarized in *Table 5.1*.

Table 5.1 Advantages and disadvantages of veterinary support intervention options

➡ Option 1: Clinical veterinary services

Sub-option	Advantages	Disadvantages
1.1 Examination & treatment of individual animals/herds	• Allows flexibility and veterinary care on a case-by-case basis • Can support existing private sector service providers, e.g. through voucher schemes • Wide coverage is possible, particularly when well-trained and supervised veterinary paraprofessional workers are used • Allows targeted or strategic prophylactic treatment or vaccination of individual animals or herds at risk • Some quantitative evidence of impact on animal mortality is available	• If provided free, coverage and duration of service likely to be limited by the budget • If provided free, risks undermining existing private sector service providers • Quality of locally available medicines may be poor
1.2 Mass medication or vaccination programmes	• Relatively easy to design and implement • Mass deworming does not require a cold chain • Cost per animal can be low • If done effectively, mass medication has the potential to enhance livestock survival and production • Mass medication has the potential to provide income for the veterinary sector; for example, through voucher schemes	• There are weak laboratory facilities in many areas for confirming disease diagnosis before targeting specific diseases • Large-scale vaccination programmes difficult to design properly without basic epidemiological information • Coverage is often determined by budget rather than technical design criteria • Free treatment and vaccination can undermine the private sector • For many vaccines, need to establish or support cold chains • Risk of poor immune response to vaccination in animals already weakened, e.g. due to lack of feed • Quality of locally available medicines may be poor

Sub-option	Advantages	Disadvantages
2.1 Veterinary public health	• Public awareness-raising is often inexpensive • Can foster collaboration between veterinary and human health sectors	• May require specialized communication expertise to design and test educational materials in local languages • If not carefully managed and timed, can divert resources away from more direct livelihoods-based assistance
2.2 Livestock disease surveillance systems	• Can complement all other veterinary interventions and assist impact assessment of these interventions • Fosters linkages between central veterinary authority and affected area • Can help to promote international livestock trade in some countries and regions	• Needs to be based on clearly defined surveillance objectives • Can easily become a data-driven rather than an action-oriented process • If not carefully managed and timed, can divert resources away from more direct livelihoods-based assistance

Timing of interventions

Support to clinical veterinary services can be appropriate in both emergency and non-emergency situations. Support to public sector veterinary functions, however, may be most appropriate during the recovery phase, when immediate threats to livestock mortality and morbidity have passed (*Table 5.2*).

Table 5.2 Possible timing of veterinary service interventions

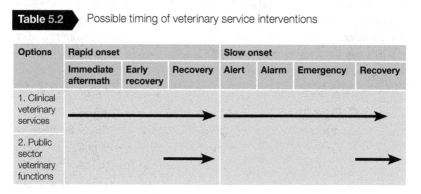

Options	Rapid onset			Slow onset			
	Immediate aftermath	Early recovery	Recovery	Alert	Alarm	Emergency	Recovery
1. Clinical veterinary services							
2. Public sector veterinary functions							

Links to other chapters

Veterinary support should be integrated with other livelihoods-based livestock interventions. Veterinary care alone does not guarantee livestock survival or productivity in emergency situations. Livestock require feed and water (*Chapters 6, Ensuring feed supplies*, and *7, Provision of water*) and, in some areas, housing (*Chapter 8, Livestock shelter and settlement*).

Clinical veterinary services and community-based animal health-care systems complement destocking (*Chapter 4, Destocking*) by helping to ensure the survival of the remaining stock. Veterinary public health inputs, such as pre-slaughter and post-mortem examinations, are important for slaughter destocking. Additional veterinary support is required during restocking (*Chapter 9, Provision of livestock*) to examine livestock before purchase and provide clinical services after livestock distribution.

Cross-cutting themes and other issues to consider

Gender and social equity

In emergencies, women are more vulnerable to food insecurity and other threats. Equitable and effective primary veterinary service delivery requires an understanding of the gender issues involved in livestock ownership and use. It is important that emergency interventions are based on understanding gender roles and responsibilities and the implications of planned activities. Women (and girls) may be responsible for small and/or young stock, including disease identification and treatment. Women should be involved in animal health interventions. Issues to consider include the following:

- In many societies, livestock care and management tasks are divided along gender lines. Men and women may have very different roles.
- In normal, non-emergency times, women tend to be overlooked by veterinary staff and by merchants who sell animal health products. Livestock extension workers and training programmes may target men. Training has lower impact when men are trained to perform women's tasks.
- In an emergency, animal health officials may prioritize protection of large species such as cattle. Women's animals may be ignored.

- It is important to identify sub-groups and consider their animals' main health problems. Vulnerable groups, such as female-headed households, may exist. Some groups may own specific types of livestock – for example, poultry, small ruminants, or donkeys.
- Women may use donkeys more than men, for example, to carry wood or water. Animal health professionals may be neither knowledgeable about nor interested in treating working equines.
- Women sometimes become responsible for all types of livestock in an emergency.

For these reasons, it is necessary to make sure that information and animal health interventions reach women and specific vulnerable groups. Women may have significant ethno-veterinary knowledge that should be taken into account in planning. Where possible and appropriate, women should be involved through specific targeting of activities and by recruiting women CAHWs.

People living with HIV and AIDS (PLHIV)

Due to their reduced immunity, it is especially important to prevent zoonotic diseases affecting PLHIV. The risk of zoonoses increases where animal and human populations live near each other. These conditions may exist in urban/ peri-urban environments and in camps with displaced people and animals. Veterinary support interventions can reduce the vulnerability of PLHIV. In addition, livestock-derived food products, such as eggs, meat, and milk, can provide significant nutrition to PLHIV. Thus, increasing livestock productivity through animal health interventions can have positive impacts.

To reduce the risks, proper handling and preparation of food is required. Veterinary public health needs to integrate veterinary interventions with human health information/services. The Sphere Handbook contains minimum standards on hygiene and human health services. These should be considered together with veterinary response plans.

Protection

CAHWs carrying cash and/or high-value medicines may invite robbery or attack. Insecurity can also have animal health implications. Animals stolen from a neighbouring group or area can introduce disease into the herd. In camps, the risk of livestock assets and associated goods being stolen is high.

Environment and climate

Vulnerable livestock keepers are susceptible to emergencies caused by extreme weather events, such as drought, severe winter, cyclones, and floods. Certain weather events are associated with increased disease. Parasitic worms may become more problematic in moist, warm conditions. Insect-borne virus diseases, such as Rift Valley fever, may follow protracted rainfall that creates favourable conditions for the mosquito vectors. Protracted droughts or winters can lead to reduced grazing, resulting in poor body condition and increased susceptibility to infectious diseases and parasites. Thus, in climate-associated crises, veterinary interventions may become a relevant addition to responses that include, for example, providing feed.

Initiatives that help to protect livestock assets, such as providing feed, water, or veterinary support, reduce mortality and may help to sustain livestock populations that natural grazing resources cannot support. The potential impact on the environment needs to be considered, particularly in an emergency that severely impacts natural resources, such as drought. However, despite common misconceptions, veterinary support is unlikely to increase herd size to the extent that unsustainably large populations of livestock are maintained. Rather, it can help to maintain a sustainable population of healthier, more productive animals.

Local capacities

Interventions that provide support to clinical veterinary services are usually community-based approaches. These approaches must recognize local people's significant capacities for primary animal health care. Livestock keepers can make important intellectual contributions to service design, assessment, and delivery. They often possess detailed indigenous knowledge about animal health problems, including disease signs, modes of disease transmission, and ways of preventing or controlling diseases. This knowledge is particularly well documented for pastoralist and agro-pastoralist communities. Training and supporting local people to become CAHWs can and should build on this knowledge. CBAH systems can also provide an effective way for veterinary support to reach the remotest rural communities and can contribute to veterinary public health and livestock disease surveillance systems.

Access

In remote areas with poor infrastructure and communications, veterinary service delivery is a challenge even in normal times. In camp-like settings, displaced livestock keepers may be beyond the reach of regular veterinary services, and access to communities may only be achieved on foot or by boat. The more remote communities tend to be more vulnerable during an emergency. In these situations, veterinary paraprofessionals are usually the most appropriate service providers because they are able to travel and function in these environments.

Although CAHWs are included as veterinary paraprofessionals in OIE international standards, they are sometimes resisted by the veterinary establishment. They may not be legally recognized owing to misconceptions about their capacity. They may also be perceived as a threat to monopolies of professional service provision (see *Core standard 7: Policy and advocacy*). Yet the potential for well-trained and supervised CAHWs should always be considered during emergencies as a form of accessible and affordable veterinary service provision.

Affordability and cost recovery

When providing veterinary support to communities, there are different approaches to cost recovery. Three options are discussed in *Box 5.1*.

Agencies responding to emergencies sometimes provide free veterinary support. This practice can threaten existing services based on cost recovery. It can confuse livestock keepers who receive services for a fee from some providers, then free from others. It can undermine the regular income of veterinary service providers, who find it difficult to charge for services that others provide free. Evidence that the provision of free clinical veterinary care either provides significant livelihood benefits to crisis-affected populations or is cost-effective or equitable is very limited. More evidence of livelihood benefits is available for veterinary paraprofessional systems based on some level of payment for services.

Increasingly, the privatization of veterinary services in developing regions has compounded issues around poorer livestock keepers' willingness and ability to pay for care. Evidence shows that poor people do make use of private clinical services based on simple, low-cost, community-based approaches.

During emergencies, veterinary service affordability is a challenge for agencies that seek to provide rapid, equitable, and effective clinical veterinary care while supporting local private service providers who require an income. Cash transfers may be an appropriate tool to implement a veterinary support intervention during emergency response.

> ## Box 5.1 ▶ Clinical veterinary service delivery in emergencies: Three options for cost recovery
>
> **1** *Services delivered free of charge.* Coverage usually depends on funding by external agencies. In many cases, only a small proportion of the disaster-affected population will be reached. If clinical services are delivered by aid agency staff, the likelihood of undermining local services, markets, and longer-term development processes is strong. Without supervision, there may be a risk that services will not be provided free at the point of delivery.
>
> **2** *Existing or newly trained veterinary paraprofessional workers.* Usually these workers are paid by their community at rates lower than for professional services. This approach helps to strengthen local capacity and support systems that can be improved over time and as the emergency wanes. It also improves accessibility and availability. On the other hand, the issue of affordability becomes important.
>
> **3** *Gradual introduction of payment for services.* In this option, services are provided free during the acute stage of an emergency, and payment is requested for services in later stages as livestock markets begin to function. The risks of this option are similar to those of the first approach. It may be difficult to persuade people that they need to pay if the service was previously provided free.

Use of cash transfers

During crises, veterinary professionals and paraprofessionals can be subcontracted to deliver veterinary support, and mechanisms such as voucher schemes can be used to provide their services. See *Chapter 3, Initial assessment and identifying responses,* for a summary of cash and voucher approaches in emergency response. Cash transfer approaches can help reach poorer and more vulnerable livestock users. They can also help to maintain private services during emergencies.

Cash and vouchers can be provided specifically for clinical veterinary services. Some public sector veterinary functions can be subsidized as a form of indirect grant. See *Case studies 5.1* and *5.2* at the end of this chapter, and *Case study 9.8* in *Chapter 9, Provision of livestock.*

Camps

Camps with displaced people and their animals create ideal conditions for the spread of disease. The risk of transmission is high where different herds and age groups mix around water troughs. Specific measures to reduce animal disease risk in camps should be taken into consideration. One way to do this is to establish quarantine areas where new arrivals are segregated from other animals for a period appropriate for the diseases of concern. Another is to provide water troughs at watering points to help reduce disease spread between animals.

In camp settings, veterinary public health activities may be particularly appropriate. Livestock keepers, for example, can be trained to recognize disease symptoms and to know to whom they should report these. They can also be trained to apply good practices to prevent disease.

The Standards

Before engaging in veterinary support, the affected populations' needs and the existing service providers' availability and capacity should be carefully considered, as highlighted in the decision-making tree (*Figure 5.1*).

Veterinary support standard 1: Assessment and planning

The crisis-affected population, including vulnerable groups, actively participates in veterinary needs assessment and prioritization.

Key actions

- With the involvement of all relevant subgroups within the crisis-affected population and in partnership with local veterinary authorities and service providers, conduct rapid participatory veterinary needs assessment and prioritization (see *Guidance note 1*).

- Within the affected area (or, for displaced communities, 'host community area'), map and analyse all existing veterinary service providers in terms of current and potential capacity if assisted by aid agencies (see *Guidance note 2*).

- Ensure the assessment includes analysis of service providers before the emergency with regard to payment for services (see *Guidance note 2*).

Figure 5.1 ▶ Decision-making tree for clinical veterinary services

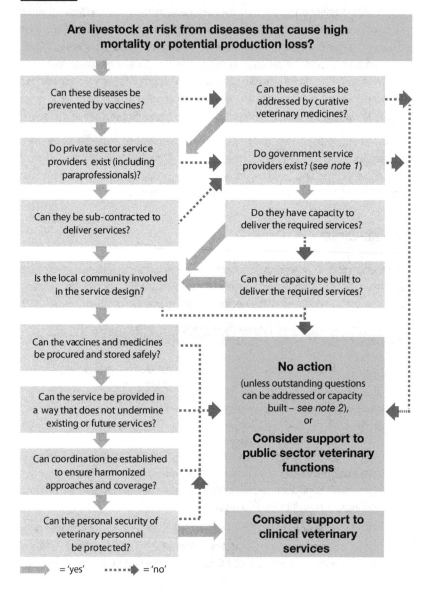

Are livestock at risk from diseases that cause high mortality or potential production loss?

Can these diseases be prevented by vaccines?

Can these diseases be addressed by curative veterinary medicines?

Do private sector service providers exist (including paraprofessionals)?

Do government service providers exist? (see note 1)

Can they be sub-contracted to deliver services?

Do they have capacity to deliver the required services?

Is the local community involved in the service design?

Can their capacity be built to deliver the required services?

Can the vaccines and medicines be procured and stored safely?

No action

(unless outstanding questions can be addressed or capacity built – see note 2), or

Can the service be provided in a way that does not undermine existing or future services?

Consider support to public sector veterinary functions

Can coordination be established to ensure harmonized approaches and coverage?

Can the personal security of veterinary personnel be protected?

Consider support to clinical veterinary services

▬▶ = 'yes'   ┅┅▶ = 'no'

Notes:
1. Where neither government nor private sector veterinary services exist (e.g. in conflict situations), an operational response by external agencies may be feasible for a limited period of time.
2. The result 'No action (unless outstanding questions can be addressed)' does not necessarily mean that no intervention should take place, but rather that further training or capacity building may be required in order to be able to answer 'yes' to the key questions.

- Ensure the assessment includes a rapid analysis of policy or legal factors that may hinder or enable specific implementation strategies (see *Guidance note 3*).

Guidance notes

1. *Rapid participatory assessment* should:
   - be conducted using experienced veterinary workers trained in participatory inquiry
   - include specific attention to the priorities of vulnerable groups
   - involve consultation with local government and private sector veterinary personnel
   - aim to identify and prioritize livestock health and welfare problems warranting immediate attention according to livestock type and vulnerable group
   - be cross-checked against secondary data when these are available and of adequate quality.[2]

   A checklist and methods for assessment are given in *Appendix 5.1* (see also *Appendix 3.2: Participatory methods* in *Chapter 3, Initial assessment and identifying responses*). Formal livestock disease surveys involving questionnaires and laboratory diagnosis are rarely feasible in emergency contexts. The modest added value of the disease information obtained is rarely justified in relation to the additional time and cost required and the need for rapid action. During protracted crises, more systematic livestock disease surveys or studies may be necessary to refine disease control strategies. In these cases, participatory epidemiological approaches should be applied as well (Catley, 2005).

2. *Mapping and analysis of veterinary service providers.* A map of existing service providers (veterinary surgeons and all types of veterinary paraprofessional workers), their activities, and coverage is needed for agencies to define their strategy for service delivery, including planned geographical coverage and access to vulnerable groups. The pricing arrangements of the different service providers should be reviewed as part of this mapping and analysis.

   Categories of veterinary paraprofessional workers vary between countries but include:
   - veterinary assistants

- animal health auxiliaries/assistants
- animal health technicians
- CAHWs, as defined in national and international veterinary legislation and codes
- informal veterinary service providers, including traditional healers and local pharmacists.

In some (usually conflict-based) emergencies, it is possible that neither the government nor the private sector can provide adequate veterinary services. In such cases, it may be appropriate for external agencies to support a community-based service through training of CAHWs and/or livestock keepers. This should be based on plans for building government and/or private sector capacity as this becomes feasible as part of a clear exit strategy.

3. *Policy and legal factors.* The assessment should include a rapid review of government and agency policies, rules, and procedures that relate to implementation options. For example:

- In some countries, certain types of veterinary paraprofessional workers are not legally recognized or else are restricted to a limited range of veterinary activities.
- Some countries may have livestock disease control policies that need to be followed; if these are not followed, alternative control methods need to be justified.
- There may also be restrictions on using certain types of veterinary products, as defined by national drug registration bodies.
- The purchase of veterinary drugs is sometimes hindered by bureaucratic requirements from some donors that prevent rapid and appropriate procurement in emergency contexts.
- Organizational/donor policy may hinder cost-recovery plans.

Understanding the policy context is vital both for recognizing potential constraints and, as appropriate, laying the foundation for associated advocacy or policy action (see *Chapter 2, Core standards common to all livestock interventions, Core standard 7: Policy and advocacy*).

Veterinary support is designed appropriately for the local social, technical, security, and policy context with the active participation of crisis-affected communities.

Key actions

- Ensure the service design process uses the information and analyses of the initial assessment, and is based on the active participation of the crisis-affected population, including vulnerable groups (see *Guidance note 1*).

- Check that the service design includes specific elements to reach vulnerable groups and, in particular, addresses challenges of accessibility and affordability (see *Guidance note 2*).

- Ensure that the service design considers disease outbreak early warning indicators linked to extreme weather events, where early warning systems are available (see *Guidance note 3*).

- Ensure that the service design considers the need for rapid procurement and availability of relevant veterinary vaccines and medicines, as well as the need for appropriate quality of products and proper storage at field level (see *Guidance note 4*).

- Check that the service design includes plans for rapid training of local service providers as necessary (see *Guidance note 5*).

- Ensure that the service design is based on local social and cultural norms, particularly in relation to gender roles (see *Guidance note 6*).

- Ensure that the service design maximizes the security of local people, veterinary service providers, and aid agency staff (see *Guidance note 7*).

- Ensure that the service design incorporates payment for services, where possible (see *Guidance note 8*).

- Ensure that the service design builds in professional supervision of veterinary paraprofessional workers (see *Guidance note 9*).

Guidance notes

1. ***Design based on assessment findings.*** Service design should aim to address the prioritized livestock health problems identified during the initial assessment. It is rarely feasible or appropriate for a primary-level veterinary

service to address all livestock health problems. In most cases, a limited range of vaccines and medicines can prevent or treat the most important diseases in a given area.

The focus of the service on prioritized livestock diseases needs to be understood and agreed by all actors, including livestock keepers. Where the priority cannot be addressed (for instance, when necessary technical support such as a cold chain is unavailable), this should be agreed with all stakeholders, including the beneficiary communities. Similarly, the appropriate timing for interventions (particularly vaccination) should be discussed and agreed with all stakeholders. The affected population should be as actively involved in the design of the service as is possible.

2. *Reaching vulnerable groups.* Service design should consider the types of livestock that vulnerable groups own or use, and should address the health problems of these types of livestock. Special attention should be given to accessibility and affordability issues in order to promote equitable access. Access to remote areas with limited infrastructure may require expensive means of transport (by air, for example), which limits coverage. Alternatively, access can be achieved by using locally based veterinary paraprofessional workers, who can travel on foot, mules, bicycles, boats, or other local means of transport. In some cases, programmes may need to provide or support local modes of transport for veterinary workers.

In rapid-onset emergencies, transport might be provided free of charge, whereas in more protracted crises, cost-share arrangements are often feasible. The payment-for-services strategy needs to take account of the need for rapid and equitable delivery while also supporting private sector veterinary workers where possible. For more vulnerable groups, private veterinary workers can be subcontracted by agencies to deliver a service for a specified short period of time. Voucher schemes may be used (see *Case studies 5.1* and *5.2*). In areas where the private veterinary sector is active or where the government charges for clinical veterinary care, normal pricing policies should be followed, with possible exemptions for targeted vulnerable groups. To avoid confusion, community participation and the agreement of community representatives on these issues will be needed, as well as clear communication with all stakeholders.

3. *Preparedness for weather-related disease outbreaks.* Many livestock diseases are associated with variations in climate, especially with the onset of rains or with heavier than usual rainfall. For example, Rift Valley fever in

East Africa has been linked to high rainfall and flooding caused by El Niño events. Emergency veterinary support interventions should take account of the developing knowledge of linkages between weather events and animal disease outbreaks in order to increase preparedness (see the section on *Links to other standards and guidelines* in the *Introduction* for links to information sources on transboundary diseases).

4. *Rapid procurement and storage.* Agencies with limited experience of veterinary drug procurement should seek expert advice. The quality of veterinary drugs and vaccines varies considerably between suppliers, whether sourced locally or internationally. Suppliers vary in their capacity to supply medicines in large volumes with appropriate expiry dates within agreed delivery times. Procurement can be further complicated by the wide range of products available. Because some veterinary vaccines require isolation of local field strains of disease pathogens, the vaccine's exact composition needs verification. Local importers, often located in capital cities, can supply readily available drugs in reasonable quantities. However, the quality, expiry dates, and drug storage conditions should be checked. At field level, many veterinary vaccines and some drugs require cold storage. They should not be purchased or used unless adequate cold-storage facilities are in place and a cold chain for transporting them can be ensured. Storage in camp-like settings may present particular challenges because of the lack of cold-chain maintenance and storage. Cold-storage facilities for human health services can sometimes be shared. However, human health professionals are sometimes unwilling to store veterinary products in human health cold chains. High-level agreement needs to be reached beforehand in order to take full advantage of expensive cold-chain facilities.

5. *Training plans.* Where some veterinary workers are already present and rapid delivery of services is required, training should be limited to short refresher courses. These should focus on 1) clinical diagnosis of the prioritized diseases, and 2) correct use of veterinary vaccines or drugs. Depending on the existing capacity of local personnel, this refresher training is not always needed. Where veterinary paraprofessional workers such as CAHWs need to be selected and trained from scratch, guidelines are available for CAHW systems in development rather than emergency programmes (see *References* and Catley et al., 2002). To enable rapid response in emergency situations, it may be necessary to streamline some

best-practice principles relating to CAHW selection and training. However, as emergencies become protracted or come to an end, further training is recommended to enhance CAHW knowledge and skills. In some countries, national technical intervention standards and guidelines for CAHW systems are available, as well as training manuals for short, practical, participatory CAHW training courses.

6. *Social and cultural norms.* The design of veterinary support needs to take into account local social and cultural norms, particularly those relating to the roles of men and women as service providers. In some communities, it is difficult for women to move freely or travel alone to more remote areas where livestock might be present. However, even in very conservative cultures, it is often possible for women to be selected and trained by women as CAHWs in order to provide a service for women. Women livestock keepers are among the most vulnerable groups.

7. *Protection.* Where livestock are very important to local economies and livelihoods, veterinary drugs are highly prized. These small-volume, high-value items are easy to steal and resell. Service design should consider the risk to veterinary personnel of violence, abduction, or theft. Livestock are often grazed away from more secure settlements. Sometimes they are moved long distances to grazing areas and water points. Veterinary workers travelling to such areas may be at risk, especially in conflict situations. Local veterinary paraprofessional workers may be appropriate in these situations because they know the area and may be familiar enough with armed groups or security forces to be able to negotiate access.

8. *Payment for service.* Based on documented evidence, service design should, where possible, incorporate payment for services. Voucher schemes should be used for the most vulnerable livestock keepers. For others, full payment for services should be rapidly resumed. Governments may consider all vaccination as a 'public good' rather than a 'private good'.[3] However, prevention of diseases not easily transmitted between animals, such as clostridial diseases, may be considered as a private good. Theoretically, the private sector is best equipped to deliver private goods.

9. *Professional supervision of veterinary paraprofessional workers.* Even where paraprofessionals such as CAHWs are working in remote areas, they should be under the overall supervision of a veterinary professional.

Professional supervision enables monitoring of the correct use of veterinary products, disease reporting from the field up the chain to the authorities, and integration of CAHWs in existing private or state veterinary services.

Clinical veterinary services standard 2: Examination and treatment

Examination and treatment are conducted appropriately with the active participation of the affected communities.

Key actions

- Clearly document the roles and responsibilities of all actors. Where appropriate and necessary, make written agreements (see *Guidance note 1*).

- Euthanize incurable sick or injured animals humanely and safely (see *Guidance note 2*).

Guidance notes

1. *Roles and responsibilities.* During emergency clinical veterinary service provision, problems may occur due to lack of stakeholder coordination. For example, problems can arise from a misunderstanding of the roles and responsibilities of different actors, from false expectations about the service's aims and coverage, or from confusion over pricing arrangements or beneficiary selection. Many of these problems can be avoided through stakeholder consultation, a commitment to community participation, and, where possible, close collaboration with local authorities and private sector actors. Roles and responsibilities should be documented in memoranda of understanding or similar agreements. These can provide useful points of reference in subsequent disputes.

2. *Euthanasia.* Animal euthanasia should follow humane standards and practices. Depending on the sickness/injury and method of slaughter, some livestock carcasses may be fit for human consumption (see *Veterinary public health standard 2: Sanitation and food hygiene*).

Men and women have access to information and services designed to prevent and control zoonotic diseases.

Key actions

- Include an assessment of zoonotic diseases and their prioritization in the initial assessment of animal health problems (see *Guidance note 1*).
- Design and implement zoonotic disease control measures either in conjunction with the provision of clinical services or as a stand-alone activity (see *Guidance note 2*).

Guidance notes

1. *Assessment.* The rapid participatory assessment conducted under *Clinical veterinary services standard 1: Service design* should include a rapid assessment of zoonotic diseases in terms of actual cases or risk. During emergencies, zoonotic disease risk may be substantially increased. Causative factors include 1) anthrax associated with abnormal movement of livestock to grazing areas that are normally avoided; 2) rabies associated with local populations of wild or domestic predators, possibly attracted to carcasses or garbage; 3) zoonotic disease associated with close contact between animals and people; 4) unhygienic conditions arising from the crowding of people and animals in camps; and 5) water supply breakdown.

2. *Zoonotic disease control.* The disease control method varies according to the zoonotic diseases in question. For some diseases, veterinary paraprofessional workers may provide information to livestock keepers verbally or by using leaflets. Such workers might also assist with organizing vaccination campaigns, for example against rabies, or with the humane control of stray dog populations. Outreach to women can be particularly important because they can play a significant role in livestock health management but are often overlooked in disease control measures. Where private workers are used on a short-term basis, payment for their services by an aid agency is usually required. Zoonotic disease control efforts should be harmonized between agencies and between areas as part of the coordination effort. Collaboration with human health agencies and programmes helps harmonize approaches and enables the sharing of

resources such as cold-storage facilities (see *Clinical veterinary services standard 1: Service design, Guidance note 4*).

Veterinary public health standard 2: Sanitation and food hygiene

Sanitary and food hygiene measures relating to the consumption of livestock products and the disposal of livestock are established.

Key actions

- Construct slaughter slabs during protracted crises (see *Guidance note 1*).
- Establish meat inspection procedures at slaughter slabs and abattoirs used by the affected population (see *Guidance note 1*).
- Publicize good food-handling practices (see *Guidance note 2*).

Guidance notes

1. *Slaughter facilities and meat inspection.* In camp-like settings or in situations in which slaughter facilities have been damaged, it may be appropriate to construct slaughter slabs to encourage humane slaughter as well as hygienic handling and inspection by trained workers. Similarly, if emergency destocking is conducted, animal welfare, health, and hygiene standards will need to be met, and either fixed or mobile slaughter slabs may need to be constructed (see *Chapter 4, Destocking*). In all these cases, consultation with local livestock workers or butchers will help to determine the correct locations for slaughter slabs and their design. Meat inspection procedures are generally well known. Safe disposal of offal from slaughtered livestock should be ensured.

2. *Public awareness.* Based on the findings of the assessment, public education campaigns should be conducted as appropriate to raise awareness of best practices in safe food handling and preparation. For example, advice can be given to control tuberculosis or brucellosis through improved hygiene when handling either animals or meat, or when preparing food, and by encouraging consumption of boiled milk.

Dead animal disposal is organized hygienically according to need.

Key actions

- Assess the needs for disposal (see *Guidance note 1*).
- Dispose of carcasses to ensure good hygiene (see *Guidance note* 2).

Guidance notes

1. *Needs assessment.* When disasters such as fire or earthquakes occur, many animals may be injured and euthanasia required. Slow-onset emergencies such as drought and severe winter may cause large numbers of animal deaths, as may widespread floods or cyclones. The question then arises: do they require hygienic disposal? Animal carcasses may spread disease, are unsightly, produce noxious odours, and attract predators and scavengers such as packs of dogs, hyenas or jackals, and crows and vultures. On the other hand, in winter emergencies animals die from undernutrition and hypothermia (with diseases like pneumonia in terminal stages) but not from diseases that remain in carcasses and pose risks to human and animal health. Also, disposal by burial may contaminate water sources and thus change a potential land fertilizer into a pollutant. A key consideration may be the psychological effect on livestock keepers for whom heaps of dead animals are a reminder of their tragic loss. On these grounds alone, it may be justifiable to organize disposal.

2. *Disposal.* Environmental and health considerations should be taken into account. Burying animals where water sources may be contaminated should be avoided. Composting can be an effective way to dispose of animal bodies that also produces useful fertilizer. Cash-for-work schemes, in which community members are paid to undertake carcass disposal, have been used effectively (see *Case study 5.6* below). See FAO, 2015 for technical details on carcass disposal, including composting.

During protracted emergencies, a livestock disease surveillance system that covers the crisis-affected population is supported.

Key actions

- Include the collection of data on important livestock diseases during routine monitoring of emergency clinical veterinary services (see *Guidance note 1*).

- Conduct livestock disease investigation in response to disease outbreaks to confirm diagnosis, trace the source of disease and where it may have spread, and instigate or modify control measures as necessary (see *Guidance note 2*).

- In protracted crises, and for livestock diseases covered by national disease surveillance policies or eradication strategies, collect information in line with these policies and strategies (see *Guidance note 3*).

- Ensure the coordination body compiles livestock disease data and submits the compiled report to the relevant veterinary authority (see *Guidance note 4*).

Guidance notes

1. *Routine monitoring.* Monitoring veterinary workers' clinical activities can contribute to a livestock disease surveillance system by recording livestock disease events and treatment or control measures. Such data are most useful if livestock morbidity and mortality by species and disease are recorded in relation to the population at risk. Monitoring tasks should be designed in collaboration with government authorities where possible.

2. *Veterinary investigation.* Veterinary programmes and agencies should have capacity to conduct investigations of disease outbreaks. Within a multi-agency programme, this task may be entrusted to a team or individual with specialist training in disease investigation, including post-mortem examination and laboratory diagnosis. In the absence of such assistance, agencies should be prepared to collect relevant samples and submit them to a diagnostic laboratory either in-country or abroad. All activities need to complement government veterinary investigation systems, where these exist, with official reporting of diagnoses by government actors. During

CH 5 Vet Support

protracted crises, agencies should consider establishing a small, local diagnostic laboratory to support the capacity of clinical veterinary workers and disease investigations. Sharing facilities with medical laboratories may be feasible. Standard recording forms with checklist questions should be used by field workers to assist with collecting relevant information for tracing disease source and spread.

3. *Animal disease surveillance.* In many countries, specific animal diseases have national or international control or eradication programmes. Standardized surveillance procedures are set by international organizations such as OIE and FAO. Where possible, livestock disease surveillance systems in protracted crises should follow these procedures. If operational constraints prevent standard surveillance procedures from being implemented, liaison with national authorities (if working) and either OIE or FAO can enable surveillance methods to be modified to suit the field conditions.

4. *Reporting.* In protracted crises, all agencies should submit regular (usually monthly) surveillance reports to the coordination body for compilation and submission to the relevant government authority. Brief reports that summarize pooled surveillance data from the region should be provided to veterinary workers who submit data from the field.

Veterinary support case studies

5.1 Process case study: Veterinary voucher scheme in Kenya

To overcome common problems associated with free distribution of veterinary drugs by emergency programmes, and also to involve the private sector, the International Committee of the Red Cross (ICRC) piloted a voucher scheme in north-western Kenya. Vouchers were given to selected families, who could exchange them for specific types of treatments provided by private CAHWs and veterinary assistants. The vouchers were valued at 1,000 Kenyan shillings (US$14) and were limited to the use of four types of drug. The CAHWs and veterinary assistants then received payment plus their service charge from a private veterinarian in exchange for the vouchers. In turn, the private veterinarian was reimbursed by ICRC and added his own service charge. The scheme covered 500 households, equivalent to around 3,000 people.

The advantages included the targeting of vulnerable households using a strong community-based process, plus delivery of the service by a relatively efficient and pre-existing private network of veterinary-supervised CAHWs. The CAHWs had received prior training according to the guidelines of the Kenya Veterinary Board.

The disadvantages included a fairly lengthy time investment at the design stage, including the need to set up detailed procedures and formats for administering and monitoring the scheme. Given the potential need to address a variety of health problems in different species of livestock, the range of drugs needs to be expanded beyond four products. In turn, this further complicates the design and administration of the scheme (*Source:* Mutungi, 2005).

5.2 Process case study: Veterinary voucher schemes in Ethiopia

Several NGOs collaborated with FAO and local government in Ethiopia on the implementation of veterinary voucher schemes during the recovery phase of a drought. The projects were in remote areas where private veterinarians did not operate, so government vets took on a supervisory role and worked with private veterinary pharmacies, CAHWs, and local communities.

The most successful model was supported by the Agency for Cooperation and Research in Development (ACORD), where people who received vouchers were still obliged to pay 30 per cent of the treatment costs provided by the CAHWs. The CAHWs were obliged to buy their initial drug stocks from a private veterinary pharmacy at full cost. Once treatment had been completed, CAHWs received the voucher worth 70 per cent of the cost of the drug and the remaining 30 per cent as cash. They returned the cash as a form of cost recovery to ACORD along with the spent voucher. ACORD then reimbursed the CAHW for the cost of the drug along with a small service payment, based on 20 per cent of the cost of the treatment. Other lessons from the voucher schemes were as follows:

- In all the voucher projects, the target population consisted of the poorest and most vulnerable households, often female-headed, as selected by the community.

- The value of the vouchers varied from project to project, but those projects that distributed vouchers with a higher value were the most successful. If the voucher value was too small, the beneficiaries complained and the process became overly bureaucratic.

- The vouchers were for the treatment of a specified range of common diseases in the areas concerned, not for any disease.

FAO completed an assessment of the programme using key indicators of availability, accessibility, and quality of service as well as intervention impacts on the existing animal health services, both public and private. The assessment concluded that in areas with strong CAHW programmes and private veterinary pharmacies and where stakeholders participate in the design, implementation, and monitoring, a treatment voucher system is effective and efficient in addressing the immediate veterinary needs of targeted beneficiaries during emergencies (*Source:* Regassa and Tola, 2010).

Save the Children USA also carried out an impact assessment of their scheme and found significantly lower livestock mortality in herds treated under the voucher system relative to control herds. They concluded that, 'Given that the veterinary voucher scheme impacted positively upon the privatised systems, upon pastoral livelihoods, and upon the health of animals in the intervention area, it is worth trying in other areas' (*Source:* Simachew, 2009, quoted in Vetwork, 2011).

5.3 Impact case study: Limitations of livestock vaccination during emergencies

Livestock vaccination has been an institutionalized response to drought in pastoralist areas of Ethiopia for many years, with millions of doses of vaccine delivered through NGOs and government. An impact assessment of this approach aimed to measure its impact on livestock asset protection, and thus compare mortality by disease between vaccinated and non-vaccinated herds in drought years in three regions of the country. For herds of cattle, camels, and small ruminants, the results showed no significant difference in mortality in vaccinated and non-vaccinated animals from those diseases covered by vaccination programmes during drought. The lack of impact from vaccination was explained by reference to a range of technical issues, but the overall conclusion was that vaccination of livestock should take place during normal, non-crisis periods.

These findings led to emergency coordination bodies and donors in Ethiopia revising their support to veterinary care during drought, and placing more emphasis on veterinary voucher schemes with the private sector. More widely, the assessment showed the importance of understanding the livelihoods impact of livestock vaccination during emergencies, and the risk of assuming that vaccination automatically protects livestock assets and that it is a cost-effective approach in emergencies (*Source:* Catley et al., 2009).

5.4 Impact case study: Limitations of mass deworming of livestock during drought in Kenya

Large-scale deworming of livestock is a common veterinary response during drought in northern Kenya. For example, during 2008–09, no fewer than 474 emergency livestock interventions took place across six countries, and mass deworming was one of the most common activities. In 2012, researchers who wanted to measure the impact of deworming during drought conducted 120 household interviews in five districts. The study design showed the technical difficulties of measuring the impact of disease caused by worms in livestock because different types of worms have different impacts on animal health. However, the study managed to conclude that 'There was clear evidence that administration (of worm medicines) within the drought itself was perceived to have little to no effect on livestock output. Although there was perceived to be an improvement in output after administration during the rains, it was not possible to attribute changes to anthelmintic [worm medicine] use because of the improvement in concurrent pasture quality and water availability'. The study report advised further impact studies to better understand the value of mass deworming of livestock during drought (*Source:* FAO, 2012: 4).

5.5 Impact case study: Veterinary interventions in Afghanistan

Over a five-year period in Afghanistan, 60–80 per cent of livestock were lost because of the conflict. In 2002–03, ICRC conducted a veterinary intervention in two districts in the central highlands that aimed to rebuild herds through improved animal health. The project planned to treat 100 per cent of the animals in order to significantly reduce parasite numbers. The project team comprised two Afghan veterinary surgeons and a team of CAHWs.

Each animal was treated free of charge with anthelmintic and acaricide in the autumn of 2002, in the spring of 2003, and again in the autumn of 2003. Every livestock owner was also given an acaricidal powder to treat the stables or sheds where the animals stayed during winter. The first treatment involved 57,000 animals, the second 154,000, and the third 248,000. The livestock belonged to a total of 5,300 families. Of the animals treated, 80 per cent were sheep or goats, 14 per cent cattle, and 6 per cent equines.

Monitoring was conducted during the treatments, and extension services were provided after the intervention. The intervention had the following impacts: herd sizes doubled, average live weight increased, herd fertility and survival of young stock improved, and the impact was so great that, after the project stopped, the two veterinary surgeons were able to earn a living treating the livestock and getting paid in full by the livestock keepers (*Source:* Oxfam, 2005).

5.6 Process case study: Carcass disposal in Mongolia

Mongolia is prone to severe winter weather as well as to drought in summer. When lack of summer rain prevents pasture growth, livestock enter the winter in poor body condition. Blizzard conditions, ice over pasture, and very low temperatures – as low as -50ºC – result in a winter emergency known as *dzud*. Horses, cattle, sheep, cashmere goats, camels, and yaks starve and freeze to death.

Dzud occurred over two consecutive winters between 1999 and 2002, and again between 2009 and 2010, leading to large-scale livestock mortality. In the 1999–2002 period, 11.2 million animals died out of around 30 million nationally according to government reports. In rural areas, a large proportion of the population were nomadic herders, and livestock mortality on this scale resulted in a great loss of livelihoods. National and international agencies responded by providing animal feed and veterinary support.

In 2010, a United Nations Development Programme (UNDP) intervention assisted in the removal of around 2.7 million animal carcasses from three *aimags* (provinces), which amounted to 20 per cent of the total *dzud*-affected territory. Individual cash-for-work (CFW) transfers to 18,605 beneficiaries and reimbursements of fuel costs, totalling $121,600, were disbursed with the assistance of a local bank that did not charge bank fees or make service charges. The CFW scheme also addressed social equity and gender equality through inclusive collective action, and helped those worst affected with overcoming the psychological trauma that they had suffered. International development agencies such as the Swiss Agency for Development and Cooperation and Mercy Corps began replicating the CFW initiative in other *aimags* in conjunction with the Government of Mongolia. The UNDP intervention complemented the Mongolian Government's carcass removal programme in the remaining *aimags* (*Sources:* Baker, 2011; UNDP, 2010).

5.7 Process case study: Emergency animal health response to drought in Kenya

Farm Africa's Northern Kenya Pastoralist Capacity Building Project works in the Marsabit and Moyale Districts of northern Kenya. During the 2005/06 drought, government veterinary officers reported livestock losses of between 65 and 85 per cent. Pasture and water were in scarce supply and livestock were exposed to starvation, and their susceptibility to disease increased.

In collaboration with government veterinary services, Farm Africa requested funds from FAO to conduct an emergency animal health initiative. The objectives were to improve the health status of core breeding livestock in the project area and reduce their parasitic load so that they might withstand stress-induced outbreaks of livestock diseases and sustain productivity. The project targeted 20 per cent of the livestock in the two districts with mass treatment and deworming.

Teams comprising Farm Africa staff, local government veterinary officers and animal health assistants, partner organization staff, and CAHWs conducted the treatment. The basic package consisted of a dewormer and a trypanocide. An optional package targeting sick or weak animals was also available, comprising multivitamins, an anti-parasitic, and antibiotics. Payment for the treatment was made in cash or kind, as shown in *Table 5.3*.

Table 5.3	Payment for treatment during 2005/06 drought	
Cost item	Payment in kind	Payment in cash
Cattle/donkeys	1 goat per 20	KSh50 (US$0.70)
Sheep/goats	1 goat per 100	KSh5 ($0.07)
Camels	1 goat per 10	KSh50 ($0.70)

KSh = Kenyan shillings

The direct beneficiaries of the project were 2,107 households in Marsabit District and 1,560 households in Moyale District – a total of approximately 27,600 people.

The anticipated impact of the project was improved livestock health over time, which in turn would contribute to higher milk and meat production, increased immunity to disease, and improved condition of draught oxen prior to the next planting season. In the longer term, it is anticipated that livestock reproduction rates will increase and that ultimately food security will improve.

In the interim, beneficiaries were positive about the intervention and felt that their livestock were stronger, more capable of withstanding the effects of drought, and likely to increase their milk production for immediate consumption (*Source:* Farm Africa, 2006).

Appendix 5.1: Assessment methods and checklist for veterinary service provision

Indicator	Useful method
1. Accessibility The physical distance between livestock keepers and the nearest trained veterinary workers	**Participatory mapping:** • Simple sketch maps of given area • Locations and owners of livestock • Nearest veterinary services/types • Distance (km, hours, etc.)
2. Availability A measure of a service's physical presence and concentration/ availability in an area	**Participatory mapping:** as above **Direct observation:** • Veterinary workers • Facilities **Interviews:** • Assess existing stocks of veterinary products • Quality of medicines and equipment • Barriers to availability on the basis of caste, gender, etc.
3. Affordability The ability of people to pay for services	**Semi-structured interviews** **Observation:** • Veterinary facilities • Livestock markets • Price lists Determines normal service costs and livestock values Allows comparison of service costs against livestock worth – if livestock markets are still functioning or if a destocking programme is taking place, it is more likely that people will be able to pay for veterinary support
4. Acceptance Relates to cultural and political acceptance of veterinary workers, which is affected by socio-cultural norms, gender issues, language capabilities, and other issues	**Interviews:** with male and female livestock keepers
5. Quality This includes veterinary workers' • Level of training • Technical knowledge and skills • Communication skills • Quality and range of veterinary medicines, vaccines, or access to equipment	**Interviews:** • Veterinary workers **Direct observation:** • Veterinary facilities • Education certificates • Licences to practice or equivalent
All indicators	**Matrix scoring:** Scoring different types of veterinary workers operational in the area against the five indicators shows the relative strengths and weaknesses of each type

CH 5 Vet Support

Appendix 5.2: Examples of monitoring and evaluation indicators for veterinary service provision

	Process indicators (measure things happening)	Impact indicators (measure the result of things happening)
Designing the system	• Completion of participatory survey and analysis • Number of meetings with community/ community representatives • Number of meetings between private veterinary workers and implementing agency	• Identification of most important animal health problems in the community according to different wealth and gender groups • Analysis of options for improving animal health **Veterinary vouchers** • Value of vouchers agreed with community and local private veterinary service providers • Beneficiary selection criteria agreed • Number of veterinary paraprofessionals linked to private veterinary drug supplier or agency • Reimbursement system for private sector workers and suppliers agreed • Field-level monitoring system agreed **Implementing agency provides medicines** • Number of veterinary paraprofessionals supplied by agency and geographical coverage
Rapid veterinary training/refresher training	• Number and gender of workers trained • Number and type of animal health problems covered in training course • Cost of training	• Improved veterinary knowledge and skills among trainees
Veterinary activities	**Veterinary vouchers** • Number of vouchers distributed by area and type of household • Number of treatments per disease per livestock type per household • Number and value of vouchers reimbursed **Medicines provided by agency** • Quantities and types of medicines supplied to veterinary workers • Cost of medicines supplied to veterinary workers	• Livestock mortality by species and disease against baseline • Geographical coverage of veterinary workers • Proportion of livestock-rearing households serviced • Proportion or number of workers functioning after training • Action taken according to disease outbreak reports • Human nutrition – consumption of animal-sourced foods in community in relation to improved animal health and according to wealth and gender groups • Income in community in relation to improved animal health and according to wealth and gender groups • Influence on policy

	Process indicators (measure things happening)	Impact indicators (measure the result of things happening)
Veterinary activities (continued)	• Number of treatments per disease per livestock type per worker per month • Number of monitoring forms submitted by veterinary workers • Number of disease outbreaks reported by veterinary workers	

Source: Catley et al., 2002

See also the LEGS Evaluation Tool available on the LEGS website: <http://www.livestock-emergency.net/resources/general-resources-legs-specific/>.

References and further reading

Admassu, B., Nega, S., Haile, T., Abera, B., Hussein A., Catley, A. (2005) 'Impact assessment of a community-based animal health project in Dollo Ado and Dollo Bay districts, southern Ethiopia', *Tropical Animal Health and Production* 37(1): 33–48 <http://dx.doi.org/10.1023/B:TROP.0000047932.70025.44>.

Aklilu, Y. (2003) 'The impact of relief aid on community-based animal health programmes: the Kenyan experience', in K. Sones and A. Catley (eds), *Primary Animal Health Care in the 21st Century: Shaping the Rules, Policies and Institutions*, proceedings of an international conference, 15–18 October 2002, Mombasa, Kenya, African Union/Interafrican Bureau for Animal Resources, Nairobi, <http://www.eldis.org/go/home&id=13563&type=Document#. U38tmbkU_Vh> [accessed 17 May 2014].

Baker, J. (2011) *5-Year Evaluation of the Central Emergency Response Fund, Country Study: Mongolia*, United Nations Office for the Coordination of Humanitarian Affairs (OCHA), Ulaan bataar. Available from: <http://www.alnap. org/resource/11664> [accessed 24 May 2014].

Burton, R. (2006) *Humane Destruction of Stock*, PrimeFact 310, New South Wales Department of Primary Industries, Orange, New South Wales. Available from: <http://www.livestock-emergency.net/resources/veterinary-services/> [accessed 23 May 2014].

Catley, A., Leyland, T. and Blakeway, S. (eds) (2002) *Community-based Animal Healthcare: A Practical Guide to Improving Primary Veterinary Services*, ITDG Publishing, London.

Catley, A., Leyland, T., Mariner, J.C., Akabwai, D.M.O., Admassu, B., Asfaw, W., Bekele, G., and Hassan, H.Sh., (2004) 'Para-veterinary professionals and the development of quality, self-sustaining community-based services', *Revue scientifique et technique de l'office international des épizooties* 23(1): 225–252 <http://sites.tufts.edu/capeipst/files/2011/03/Catley-et-al-OIE-Apr-04.pdf> [accessed 18 May 2014].

Catley, A. (2005) *Participatory Epidemiology: A Guide for Trainers*, African Union/Interafrican Bureau for Animal Resources, Nairobi, <http://www. participatoryepidemiology.info/PE%20Guide%20electronic%20copy.pdf> [accessed 18 May 2014].

Catley, A., Abebe, D., Admassu, B., Bekele, G., Abera, B., Eshete, G., Rufael, T. and Haile, T. (2009) 'Impact of drought-related livestock vaccination in pastoralist areas of Ethiopia', *Disasters* 33(4): 665–685 <http://dx.doi.org/10.1111 /j.1467-7717.2009.01103.x>.

FAO (Food and Agriculture Organization of the United Nations) (2012) *An Assessment of the Impact of Emergency De-worming Activities'*, FAO report OSRO/ KEN/104/EC – FAOR/LOA NO. 008/2012, FAO, Nairobi.

FAO (2015) *Technical Interventions for Livestock Emergencies: The How-to-do-it Guide,* Animal Production and Health Division Guidelines Series, FAO, Rome.

Farm Africa (2006) *Immediate Support to Agro-Pastoral Communities as a Drought Mitigation Response: Marsabit and Moyale Districts*, Final Report to FAO, OSRO/RAF/608/NET (CERF2), Farm Africa, Nairobi.

Heath, S.E., Kenyon, S.J., and Zepeda Sein, C.A. (1999) 'Emergency management of disasters involving livestock in developing countries', *Revue scientifique et technique de l'office international des épizooties* 18(1): 256–271.

Iles, K. (2002) 'Participative training approaches and methods' and 'How to design and implement training courses', in A. Catley, T. Leyland, and S. Blakeway (eds), *Community-based Animal Healthcare: A Practical Guide to Improving Primary Veterinary Services,* ITDG Publishing, Rugby.

Leyland, T. (1996) 'The case for a community-based approach, with reference to Southern Sudan', in *The World Without Rinderpest*, pp. 109–120, FAO Animal Health and Production Paper 129, FAO, Rome, <http://www.fao.org/docrep/003/w3246e/W3246E09.htm> [accessed 18 May 2014].

Leyland, T., Lotira, R., Abebe, D., Bekele, G. and Catley, A. (2014) *Community-based Animal Health Care in the Horn of Africa: An Evaluation for the US Office for Foreign Disaster Assistance*, Feinstein International Center, Tufts University, Addis Ababa and Vetwork UK, Great Holland.

Linnabary, R.D., New, J.C. and Casper, J. (1993) 'Environmental disasters and veterinarians' response', *Journal of the American Veterinary Medical Association* 202(7): 1091–1093.

Mariner, J.C. (2002) 'Community-based animal health workers and disease surveillance', in A. Catley, T. Leyland, and S. Blakeway (eds), *Community-based Animal Healthcare: A Practical Guide to Improving Primary Veterinary Services,* ITDG Publishing, Rugby.

Mutungi, P.M. (2005) *External Evaluation of the ICRC Veterinary Vouchers System for Emergency Intervention in Turkana and West Pokot Districts*, International Committee of the Red Cross (ICRC), Nairobi.

Oxfam (2005) *Livestock Programming in Emergencies Guidelines*, unpublished draft, Oxfam, Oxford.

Regassa, G. and Tola, T. (2010) *Livestock Emergency Responses: The Case of Treatment Voucher Schemes in Ethiopia*, FAO, Addis Ababa, <http://www.disasterriskreduction.net/fileadmin/user_upload/drought/docs/Livestock%20Treatment%20Voucher%20Experience%20in%20Ethiopia.pdf> [accessed 20 May 2014].

Schreuder, B.E.C., Moll, H.A.J., Noorman, N., Halimi, M., Kroese, A.H., and Wassink, G. (1995) 'A benefit-cost analysis of veterinary interventions in Afghanistan based on a livestock mortality study', *Preventive Veterinary Medicine* 26: 303–314 <http://dx.doi.org/10.1016/0167-5877(95)00542-0>.

Simachew, K. (2009) *Veterinary Voucher Schemes: An Emergency Livestock Health Intervention – Case Studies from Somali Regional State, Ethiopia*, Save the Children USA, Addis Ababa.

UNDP (United Nations Development Programme) (2010) *2010 Dzud Early Recovery Programme,* UNDP Project Document, United Nations Development Programme, Ulaan bataar, <http://www.undp.org/content/dam/undp/

documents/projects/MNG/00059396/Dzud%20early%20recovery_ProDoc.
pdf> [accessed 18 May 2014].

Vetwork (2011) *The Use of Cash Transfers in Livestock Emergencies and their Incorporation into the Livestock Emergency Guidelines and Standards (LEGS)*, Animal Production and Health Working Paper No. 1, FAO, Rome. Available from: <http://www.livestock-emergency.net/resources/general-resources-legs-specific/> [accessed 18 May 2014].

Notes

1. Leyland, T., Lotira, R., Abebe, D., Bekele, G. and Catley, A. (2014) *Community-based Animal Health Care in the Horn of Africa: An Evaluation for the US Office for Foreign Disaster Assistance*, Feinstein International Center, Tufts University, Addis Ababa and Vetwork UK, Great Holland.

2. Secondary data sources are, for example, government disease surveillance reports, disease studies from local research institutes, and published data.

3. In the case of a 'private good', the person who paid for the good or service benefits exclusively from it (for example, treatment of an animal's injury). With a 'public good', an individual's consumption does not reduce its entitlement for others; the person who pays for the service cannot exclude access by others (for example, meat inspection).

CHAPTER 6

Technical standards
for ensuring feed supplies

Ensuring feed supplies

```
┌─────────────────────────────┐
│        Standard 1           │
│   Assessment and planning   │
└─────────────────────────────┘
              │
              ▼
┌─────────────────────────────┐
│        Standard 2           │
│      Feeding levels         │
└─────────────────────────────┘
              │
              ▼
┌─────────────────────────────┐
│        Standard 3           │
│        Feed safety          │
└─────────────────────────────┘
              │
              ▼
┌─────────────────────────────┐
│        Standard 4           │
│  Sources and distribution   │
└─────────────────────────────┘
```

Introduction

Several kinds of emergency can affect livestock's access to feed. During a drought, feed is in short supply because of a lack of rainfall. In conflict, normal feed sources may not be accessible. After a severe flood, natural resources may have been lost. This chapter discusses the importance of ensuring feed supplies in emergency response. It presents the options for feed interventions together with tools to determine their appropriateness. The Standards, Key actions, and Guidance notes follow each option. Case studies are found at the end of the chapter. They are followed by appendices containing checklists for assessment and monitoring and evaluation. Key references are listed at the end.

Links to the LEGS livelihoods objectives

Ensuring feed supplies in emergency situations relates largely to the second and third LEGS livelihoods objectives:

- to protect the key livestock assets of crisis-affected communities
- to rebuild key livestock assets among crisis-affected communities.

If livestock can be protected and kept alive by ensuring feed supplies, animal stocks can eventually be rebuilt. The provision of feed can also have an impact on the first LEGS livelihoods objective – *to provide immediate benefits to crisis-affected communities using existing livestock resources* – to the extent that keeping stock alive contributes to the immediate household food supply.

The importance of ensuring feed supplies in emergency response

Livestock are particularly vulnerable to short-term disruption of the resources on which they depend for their survival. In particular they need to be supplied with adequate feed and water. Any emergency response that aims to maintain livestock populations in an affected area must therefore make adequate provision for the continuing supply of feed resources.

This may be particularly important in cases of drought, when excessive livestock deaths are due to starvation rather than disease (Catley et al., 2014). In floods, the failure to get feed to stranded animals may result in their deaths, and in conflict situations access to pasture is restricted because of insecurity. Where feed stores have been destroyed by an emergency (such as a cyclone, earthquake, or flood), there may be an urgent need to replenish feed reserves and to rebuild storage facilities to enable livestock to survive in the short to medium term.

Ensuring feed supplies for livestock in emergencies is often prioritized by livestock keepers themselves. It is not uncommon to find that livestock keepers feed their animals a portion of the food aid they have received for themselves, or to discover that they have exchanged it for animal feed. For example, many refugees from Darfur who managed to reach camps in eastern Chad brought their livestock with them, but found little water and pasture available. A number of them used some of the food rations they received to keep their animals alive (SPANA Press release, 2007).

While external agency support for animal feed provision may prove contentious if it is considered to be taking resources (for example, transport) that could be used to support the provision of human food, animal feed in emergencies may be a top priority for livestock-owning communities.

Ensuring feed supplies also contributes to the first of the animal welfare 'five freedoms' described in the *Introduction*; namely, *'freedom from hunger and thirst* – through ready access to fresh water and a diet to maintain full health and vigour'.

The relative costs of keeping livestock alive during an emergency (particularly a drought) need to be set against the alternatives, such as the provision of livestock for herd replacement after the emergency is over. One study in pastoralist areas in northern Kenya and eastern Ethiopia found that it was between three and six times more expensive to restock a core herd of livestock following a drought than to keep the animals alive through feeding (Catley, 2007). A cost–benefit analysis will indicate the relevance of a proposed feed intervention compared with other options, as any intervention will be dependent on distance or feed price.

➡ Options for ensuring feed supplies

Emergency feeding provides a substitute when feed resources are unavailable in adequate quantities due to an emergency. Such emergency feeding may be initiated by livestock keepers themselves, who resort to the use of non-traditional, collected or purchased feeds, or to traditional fodder banks that have been preserved in anticipation of scarcity. Sometimes these options are not open to livestock keepers, who may be unable to support the current needs of their animals. In such cases, externally managed emergency feeding programmes may be able to assist through the provision of forage, concentrates, or multi-nutrient blocks.

Emergency feeding strategies vary depending on the role of livestock in livelihoods. In pastoralist areas, feeding focuses only on maintaining a core breeding herd, rather than feeding all animals. In other areas, where households may own a small number of animals, feeding programmes may target all the livestock in the community. Where significant feed reserves have been destroyed in the emergency, feeding programmes may also consider replenishment of these stores as well as the rebuilding of storage facilities.

However, emergency feeding usually implies transportation over long distances, with all the security and logistical constraints this implies. Such programmes are input-intensive. Clear exit strategies are therefore required to ensure that the feeding programme can be sustained for the duration of the emergency and phased out appropriately. Livestock, particularly large ruminants, require large quantities of feed over an extended period of time, and this volume of feed will often have to be transported from outside the area. Where large herds are involved, it may be important to consider implementation of parallel destocking programmes to maintain the ecological balance of the affected region, or to address resource constraints by targeting the most valuable livestock.

This chapter covers two ways of ensuring supplies of feed in an emergency: emergency feeding in situ; and emergency feeding in feed camps.

Box 6.1   External support to indigenous mobility and relocation

In many pastoral societies, mobility is a key strategy for accessing dispersed grazing and water over large areas. In times of stress such as drought, this pattern may be further extended to involve specific drought reserves and/or new territories. In some countries (for example, in certain West African states, including Cameroon), these mobility rights are enshrined in law through pastoral codes and the demarcation of stocking routes. Such routes also exist in a few developed countries such as Spain and Australia (IIED and SOS Sahel UK, 2010; Cripps, 2013). During an emergency, these mobility strategies become even more important for the survival of livestock and, at the least, livestock keepers should be able to continue to use them.

Although there is not yet any evidence base demonstrating impact, it may be possible for external agencies to intervene when indigenous relocation strategies are restricted. This could involve, for example, supporting discussions between national governments or regional authorities with regard to permitting livestock keepers and their animals to move across borders (see also *Core standard 7: Policy and advocacy*) or facilitating access to drought reserves restricted by conflict. It could also involve giving practical supplementary support, such as the provision of water, feed, or veterinary support en route. Any support of this nature would need to take into account issues such as personal security risks for livestock keepers, relationships with host communities, increased disease risk, potential reduction in access to livestock products for vulnerable groups, and impact on other livelihood activities if labour is withdrawn to supervise stock in a distant place. External support to indigenous relocation strategies therefore requires further investigation and analysis before it can be promoted as a good practice intervention. For issues relating to displaced people and their livestock needs, see *Chapter 9, Livestock shelter and settlement* (Livestock and Emergency Guidelines and Standards, 2014).

Option 1: Emergency feeding in situ

Emergency feed is preferably distributed in situ. The feed is transported and distributed to individuals/households, who collect it and take it home. Conditional cash grants and voucher schemes can be effective mechanisms for emergency feeding in situ and should be considered where markets are functioning (see *Chapter 3, Initial assessment and identifying responses*).

Option 2: Emergency feeding in feed camps

Where distribution in situ is not possible, feed camps may be established to which livestock keepers can bring their endangered livestock. For example, during conflict situations feed camps may be established in resource-poor but safe areas because feed can be transported with less risk than the animals themselves. Feed camps may also provide the opportunity to link with food- or cash-for-work programmes for the guarding and supervision of the camp. Two feed camp systems can be used:

- *The 'in-out' feed camp system.* An agreed number and type of livestock (e.g. two lactating cows per household) are brought on a daily basis to a feed camp, where they receive their feed ration. Marking the animals makes sure they continue to be fed.
- *The 'residential' feed camp system.* An agreed number and type of livestock are brought to a camp, where they remain until the crisis is over.

The advantage of feed camps is that the organizers can control the use of the feed and also target key stock types according to objectives. The logistics involved and administration costs are obviously greater than those of in situ distribution.

A summary of the key advantages and disadvantages of these two options is presented in *Table 6.1*.

| Table 6.1 | Advantages and disadvantages of feed provision options |

Option	Advantages	Disadvantages
1. Emergency feeding in situ	• Rapid response to keep at-risk animals alive • Can exploit fodder banks established previously as part of emergency preparedness • May generate knock-on benefits in the local economy where opportunities for local sourcing exist • Can target core breeding stock • Potential to replenish feed stocks lost in the emergency	• Input-intensive and expensive • Needs to be able to continue for the duration of the emergency • Not sustainable in the longer term • Requires safe facilities for storage and transport • Carries risk of importing diseases, pests, and vectors from outside • Sourcing feed from outside the area may disrupt local markets • Requires supervision and management
2. Emergency feeding in feed camps	• As above, also: • Increased security for stock and people • If resources are limited in the area, feed can be transported to the camp from elsewhere • Provides income-generating opportunities for caretakers/guards	• As above, also: • Requires a suitable site with shelter/enclosure, water, and feed • Requires more organization and management than feeding in situ as well as resources for salaries, feed, etc. • Requires organized labour to supervise and guard the stock • Livestock need to be healthy enough to travel to the camp

Timing of interventions

Emergency feeding is costly and input-intensive. As such, it is generally a short-term measure, implemented in the immediate aftermath or emergency phases of a rapid- or slow-onset emergency in order to maintain livestock assets until longer-term measures can be effected or until natural resources recover. In this respect, seasonality needs to be taken into account in planning an emergency response, including an estimate of when feed resources may become available again post-emergency (*Table 6.2*).

Table 6.2 Possible timing of feed interventions

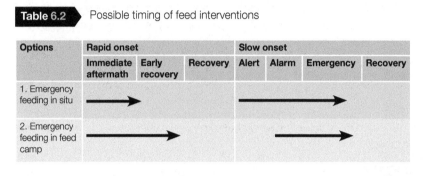

Options	Rapid onset			Slow onset			
	Immediate aftermath	Early recovery	Recovery	Alert	Alarm	Emergency	Recovery
1. Emergency feeding in situ	⟶			⟶			
2. Emergency feeding in feed camp	⟶			⟶			

Links to other chapters

Ensuring feed supplies may complement other livestock-based emergency responses, particularly destocking (see *Chapter 4, Destocking*; see also *Case study 4.7* at the end of *Chapter 4*), whereby some animals are taken out of the production system, and efforts, such as the provision of feed and water, are made to ensure the survival, and ideally improvement, of the remaining stock. Coordination between initiatives and between agencies is therefore paramount to avoid one activity undermining another (see also *Chapter 2, Core standards common to all livestock interventions, Core standard 8: Coordination*). Feed initiatives may also supply additional support to livestock provision for crisis-affected households (see *Chapter 9, Provision of livestock*).

Cross-cutting themes and other issues to consider

Gender and social equity

As for all livestock-based initiatives in emergencies, specific gender roles in relation to livestock care and production should be taken into account when designing interventions (see, for example, *Case study 6.1* at the end of this chapter). Consideration should be given to gender division of labour both before and during emergencies. In some societies, many of the activities relating to livestock management are undertaken by women, who are not always able to reap an equitable share of the benefits derived from these activities. Milking of dairy and dual-purpose animals and cleaning of animal housing are often tasks that fall disproportionately upon female members of the household. In addition, the collection and management of feeds can confer particularly onerous duties on women and girls. For this reason, emergency programmes with components directed at ensuring supplies of feed resources should take particular care that the extra management activities that interventions may require do not compromise the interests of women or adversely affect the daily workload of women or any vulnerable group in affected communities. Women are often responsible for procuring animal feed during normal times, and this task may become more difficult during emergencies. Armed conflict can make normal routes to feed resources treacherous. Women's workload increases when they have to walk farther or spend more time trying to gather poor-quality feed, such as seed pods.

When supplying emergency feed, women may require additional assistance to transport it back to the settlement. Donkeys and pack animals may therefore be especially important.

PLHIV

In families affected by HIV/AIDS, labour availability may be severely reduced. In these cases, the introduction of supplementary feed activities may require labour inputs that affected families cannot provide. Alternatively, as with other livestock-based interventions discussed in this Handbook, ensuring the survival of family stock can help to maintain a nutritious diet for affected people through the provision of livestock products.

Protection

Emergencies may be plagued by lawlessness and civil strife even when they have not arisen directly as a result of conflict. Successful livestock feeding programmes should result in livestock that regain or increase their original value, which may therefore make them more attractive for looting. Feed camps involving the concentration of large numbers of livestock may attract thieves, particularly in insecure areas. The poorest livestock keepers may not be equipped to deal with theft of their stock, so programmes should carefully consider how the continuing protection of the animals can be ensured. Where such protection cannot be reasonably guaranteed, other options for interventions, such as destocking, may be more appropriate. Where large numbers of people and their livestock have been displaced and moved into camps, grazing may be available outside the camp but at the risk of violence or personal insecurity, in which case the provision of feed to the camp or to a nearby area may be appropriate.

Environment

The impact on the environment of planned feed initiatives should also be taken into account. Livestock, to a greater or lesser degree, place a burden on the ecosystem in which they live through their consumption of feed resources and, in the case of more intensive systems, through the generation of waste products. When these ecosystems have been severely affected by an emergency, the impacts may well be exacerbated both in the short term and during recovery. In such situations, it may be questionable whether people's livelihoods are best served by programmes that involve improvements in feeding to encourage the rapid re-establishment of livestock populations. Moreover, the environmental costs of transporting feed should be taken into account when considering environmental impact. Initiatives to provide feed should also take into account the availability of water necessary to support the livestock (see *Chapter 7, Provision of water*).

Targeting vulnerable groups

In all emergency interventions, challenges exist in ensuring that initiatives are targeted at the most needy. Because feed resources are a commodity (the more so when they are in short supply), logistical arrangements need to ensure that they arrive at their intended destinations. Where such controls are inadequate, the wealthiest and most powerful individuals in a community may appropriate a disproportionate quantity of resources for feeding their own livestock, which are at less risk, and shipments of feed may be diverted and sold for profit by non-livestock keepers.

Families that have survived for generations as livestock keepers may be affected to such an extent that livestock are no longer a viable option for them in the post-recovery period. Intervention programmes need carefully to consider the livelihood enterprises that families are likely to be able to pursue in future. This is best done through consultation with families, and applies particularly to those interventions, such as the provision of feed resources, that aim to preserve livestock assets over a crisis period. There is little benefit to be gained by feeding animals during an emergency if the only post-emergency option open to the household is the dispersal of their holding.

Management capacities

Even in communities with a long tradition of livestock keeping, management capacities may have been eroded as a result of an emergency. Family members may have migrated or been killed, or may no longer be healthy enough to provide labour inputs or managerial expertise. This situation may be compounded by the introduction of unfamiliar management options, such as the feeding of concentrates or multi-nutrient blocks. Intervention programmes need to consider whether these factors are likely to impede their success and whether they can realistically provide adequate support for building managerial and other manpower capacity (training programmes and encouraging external labour forces).

Local capacities and indigenous coping strategies

Livestock-owning communities affected by an emergency can also draw on their indigenous knowledge and capacities to respond to the emergency, and at times to anticipate it using indigenous early warning mechanisms. Their knowledge and skills in livestock management enable them to select appropriate animals that can benefit from feeding programmes and therefore to preserve a core breeding herd. They may have extensive knowledge of feed availability and the most suitable types of feed for purchase or storage, or both. They may also be able to negotiate access to neighbouring grazing lands through social networks. In many parts of the world, people have had to face the consequences of emergency situations since long before the advent of external assistance programmes. While there is clearly a role for external support, agencies should not ignore these strategies that communities have developed for themselves, as they will usually be well focused on the key objectives that affected people have for recovery. For example, pastoralists commonly keep some areas of rangeland in reserve for use in leaner times (see also *Box 6.1*). Further specific examples of indigenous coping strategies are highlighted in the *Key actions* and *Guidance notes* below.

Introduction of pests, diseases, and vectors

When feedstuffs are transported from outside an affected area, there is a risk that diseases and pests may be imported with them. Proper phytosanitary management is of great importance in ensuring that these risks are minimized. It is therefore common practice to conduct an independent laboratory analysis for nutrients (energy and protein), dry matter, acid-insoluble ash, inert additives, and moulds or toxins, together with thorough quality control at delivery.

Disruption of local markets

Occasionally, transporting feed resources into an affected area may be perceived as an 'easy' option, at least logistically. In fact, it should not be considered until the possibility of local sourcing has been ruled out. In addition to the disease risks discussed above, resources brought from elsewhere may replace feeds that could have been provided by local farmers and traders. Local sourcing spreads the benefits of the intervention more widely in the affected area. In purchasing from local markets, it may also be helpful to stagger the purchase of feed in order to limit the impact on market systems (and avoid possible opportunistic price hiking). Public consultation and a proper assessment of potential impact are essential in order to evaluate and control the risk of price hiking. A market assessment is also necessary if vouchers are being considered as a means to support emergency feeding.

Camps

When people move into camps with their livestock, specific planning issues are raised with regard to feed and grazing (as well as other requirements, such as water; see *Chapter 7, Provision of water*). Hosting a camp population can put considerable social, economic, environmental, and cultural pressure on a host population, who may themselves be poor and under-resourced. Competition and consequently tension may develop around the sharing of common resources such as feed, grazing, and water. When selecting and planning sites, these resources should be thoroughly assessed to ensure that they will meet the needs of both the host community and the displaced population. Where displaced people are accompanied by their livestock, site selection should also take into account the need for space for livestock within the camp (see *Chapter 8, Livestock shelter and settlement*).

The Standards

Before emergency feed initiatives are embarked upon, careful consideration needs to be given to the feasibility of the different options, as highlighted in *Figure 6.1*, as well as to the most appropriate stock to be targeted.

Figure 6.1 Decision-making tree for feed options

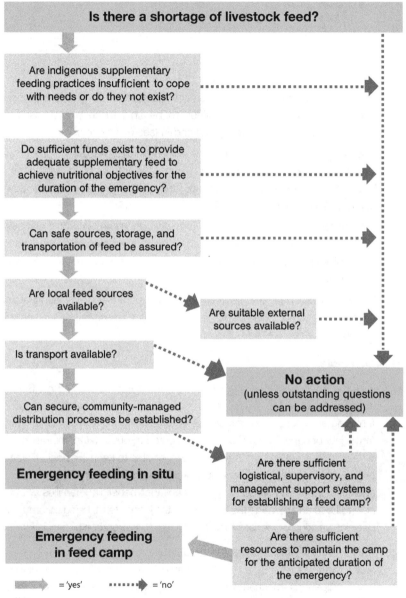

Is there a shortage of livestock feed?

Are indigenous supplementary feeding practices insufficient to cope with needs or do they not exist?

Do sufficient funds exist to provide adequate supplementary feed to achieve nutritional objectives for the duration of the emergency?

Can safe sources, storage, and transportation of feed be assured?

Are local feed sources available?

Are suitable external sources available?

Is transport available?

No action
(unless outstanding questions can be addressed)

Can secure, community-managed distribution processes be established?

Emergency feeding in situ

Are there sufficient logistical, supervisory, and management support systems for establishing a feed camp?

Emergency feeding in feed camp

Are there sufficient resources to maintain the camp for the anticipated duration of the emergency?

→ = 'yes'   ┈┈▶ = 'no'

Note
The result 'No action (unless outstanding questions can be addressed)' does not necessarily mean that no intervention should take place, but rather that further training or capacity building may be required in order to be able to answer 'yes' to the key questions.

CH 6 Feed

The options for ensuring supplies of feed resources are assessed on the basis of local needs, practices, and opportunities.

Key actions

- Initiate feed provision activities only where there is a significant chance that the beneficiaries will continue to be able to keep and manage livestock after the emergency has ended (see *Guidance note 1*).

- Ensure plans based on the options outlined in this chapter are produced with full stakeholder participation and take into account indigenous coping strategies, local sourcing, and potential disruption to local markets (see *Guidance note 2*).

- Base targeting of stock for feed provision on an analysis of the status of the animals, their chances of surviving the emergency, and their usefulness in rebuilding livestock assets in the future (see *Guidance note 3*).

- Take into account the policy context and potential policy constraints affecting access to feed and pasture during assessment and planning (see *Guidance note 4*).

Guidance notes

1. ***Beneficiaries can keep and manage livestock in the future.*** Some households may be at long-term risk of losing their livestock assets following an emergency – either they have lost too many livestock or their family labour capacity may have been affected through death, migration, or ill health to the extent that they are no longer able to keep livestock. Before engaging in interventions that help to keep livestock alive in the short term, agencies should be reasonably confident that beneficiary families will be able to keep and manage the livestock in the longer term, using community decision-making processes to target the most appropriate beneficiaries.

2. ***Participatory plans based on indigenous coping strategies and local markets.*** As noted earlier, many livestock-owning communities have indigenous mechanisms for coping with feed shortages. These should be taken into account as well as strengthened and built on where possible, which will contribute to better ownership of interventions and

active participation by the community (see *Case study 6.3*). Where coping mechanisms exist but are not being used, the reasons for this problem should be carefully analysed before interventions are taken forward. Local markets should also be supported and not undermined by any purchase or transporting of feed. Local fodder production sources should be assessed ideally as part of preparedness before the emergency begins (see *Chapter 2, Core standards common to all livestock interventions, Core standard 2: Preparedness*). In some cases, community feed banks are established as part of emergency preparedness initiatives and can provide a valuable local source of feed in emergencies (see *Case study 6.3*). *Appendix 6.1* contains a checklist to guide the assessment and planning process.

3. ***Targeting livestock.*** Some types of animal are better adapted to coping with and recovering from feed or water shortages than others. Some may be deemed capable of surviving the emergency without assistance; others may be regarded as a better target for assistance; while other more vulnerable animals may be unlikely to survive even with support. Resources for implementing feed-related interventions during emergencies will almost always be very limited. As a result, it will rarely be possible to address the needs of all animals in the herd, and therefore only the most valuable animals should be targeted. In practice, this means quality breeding stock and possibly working animals or animals that could attain a reasonable market value with minimal inputs of feed. This targeting should be based on participatory planning with beneficiary communities to ensure that the species and class of animals selected reflect the needs of vulnerable groups and ethnicities, who may be affected differently by a shortage of feed.

4. ***Policy context.*** The initial assessment should analyse the policy context with regard to access to feed. This may include obstacles to the movement or purchase of feed (for example, internal procedures governing commercial purchase). This analysis should inform implementation plans and, as appropriate, also form the basis for any relevant advocacy activities (see *Chapter 2, Core standard 7: Policy and advocacy*).

Levels of feeding supported by the programme should enable appropriate production outcomes and be sustainable over the life of the programme.

Key actions

- Determine feeding levels for the programme with reference to a clearly defined set of production objectives (see *Guidance notes 1* and *2*).

- Ensure levels of feeding implemented by the programme are both attainable and sustainable (see *Guidance note 2*).

- Where the loss of feed reserves represents an immediate threat to livestock, ensure reserves are replenished as part of the feed programme (see *Guidance note 3*).

Guidance notes

1. *The concept of nutritional adequacy.* It is important to realize that the concept of nutritional adequacy does not imply any absolute standards of feeding. A diet that is nutritionally adequate for keeping an animal alive during a two-month drought will not be adequate for a cow producing 25 litres of milk every day on a peri-urban dairy farm. Therefore, it is important to establish early on what constitutes an adequate nutritional outcome for the current situation, whether it be 'survival rations', stabilization of body weight, increase in body weight, re-establishment of reproductive performance, etc. This information should then be used to inform the selection of options and the development of the technical and logistical details of the intervention.

2. *Feed budgeting.* Planning the quantities of feeds needed by the programme requires balancing the consumption by participating animals and the feeds that can feasibly be delivered to the point of use. Broadly, this requires estimates of:

    - daily feed requirements of the different types of participating animals, based on the desired objective as described under *Guidance note 1*

    - quantities of available feeds that can be sourced within the programme's budget

    - distance from the source of feed

- duration of the proposed programme

- number of animals that can realistically participate.

If resources are inadequate for the number of participating animals, then the programme may need to re-evaluate its overall objective (for example, accept that it can only stabilize live weight in most animals rather than re-establishing gain) or seek additional funding.

3. **Feed stores replenishment.** In many rapid-onset emergencies, feed stores may be destroyed. If the loss of these reserves threatens the immediate survival of livestock, emergency feeding programmes should include replenishment of these supplies (together with the reconstruction of the necessary storage facilities) to ensure protection of livestock assets.

Feed standard 3: Feed safety

Where feeds are imported into the affected area, proper attention is given to sanitary, phytosanitary, and other aspects of feed safety.

Key actions

- Adequately assess the vulnerability of local livestock populations and feed sources to imported pests, diseases, and vectors (see *Guidance note 1*).

- Screen feed materials brought into the affected area for significant sources of contamination (see *Guidance note 2*).

- Implement satisfactory measures to ensure that vehicles and storage facilities are clean and sanitary; where appropriate storage is unavailable, explore voucher schemes (see *Guidance notes 3* and *4*).

Guidance notes

1. **Risk assessments.** During emergencies, detailed risk assessments may be difficult to accomplish. Nevertheless, it is important to identify the most significant risks that might compromise the recovery phase before the feed imports are finalized. Previous problems in an affected area may provide useful indicators of where future risks may lie. Where risks are deemed to be high, importing a particular feedstuff into an area may still be considered if there is an acceptable level of confidence in the measures in place for screening and management of the feedstuffs involved.

CH 6 Feed

2. *Quality control of feeds to be imported.* Feed materials imported into an affected area must always be subjected to adequate quality control before delivery. This can include visual inspections, either by naked eye or microscope, for pest and disease contamination. For certain types of feed it may also be appropriate to include further laboratory analysis to detect the presence of toxins. For example, maize grains or meals can be at significant risk of contamination with fungal aflatoxins, particularly when they may have been subject to long periods of transport and storage.

3. *Cleanliness and sanitary procedures.* It is generally neither possible nor desirable for exhaustive quality control procedures to be implemented at the point of delivery. As a result, it is particularly important that any staff who handle feeds or transport them into an affected area after quality controls have been undertaken should use procedures that minimize the risk of further contamination or deterioration. These should include:

- proper washing and cleaning of storage bins and trucks between loads (ideally by steam cleaning)
- proper drying of storage bins and lorries after cleaning
- proper record keeping of materials carried to avoid risk of cross-contamination – feedstuffs should never be transported in trucks previously used to transport hazardous materials such as agrochemicals, glass, or scrap metal
- minimal staff contact with the material they are storing or transporting – for example, drivers should never walk on top of open loads of feed
- the covering of open loads of feed with tarpaulins
- transport and storage times kept to a minimum.

4. *Voucher schemes.* Voucher schemes are particularly useful where households lack storage facilities. The feed can be stored properly at a central facility and vouchers used when feed is required.

Feed standard 4: Sources and distribution of feed resources

Feed resources are procured locally where possible, distributed safely, and in a manner that causes minimal disruption to local and national markets.

Key actions

- Ensure supporting agencies have or can adapt administrative systems and procurement processes to allow them to purchase feed quickly (see *Guidance note 1*).

- Conduct assessments of the local availability of suitable feed resources for inclusion in an emergency feeding programme (see *Guidance note 2*).

- Include the option of using cash transfers to supply feed during assessments (see *Guidance note 3*).

- Where feeds must be brought in from outside the affected area, obtain them from reliable and sustainable sources (see *Guidance note 4*).

- Conduct proper security assessments for the proposed feed distribution network (see *Guidance note 5*).

- Build distribution mechanisms on indigenous community structures where possible (see *Guidance note 6*).

- Where distribution in situ is not possible and feed camps are established, ensure that the security of stock and people is addressed, that logistics and resources are sufficient to support the camp for the duration of the emergency, and that management of the camp promotes rapid re-establishment of sustainable practices (see *Guidance note 7*).

Guidance notes

1. *Administrative systems.* Some organizations do not have the appropriate systems or internal policies to allow them to purchase feed from private traders, for example. Systems should be put in place before the onset of an emergency to enable such transactions to take place. This may include a list of potential suppliers of feed as part of agency emergency preparedness planning (see *Chapter 2, Core standards common to all livestock interventions, Core standard 2: Preparedness*; and *Core standard 7: Policy and advocacy*).

2. *Locally available feeds.* The use of locally available feeds offers a number of significant advantages in emergency feeding programmes:

   - Transport costs are considerably lower, although purchase costs may be higher in the affected area.

   - Shorter transport distances make losses to pilfering less likely.

CH 6 Feed

- Disruptions that may result from the percolation of imported feeds into the local market can be avoided ('imported' in this context refers to goods from outside the affected area but not necessarily from outside the country).
- Cash may be injected into the local economy through feed purchases.
- There may be significant opportunities for the use of local labour in the transportation, handling, and distribution of feeds.

Alternatively, local procurement can lead to implementing agencies effectively competing with other local livestock keepers for resources, thus increasing their vulnerability and inflating market prices. A pre-intervention assessment is required to identify the risk of market disruption.

3. *Using cash transfer mechanisms.* Feed may be supplied by cash transfer, notably vouchers, with the proviso that the required feed resources are available at an acceptable quality and quantity in the local market. A fair redemption value for the vouchers needs to be determined. The price of feed can fluctuate and is determined by the price of the ingredients, which in turn is affected by supply and demand as well as seasonal changes. The local market price of some feeds may not necessarily be a fair price: where there is short supply and high demand, local traders may try to exploit the situation. Furthermore, the transaction costs of bringing relatively small quantities (a few bags) of animal feed to remote areas can be high. The wholesale price for the feed, an estimate of the transaction costs (transportation, handling, and storage), and an acceptable profit margin should first be obtained to determine a fair value for the feed. It may be appropriate to add an additional small financial incentive for traders to accept the extra risks and costs involved with accepting vouchers.

4. *Sourcing feeds externally.* Some emergency feeding programmes may require the use of feeds that cannot be provided from local sources. These may include concentrate feeds with specific nutritional formulations or multi-nutrient blocks. In some cases, these may have to be sourced from outside the affected country or countries. In any of these cases, adequate transport systems and infrastructure must be in place. In general, the greater the separation between the points of supply and consumption, the greater the risk of interruptions to supplies. In order to minimize these risks, programmes should consider:

- arranging adequate in-country storage facilities that allow stockpiling to cover for interruptions to deliveries; it should be noted that this is not without risks because of the possibility of pilfering or degradation of feeds in store

- identifying and using more than one supply chain so that the failure of one does not completely halt the programme

- assessing the availability of local alternatives for short-term use as stopgaps; for example, high-protein straight feeds such as cottonseed or other oilseed cakes might substitute for specially formulated concentrates for a limited period

- backloading for the transport of feed into an affected area – for example, when undertaken in conjunction with a commercial destocking initiative, stock may be taken out of the area in the same trucks that bring in feed

- adopting more modest objectives for an emergency feeding programme that might be satisfied by the use of locally available feed, bearing in mind the potential negative impact on local markets of importing feed.

5. *Establishing a safe distribution network.* The risks to the personal safety of staff employed in transporting feeds for use in emergency programmes should always be of paramount importance. The disruption caused by emergencies is very often associated with a degree of lawlessness, and the cargo and trucks used by distribution networks can offer a tempting target for robbery. Most international relief agencies have well-established security guidelines that take this into account and are generally able to implement them effectively, often in collaboration with local or other security agencies. However, it may be difficult for small-scale local initiatives with limited resources to achieve a similar level of protection.

6. *Indigenous distribution structures.* Where possible and appropriate, distribution should be managed and coordinated by existing (or created) local structures. Such mechanisms – such as community distribution committees established specifically for this purpose, or existing village elders or leadership structures – facilitate the equitable distribution of resources and targeting of vulnerable households.

7. *Feed camps.* Feed camps should be planned and established with potential beneficiaries, taking into account key issues such as accessibility, security, and cost implications for both beneficiaries and supporting agencies. Given the considerable investment involved (movement of

animals, provision of feed and water, provision of animal health services, infrastructure, and staffing costs), feed camps should only be established if resources are sufficient for the anticipated duration of the emergency. Feed camps should target livestock keepers at greatest risk and the most valuable types of livestock. Management and staffing should be planned in advance, and the possibility of local community or local institutional control of the camp should be explored (see *Case study 6.1*).

Ensuring feed supplies case studies

6.1 Process case study: Women help manage a nucleus herd feeding programme in Ethiopia

One Save the Children USA intervention during the Ethiopian drought in early 2006 was a feeding project to help the most vulnerable members of pastoralist communities to protect an essential component of their livelihoods by preserving a nucleus breeding herd. Feed camps were established at three sites in Moyale District for feeding, treating, and vaccinating a selected group of productive livestock. In total, about 1,000 sheep and goats and 400 cattle were kept in the feed camps during the peak of the drought, and then returned to their owners.

Efforts were made to ensure that female-headed households were able to participate fully and benefit from the project. At the same time, women were also involved in the management of the feed camps, which included employment as caretakers to look after the stock during the day. The involvement of women in these tasks was first discussed and agreed with community leaders, building on Somali women's roles as the prime carers of sheep and goats (*Source:* Nejat Abdi Mohammed, personal communication, 2008).

6.2 Impact case study: Measuring the impacts of cattle supplementary feeding in Ethiopia

Drawing on experiences from livestock feeding in 2006, Save the Children USA expanded their livestock feed support during another drought in early 2008. This programme set up 10 feeding centres, targeting 6,750 cattle. While some animals were fed in the centres, others were left to graze and did not receive the supplementary feed.

In May 2008, an impact assessment was conducted to measure possible changes in mortality in cattle *receiving* and *not receiving* the supplementary feed. Two feeding centres, in areas where the drought had varied in severity, were selected for the impact assessment. In each, different durations of feeding had been used. In Bulbul centre, 1,000 cows were fed for 22 days, whereas in Web centre, 800 cows were fed for 67 days. The impact assessment studied mortality rates among a sample of households (*Table 6.3*).

Location/Group	Mortality	
Bulbul area: affected by moderate drought; 22-day feeding programme started on 15 March 2008		
Unfed cattle moved to grazing areas	108/425	(25.4%)
Cows fed using Save the Children USA feed	13/161	(8.1%)
Web area: affected by severe drought; 67-day feeding programme began on 9 February 2008		
Unfed cattle moved to grazing areas	139/407	(34.2%)
Cows fed using Save the Children USA feed	49/231	(21.2%)

Table 6.3 Impacts recorded in two feeding centres

- *Mortality.* Relative to unfed cattle, mortality was significantly lower in cows in both feeding centres.

- *Body condition.* Relative to unfed cattle, cows in the feeding centres gained body condition, with up to 70 per cent of cows moving from 'poor' to 'moderate' body condition.

- *Milk and calves.* Some cows gave birth in the feeding centres and were able to rear calves until the start of the rains. A total of 198 calves survived in the two centres. Some cows maintained lactation, and this milk – amounting to 5,640 litres – was fed to children.

- *Benefit–cost analyses.* In Bulbul the benefit–cost ratio of the intervention was 1.6:1 whereas in Web the benefit–cost was 1.9:1. Sensitivity analysis showed that the intervention was robust and that the benefit–cost ratio was not unduly affected by moderate to high changes in market conditions (*Source:* Bekele and Abera, 2008).

6.3 Process case study: Animal feed banks in Niger for drought preparedness

The Pastoralist Survival and Recovery Project in the Dakoro region, Niger, was run by Lutheran World Relief (LWR) with its partner Contribution à l'Education de Base (CEB). The project followed LWR's emergency food relief intervention during the Niger famine in 2005. It aimed to increase the preparedness of affected communities to cope with future droughts and famine. Based on discussions with communities, four key interventions were identified:

- provision of livestock ('re-stocking')
- feed banks
- water point development
- community forums to facilitate participation in all aspects of the project, to address issues such as conflict between farming and herding communities, and to raise awareness of rights.

The community-run feed banks aimed to ensure year-round access to reasonably priced animal feed. Each of the six banks served as a storage facility, a cooperative, and a financial institution combined, and each was supported by a warehouse and a bank account. The banks were owned by herder associations, which bought feed in bulk when prices were low during and after the harvest, and then sold the feed back to members during the year at cost, plus a management fee. This improved the pastoralists' terms of trade between feed costs and animal sales because it both decreased the cost of inputs and, with better feed, increased the sale price of animals, increasing their income and their ability to purchase food for their families.

The feed banks were established in sites selected by the local herders for accessibility, security, and visibility: generally a herders' meeting point in a village or a temporary settlement along migratory paths. Community members contributed labour and locally available building materials, such as sand and gravel, under the management of a committee elected by the herder association.

Communities anticipated short- to medium-term livelihood benefits in addition to drought protection; namely, improved animal health and an increase in milk production, with the latter leading to better nutrition and/or increased income. The feed banks were expected to reduce livestock deaths in case of drought and also to reduce stress sales of livestock.

The combination of the feed banks and the provision of livestock based on a traditional restocking system (see *Case study 9.2* in *Chapter 9, Provision of livestock*) was seen as having a positive effect on the terms of trade for livestock keepers in the Dakoro region (*Sources*: LWR, 2005; Burns, 2006; Evariste Karangwa, Meghan Armisted and Mahamadou Ouhoumoudou, personal communication, 2008).

6.4 Process case study: Building on existing feed supply lines and distribution points in India

When a major earthquake occurred in 2001, Gujarat State in India had already been experiencing a drought for two years. As such, the government already had a national committee in place to monitor and implement drought mitigation activities. The railway and truck supply lines that were used to bring concentrate and fodder to livestock in drought-stricken areas were therefore also used to deliver feed to distribution points in the weeks following the earthquake. Local NGOs and village institutions were able to assist in providing temporary shelters and secure holding areas for livestock, along with feed and water. These groups also helped to coordinate the receipt and distribution of feed sent to the earthquake-affected area by private organizations and NGOs from outside the state (*Sources:* Goe, 2001a; Goe, 2001b).

6.5 Impact case study: Human nutrition impacts of livestock supplementary feed during drought in Ethiopia

In the Somali Region of Ethiopia, the main risk period for child malnutrition is towards the end of the long dry season, when livestock milk supply becomes limited as grazing is less available. A research project run by Tufts University and Save the Children aimed to test approaches for prolonging the supply of animal milk to children during this critical period. Based on discussions with local women, it was decided to provide supplementary feed and preventive veterinary care to milking cows and goats near homesteads during the main dry season, and then measure the amounts of milk fed to children over time.

As the project was implemented, a drought affected the research sites and so the context shifted from 'normal dry season' to 'drought period'. The changes in milk offtake in goats and cows in two of the project sites are summarized in *Table 6.4.*

Table 6.4 Changes in milk offtake in goats and cows

Livestock type	Stage of lactation	Average milk offtake (mL)	
		Dry season with no intervention, normal year 2010	Dry season with intervention, drought year 2011
Goat (n=352)	Early	224	628
	Middle	54	567
	Late	8	382
Cattle (n=112)	Early	638	2197
	Middle	293	2251
	Late	46	860

Women reported that all the additional milk was used for household consumption, especially for children. Monitoring of children showed that their nutritional status was maintained during the drought, whereas the condition of children in control sites declined during the same period (*Source:* Sadler et al., 2012).

6.6 Process case study: Using invasive plants for animal feed in Sudan

Over the past thirty years, Kassala State in eastern Sudan has experienced a range of humanitarian emergencies, including drought and food insecurity, flooding and wildfires, complex emergencies associated with conflict, forced displacements, and refugee crises. The economy of Kassala is based on agriculture; this includes both rainfed and irrigated cultivation as well as pastoralist livestock production that involves seasonal movements across the state. Drought contributed to a livestock fodder gap in the late dry season, and the Sudanese Red Crescent Society (SRCS) implemented an approach that produced dry season fodder from an invasive rangeland plant called *Prosopis* (mesquite). The dual aim was to support livestock while also contributing to *Prosopis* control.

The *Prosopis* tree produces pods, and these were collected. SRCS installed a grinding machine for processing the pods and developed guidelines for *Prosopis* management in the eastern Atbara River region. There was dense coverage of the plant in both the main agricultural land and in the adjacent forest areas. Ground pods were a welcome feed intervention by the beneficiaries. In other countries, including Kenya and Ethiopia, ground *Prosopis* pods were also fed to animals, particularly goats, as a supplemental feed (*Source:* Gebru et al., 2013).

6.7 Process case study: Feed provision in severe winter in Bolivia

Communities in the Andean highlands in Bolivia depend mainly on their livestock – chiefly llamas and sheep – for their livelihood. In June and July of 2011, the Potosí region suffered snowstorms, resulting in a metre of snow in some areas and extreme temperatures as low as -20 °C. Over 1,200 llamas were killed, and many became emaciated due to loss of forage as well as disease. Communities living above 3,600 m above sea level were particularly badly affected.

In response to the crisis, the United Nations Food and Agriculture Organization (FAO) implemented a supplementary feed programme, providing forage and mineral supplements to 140,000 llamas belonging to 1,800 families. This activity was complemented by capacity building and other activities to increase resilience against future severe weather events, including forage and food crop seed reserves and the introduction of improved forage crops, short-cycle varieties, and grass production in protected underground nurseries or ditches.

The activities focused specifically on women as they are the main livestock keepers because of the steady outmigration of men to urban areas in search of employment. The project worked in conjunction with the local authorities and representatives from community-based organizations in the selection of targeted beneficiaries and the distribution of the feed and other inputs (*Source:* Einstein Tejada, personal communication, 2014).

Appendix 6.1: Assessment checklist for feed provision

This checklist is intended as an aid to rapid assessment for ensuring supplies of feed resources. It provides a framework for targeting expert opinion from both the local community and those involved in delivering emergency assistance. In addition to the topics considered in this checklist, more detailed evaluation of key issues may be required, such as local acceptability, resource availability, and logistics.

Emergency feeding: In situ

Feed allowances and nutritional quality

- Have feeding regimes and allowances been developed that are appropriate to the specific objectives of the feeding programme?
- Do these feeding regimes take realistic account of the logistical difficulties that may be encountered when attempting to deliver them to target beneficiaries?
- Do these feeding regimes take realistic account of available budgets?

Feed safety

- Have risk assessments been conducted for possible feed contaminants that might put livestock in danger?
- Are the quality control measures used in the programme for screening feeds adequate?
- Are storage times for feeds consistent with maintaining feed safety and quality?
- Are proper procedures in place for ensuring adequate standards of cleanliness both for vehicles used for transporting feeds and for storage facilities?

Sourcing and distribution of feeds

- Are the agencies' administrative systems flexible enough to meet the needs of a continuing feed supply programme?
- Where possible, has feed been sourced locally to minimize transport costs and support local traders and other businesses?

- Where feeds are sourced locally, have steps been taken to ensure that other stakeholder groups are not put at risk as a result?
- Has provision been made for the replenishment of depleted feed stores during the recovery phase?
- Can opportunities for backloading (ensuring trucks carry loads both in and out of affected areas) be identified to increase the efficiency of the distribution system?
- Are distribution networks adequately protected from security risks?

Emergency feeding: Feed camps

In addition to the above:

Acceptability of feed camp and identification of beneficiaries

- Can a proper assessment be made of the capacity of the feed camp to meet the immediate and longer-terms needs of the various groups of target beneficiaries?
- Have proper procedures been put in place for informing beneficiary groups about what the feed camp can – and cannot – offer, and the terms under which they would participate?
- Have potential beneficiaries been properly informed about the risks to which they might be exposed as a result of participating in the initiative?
- Are potential beneficiaries likely to be able to meet the demands of participating in the feed camp (such as providing labour for overseeing animals)?
- Are proper procedures in place for identifying the beneficiary groups and the most appropriate animal types to be targeted by the establishment of a feed camp?

Logistics and management

- Can construction and other materials necessary for establishing the feed camp be sourced locally or transported to the site at an acceptable cost and risk?
- Are adequate supplies of feed and water available or deliverable for the level of occupancy envisaged for the camp?
- Can appropriate support services be provided, such as animal health?

- Are managers with appropriate levels of skills available to run the camp?
- Are management structures in place that can address the needs and concerns of all local stakeholders?
- Can adequate levels of staffing be put in place for the camp? Where possible, labour inputs should include participating beneficiaries.

Appendix 6.2: Examples of monitoring and evaluation indicators for livestock feed interventions

	Process indicators (measure things happening)	Impact indicators (measure the result of things happening)

Designing the system	• Number of meetings with community/community representatives and other stakeholders, including private sector suppliers, where relevant	• Meeting reports with analysis of options for providing livestock feed
		• Action plan including:
		  - roles and responsibilities of different actors
		  - approach for feed provision, including procurement, transport, and distribution of feed
		  - community involvement in selecting beneficiary households and number and type of livestock to receive feed
		  - community involvement in managing livestock to receive feed, e.g. in village-based feeding centres

Provision of livestock feed	• Amount and value of feed procured and delivered to project sites • Number and type of livestock receiving project feed • Amount of feed by feed type per animal per day • Duration of feeding	• Mortality in animals receiving project feed vs. animals not receiving project feed • Human nutrition – consumption of animal-sourced foods (e.g. milk) derived from project animals per household and family member • Body condition of animals receiving project feed vs. animals not receiving feed • Increase or decrease in women's and girls' labour burden to collect livestock feed • Influence on policy

See also the LEGS Evaluation Tool available on the LEGS website:
<http://www.livestock-emergency.net/resources/general-resources-legs-specific/>.

References and further reading

Ayantunde, A.A., Fernández-Rivera, S., and McCrabb, G. (eds) (2005) *Coping with Feed Scarcity in Smallholder Livestock Systems in Developing Countries*, International Livestock Research Institute (ILRI), Nairobi, <http://mahider.ilri.org/handle/10568/855> [accessed 18 May 2014].

Bekele, G. and Abera, T. (2008) *Livelihoods-Based Drought Response in Ethiopia: Impact Assessment of Livestock Feed Supplementation*, Feinstein International Center, Tufts University, Digital Collections and Archives, Medford, MA <http://hdl.handle.net/10427/71144> [accessed 18 May 2014].

Blackwood, I. (2006) *Survival Feeding in Drought*, PrimeFact 286, New South Wales Department of Primary Industries, New South Wales. Available from: <http://www.livestock-emergency.net/resources/feed-supply/> [accessed 18 May 2014].

Blackwood, I. and Clayton, E. (2006) *Supplementary Feeding Principles,* PrimeFact 287, New South Wales Department of Primary Industries, New South Wales. Available from: <http://www.livestock-emergency.net/resources/feed-supply/> [accessed 18 May 2014].

Burns, J. (2006) *ARVIP Baseline* Survey and *Mid-Term Visit Report*, Feinstein International Center, Tufts University, Medford, MA.

Catley, A. (ed.) (2007) *Impact Assessment of Livelihoods-Based Drought Interventions in Moyale and Dire Woredas, Ethiopia*, Pastoralists Livelihoods Initiative, Feinstein International Center, Tufts University, Medford, MA, together with CARE, Save the Children USA, ad USAID-Ethiopia, <https://wikis.uit.tufts.edu/confluence/download/attachments/14553622/IMPACT~1.PDF?version=1> [accessed 17 May 2014].

Catley, A., Admassu, B., Bekele, G. and Abebe, D. (2014) 'Livestock mortality in pastoralist herds in Ethiopia and implications for drought response', *Disasters* 38(3): 500–516 <http://dx.doi.org/10.1111/disa.12060>.

Cripps, S. (2013) 'Brinkworth drove stops Surat' in *Queensland Country Life*, <http://www.queenslandcountrylife.com.au/news/agriculture/cattle/beef/brinkworth-drove-stops-surat/2668776.aspx> [accessed 20 May 2013].

Gebru, G., Yousif, H., Mohamed, A., Negesse, B. and Young, H. (2013) *Livestock, Livelihoods, and Disaster Response, Part Two: Three Case Studies of Livestock Emergency Programmes in Sudan, and Lessons Learned*, Feinstein International Center, Tufts University, Medford, MA, <http://fic.tufts.edu/publication-item/livestock-livelihoods-and-disaster-response-part-two-2/> [accessed 18 May 2014].

Goe, M.R. (2001a) *Assessment of the Scope of Earthquake Damage to the Livestock Sector in Gujarat State, India*, Consultancy Mission Report, Food and Agriculture Organization of the United Nations (FAO), Bangkok/Rome.

Goe, M.R. (2001b) *Relief and Rehabilitation Activities for the Livestock Sector in Earthquake Affected Areas of Kachchh District, Gujarat State, India*, Technical Cooperation Project Proposal, FAO, Rome/Bangkok.

IIED (International Institute for Environment and Development) and SOS Sahel UK (2010) *Modern and Mobile: The Future of Livestock Production in Africa's Drylands,* IIED and SOS Sahel UK, London, <http://pubs.iied.org/12565IIED.html?c=drylands/pastoral&r=p> [accessed 18 May 2014].

LEGS (Livestock Emergency Guidelines and Standards) (2014), *Livestock Emergency Guidelines and Standards, 2nd Edition*, Practical Action Publishing: Rugby.

LWR (Lutheran World Relief) (2005) *Lutheran World Relief Pastoralist Survival and Recovery Program (ARVIP)*, Proposal 2005, Lutheran World Relief, Niamey.

Sadler, K., Mitchard, E., Abdulahi, A., Shiferaw, Y., Bekele, G. and Catley, A. (2012) *Milk Matters: The Impact of Dry Season Livestock Support on Milk Supply and Child Nutrition in Somali Region, Ethiopia*, Feinstein International Center, Tufts University and Save the Children, Addis Ababa, <http://fic.tufts.edu/publication-item/milk-matters/> [accessed 18 May 2014].

CH 6 Feed

CHAPTER 7

Technical standards for the provision of water

Provision of water

```
┌─────────────────────────┐
│        Standard 1        │
│  Assessment and planning │
└─────────────────────────┘
              │
              ▼
┌──────────────────┐   ┌──────────────────┐
│   Water points   │   │  Water trucking  │
└──────────────────┘   └──────────────────┘
         │                      │
         ▼                      ▼
┌──────────────────┐   ┌──────────────────────┐
│    Standard 1    │   │      Standard 1      │
│ Location of      │   │ Water sources and    │
│ water points     │   │ quality              │
└──────────────────┘   └──────────────────────┘
         │                      │
         ▼                      ▼
┌──────────────────┐   ┌──────────────────────┐
│    Standard 2    │   │      Standard 2      │
│ Rehabilitation   │   │ Logistics and        │
│ and              │   │ distribution         │
│ establishment    │   │                      │
└──────────────────┘   └──────────────────────┘
```

Introduction

This chapter discusses the importance of the provision of water in emergency response. It presents the options for water interventions together with tools to determine their appropriateness. The Standards, Key actions, and Guidance notes follow each option. Case studies are found at the end of the chapter. They are followed by appendices containing checklists for assessment and monitoring and evaluation. Key references are listed at the end.

Links to the LEGS livelihoods objectives

The provision of water for livestock in an emergency focuses on the survival of livestock assets during and beyond the emergency and, as such, relates largely to the second and third LEGS livelihoods objectives:

- to protect the key livestock assets of crisis-affected communities
- to rebuild key livestock assets among crisis-affected communities.

In this way (as with the provision of feed – see *Chapter 6, Ensuring feed supplies*), livestock vital to livelihoods are kept alive by the provision of water and, after a time, animal stocks can be rebuilt. The provision of water also impacts on the first LEGS livelihoods objective – to provide immediate benefits to crisis-affected communities using existing livestock resources – to the extent that keeping stock alive contributes to the immediate household food supply.

The importance of the provision of water for livestock in emergency response

Alongside the provision of veterinary care for traumatized or acutely diseased animals, the provision of water in an emergency is probably the intervention with the most immediate and indispensable impacts for livestock keepers. In the absence of water, animals (with the exception of some camelids) cannot survive for more than a few days. Therefore in emergency situations where water sources have been seriously compromised, the provision of alternatives is of the highest priority. Even where water is currently available, relief programmes need to assess and, if necessary, implement appropriate responses to potential and future threats to water sources to ensure that other relief efforts are not undermined by water shortages. While water for livestock must meet some basic quality requirements, the quality standard is not as high as for human consumption. In other words, livestock can make use of water unfit for humans.

The provision of water also contributes to the first of the animal welfare 'five freedoms' described in the *Introduction*; namely, *'freedom from hunger and thirst* – by ready access to fresh water and a diet to maintain full health and vigour'.

➡ Options for water provision

Water is a homogeneous commodity, but it may be available from a range of sources and deliverable by a number of methods. This can complicate the selection of appropriate interventions that seek to match supply with demand. As a rule, the most cost-effective and sustainable options should be selected. However, the need to deliver water is often acute, and expensive and unsustainable methods such as water trucking may have to be considered at least for the short term. Cash options such as the provision of vouchers for the purchase of livestock water supplies may be appropriate and cost-effective, depending on the market and availability (see *Chapter 3, Initial assessment and identifying responses,* for more details on cash and voucher responses).

Option 1: Water points

Providing water points will almost invariably offer the most viable, long-term solution to the problem of water shortages, assuming that it is feasible to implement a sustainable management plan for their use. Water distribution points may take a number of different forms, including wells, boreholes, and surface water harvesting systems (for example, check dams and storage tanks). However, the principles underlying their establishment and the issues that must be addressed in managing them effectively are broadly similar.

During an emergency, access to water points may be provided for livestock keepers in one of three ways:

1.1 changing the management of existing water points to provide broader access to affected populations

1.2 rehabilitating existing but degraded water points

1.3 establishing new water points.

The first of these approaches could normally be implemented at the lowest cost but may not be feasible due to lack of adequate water or because of the complexities of meeting the needs of both existing and new users. In slow-onset emergencies, rehabilitation and establishment of water points may be best considered as preparedness interventions rather than emergency response activities.

Conflicts between the demands of human populations and their associated livestock for water may also be an issue. However, this is likely to represent a less difficult problem than when trucking water. With proper planning and management, it should be possible to create a network of distribution points that can meet the needs of both humans and animals.

Option 2: Water trucking

Water trucking should generally be regarded as a last resort and only used during the first stages of an emergency. It is expensive, resource-inefficient, and labour-intensive. However, due to the critical nature of the impact of dehydration on livestock, it is sometimes the only option that can be implemented rapidly to keep animals alive in the short term. As a rule, therefore, trucking should be regarded as a temporary intervention that will be replaced as soon as possible by other means of water provision.

Water trucking requires major logistical inputs. Accordingly, great care and attention need to be given to the planning and management of trucking operations. This includes the need to monitor the evolving situation, making sure that routes remain open, protecting drivers and other crew from changes in the security situation, and maintaining the tankers effectively.

The advantages and disadvantages of the different options for the provision of water are summarized in *Table 7.1*.

Table 7.1 Advantages and disadvantages of water provision options

Option	Advantages	Disadvantages
1.1 Changing management of existing water sources	• Relatively cheap option making maximum use of existing opportunities and resources • Can normally be implemented rapidly in response to an emergency	• Often limited opportunities on the ground to achieve this • Can introduce potential for conflict among groups of new users[1]
1.2 Rehabilitating existing water sources	• Potentially cheaper than other water provision options • Management structures and systems for the water source may already exist • Long-term solution that can outlast the emergency	• Reasons for original degradation may still apply or recur

Option	Advantages	Disadvantages
(continued) 1.2 Rehabilitating existing water sources	• Potential to provide water for both livestock and human needs • Support of vulnerable households through cash-for-work (CFW) projects (e.g. dam de-silting, cleaning natural water catchments, rehabilitation of existing pan)	
1.3 Establishing new water sources	• Potential to provide sustainable new water sources for emergency and post-emergency populations in immediate locality of need • Potential to provide water for both livestock and human needs	• More costly than rehabilitation; requires very high capital investment • Appropriate siting may be difficult in short (emergency) time frame • Locally based and agreed management systems need to be established to prevent conflict and ensure equitable access, and to ensure sustainable use of the water resource and the surrounding environment • Potential negative consequences (conflict, environmental degradation) of making new areas accessible to people and livestock • Risks due to modification of the usual grazing pattern (easy access to dry-season pastures, modification of migration routes, land tenure disputes, etc.)
2. Water trucking	• Can respond rapidly to immediate water needs • May make use of water of insufficient quality for human consumption	• Expensive and resource-inefficient – relocating livestock to water sources may be more appropriate • Labour-intensive and logistically complex • Not sustainable – temporary solution only • Greatest potential for conflict between human and livestock water needs • Requires locally based management structure to ensure equitable access to water • Potential conflict with existing users of water source

Timing of interventions

As noted above, water trucking is a short-term measure that may be appropriate in the immediate aftermath (rapid onset) or emergency (slow onset) phases of an emergency but which should not be continued beyond these stages, as it is a costly and unsustainable intervention. The rehabilitation or establishment of water sources, in contrast, may also be carried out in the subsequent stages, and indeed should ideally link with longer-term water development programmes in the area, as should the improved management of water points. The establishment of new water sources should only be considered when existing degraded water sources are insufficient or unsuitable for rehabilitation (*Table 7.2*).

Table 7.2 Possible timing of water interventions

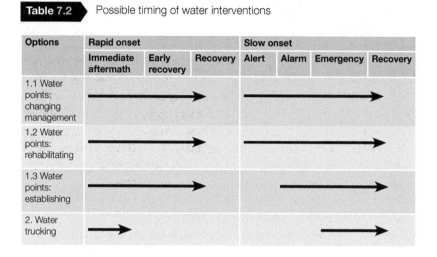

Options	Rapid onset			Slow onset			
	Immediate aftermath	Early recovery	Recovery	Alert	Alarm	Emergency	Recovery
1.1 Water points: changing management							
1.2 Water points: rehabilitating							
1.3 Water points: establishing							
2. Water trucking							

Links to Sphere and other LEGS chapters

The provision of water may be complementary to other livestock-based emergency responses, particularly supplementary feeding (see *Chapter 6, Ensuring feed supplies*) and destocking (see *Chapter 4, Destocking*), whereby some animals are taken out of the production system, and efforts such as the provision of water and feed are made in order to ensure the survival of the remaining stock. Coordination between initiatives and between agencies is therefore paramount to avoid one activity undermining another (see *Chapter 2, Core standards common to all livestock interventions, Core standard 8: Coordination*).

The provision of water for livestock may also be complementary to human water provision, particularly where the rehabilitation or establishment of water sources provides water of a suitable quality for both animals and humans. Water trucking for livestock, in contrast, may compete with human water supplies unless carefully managed. For further information on human water supplies, see the Sphere Handbook's chapter on 'Water supply, sanitation and hygiene promotion' (Sphere, 2011). The need to ensure coordination between human and livestock water supply may become particularly important in camp settings, where space and water sources may both be limited.

Cross-cutting themes and other issues to consider

Gender and vulnerable groups

As with the provision of feed (*Chapter 6, Ensuring feed supplies*), ensuring that the water provided for livestock during an emergency reaches the most vulnerable presents a number of challenges. For example, wealthier livestock keepers may be able to secure private means to provide water for their animals – an option unavailable to poorer households. Land rights, ethnicity, and local politics may all affect the access of certain groups to water. Interventions should therefore take into account the constraints facing vulnerable groups within the community to ensure that access is as equitable as possible. Gender roles and implications should be assessed, particularly for poorer women and girls, who may be at risk of violent assault if they have to travel over distance to bring water for stock, or who may suffer exploitation or inequitable access to water.

Protection

The personal security and protection of water users should be taken into account. For example, people watering animals at water points may be vulnerable to livestock rustling, robbery, or attack, especially women. Failure to involve existing water management structures (whether community or local government) may lead to friction with new water users or other institutions. Water point management must therefore be addressed prior to rehabilitation or establishment in order to avoid ownership conflicts as well as to ensure equitable access and sustainable systems for the future. Issues of water management are particularly important because of the need to ensure the protection of water users around camps. For example, camp residents who need access to water points outside the camp for their livestock may come into conflict with the host populations. Early negotiation with all stakeholders can help to minimize potential conflicts.

Environment

Environmental considerations in the provision of water for livestock in emergencies include the importance of avoiding the following: excessive extraction (either through density of water sources or high extraction rates) that would affect the water table; and high concentration of livestock around water points that could lead to environmental degradation. Alternatively, in some situations (for example, in pastoral societies) the provision of water in accordance with existing natural resource management strategies may have a positive impact on the environment by supporting balanced and effective natural resource use. It is also important to ensure that human water supplies are not contaminated by livestock and that contaminated water supplies do not lead to disease transmission to wild species, which can endanger wildlife and also lead to further contamination of livestock.

Local capacities

Crisis-affected communities also draw on their own capacities to respond to emergencies; for example, their indigenous knowledge of natural resources, and, in particular, the relationship between water sources and natural resource management. Local water management systems and indigenous institutions may also play a significant role in the management of water points and the avoidance of conflict.

The Standards

Before engaging in water provision initiatives, the feasibility and costs of the different options should be carefully considered, as highlighted in *Figure 7.1*.

Water standard 1: Assessment and planning

Water provision for livestock is based on an analysis of needs, opportunities, and local water management systems.

CH 7 Water

Key actions

- Starting with an assessment of existing water source management systems, conduct an analysis of different water provision options that can be used to form the basis for water provision activities (see *Guidance note 1*).

- Assess existing and degraded water sources for water quantity and quality (see *Guidance notes 2 and 3*).

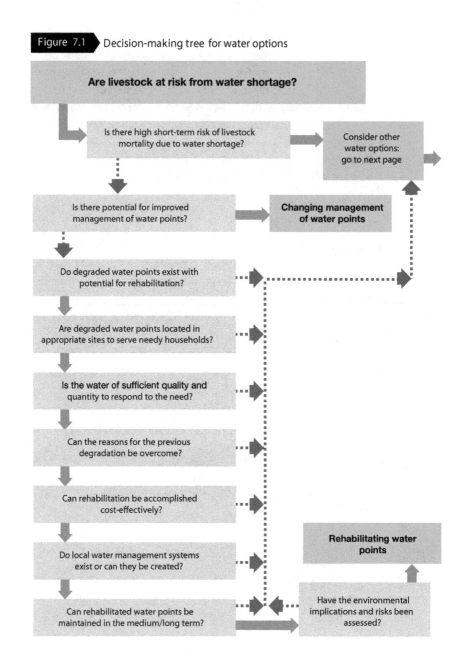

Figure 7.1 Decision-making tree for water options

Are livestock at risk from water shortage?

Is there high short-term risk of livestock mortality due to water shortage?

Consider other water options: go to next page

Is there potential for improved management of water points?

Changing management of water points

Do degraded water points exist with potential for rehabilitation?

Are degraded water points located in appropriate sites to serve needy households?

Is the water of sufficient quality and quantity to respond to the need?

Can the reasons for the previous degradation be overcome?

Can rehabilitation be accomplished cost-effectively?

Rehabilitating water points

Do local water management systems exist or can they be created?

Can rehabilitated water points be maintained in the medium/long term?

Have the environmental implications and risks been assessed?

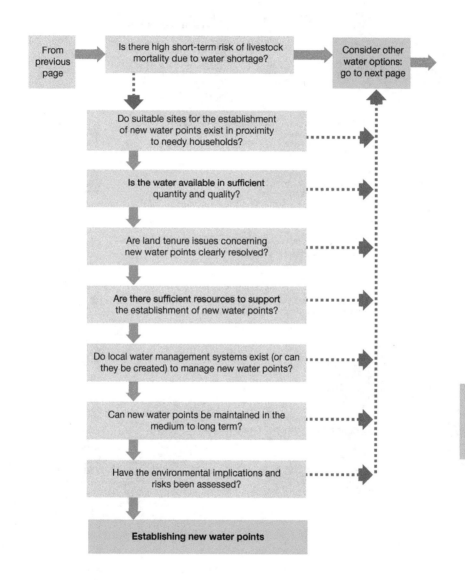

From previous page → Is there high short-term risk of livestock mortality due to water shortage? → Consider other water options: go to next page →

Do suitable sites for the establishment of new water points exist in proximity to needy households? → ▶

Is the water available in sufficient quantity and quality? → ▶

Are land tenure issues concerning new water points clearly resolved? → ▶

Are there sufficient resources to support the establishment of new water points? → ▶

Do local water management systems exist (or can they be created) to manage new water points? → ▶

Can new water points be maintained in the medium to long term? → ▶

Have the environmental implications and risks been assessed? → ▶

Establishing new water points

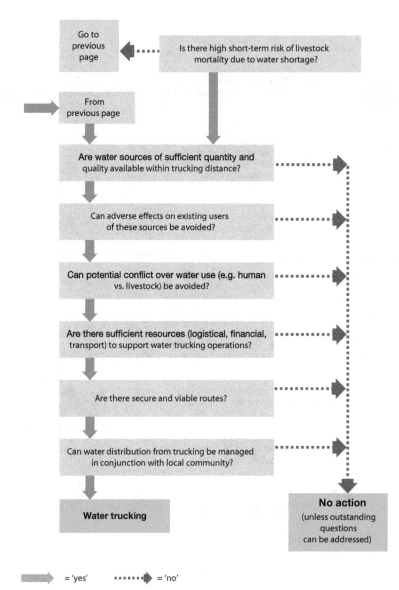

Go to previous page	Is there high short-term risk of livestock mortality due to water shortage?

From previous page

Are water sources of sufficient quantity and quality available within trucking distance?

Can adverse effects on existing users of these sources be avoided?

Can potential conflict over water use (e.g. human vs. livestock) be avoided?

Are there sufficient resources (logistical, financial, transport) to support water trucking operations?

Are there secure and viable routes?

Can water distribution from trucking be managed in conjunction with local community?

Water trucking

No action
(unless outstanding questions can be addressed)

➡ = 'yes'   ┅┅► = 'no'

Note
The result *'No action (unless outstanding questions can be addressed)'* does not necessarily mean that no intervention should take place, but rather that further training or capacity building may be required in order to be able to answer 'yes' to the key questions.

- Identify effective management systems to ensure continued provision of water of acceptable quality without conflict, thus addressing the needs of the different user groups (see *Guidance note 4*).

- Analyse policy constraints to water access and take appropriate action to address them (see *Guidance note 5*).

Guidance notes

1. *Analysis of options, and assessment of existing water sources.* The planning of water provision activities should begin with an assessment of existing water sources to review the quantity and quality of available water, including water sources that have fallen into disrepair and are no longer used. Organizations on the ground may already have this information (see *Chapter 2, Core standards common to all livestock interventions, Core standard 2: Preparedness*). This helps to ensure that water interventions build on existing infrastructure and contribute to low cost and sustainability. *Appendix 7.1* contains a checklist for assisting with rapid water point assessment. The assessment should consider the impact on the environment of the location and capacity of any potential water source. The siting of water sources can have a negative environmental impact; conversely, when water points are planned in conjunction with natural resource management strategies, the impact on the environment and on the natural resources available for livestock can be beneficial. Because the cost of water trucking is very high, other options should be explored first, including the relocation of livestock to existing water sources. The needs for human water supply should also form part of this analysis (see *Water points standard 1* below).

2. *Water quality.* Although water quality for livestock is generally a much less critical issue than water quality for humans, animals can also be affected by water-borne diseases such as salmonella, anthrax, and colibacillosis. In the absence of a recognized field test to assess the bacterial content of water, a basic investigation is recommended concerning possible chemical contamination (nearby factories) and bacteriological/organic contamination (human settlements), including consultation with the local community (see *Appendix 7.1*).

3. *Contamination of water sources.* Where livestock and humans share water sources, the water may easily become contaminated by the stock and affect human health and well-being. Simple management measures

can be put in place to ensure that this does not happen, including the use of troughs or pans for livestock watering. Protection of water sources may also be necessary to prevent the water becoming contaminated with acaricides and other chemicals.

4. *Analysis of existing water management systems.* Boreholes as well as shallow and deep wells are usually managed by local (often customary) institutional arrangements. The rehabilitation of existing water sources or the establishment of new sources should take into account these management systems, and the involvement of women is recommended to strengthen sustainable and equitable water use. The management of water distribution in water trucking activities can also build on local water management systems to help ensure equitable distribution and access within communities. Where camp residents need access to water for their livestock and must share resources with the host community, prior negotiations can help avoid conflict. Establishing clear and equitable management systems for water sources is also important for the longer term – into the recovery phase and beyond. Experience has shown that unless these issues are considered at the beginning of the intervention, water sources may fall into disrepair after the emergency is over.

5. *Policy constraints.* Water sources may exist, but access may be limited or restricted because of formal or informal policy constraints. These constraints should be analysed during the assessment, and appropriate action should be planned to address them (see *Chapter 2, Core standards common to all livestock interventions, Core standard 7*).

Water points standard 1: Location of water points

Water source rehabilitation and establishment programmes are carefully located to ensure equitable access to water for the livestock of the most vulnerable households in the affected areas.

Key actions

- Base the location of water points on a sound assessment of current and future demands of both local human and livestock populations (see *Guidance note 1*).

- On the supply side, ensure that the capacities of the water sources used can reasonably be expected to meet needs throughout the period of the emergency and beyond (see *Guidance note 2*).

- When making arrangements for access to water points and distribution of water to users, take into account the need to ensure equity among all vulnerable groups (see *Guidance note 3*).

- Make proper arrangements to protect the personal safety of users and their livestock while they use the water point (see *Guidance note 4*).

- Organize siting and management of water points in conjunction with community leaders, preferably building on existing indigenous water management systems (see *Guidance note 5*).

Guidance notes

1. *Assessment of demand for water.* Demand assessments should be based on the best estimates derived from livestock population censuses, local authority records, and consultation with local populations. In addition, livestock traders and middlemen may be able to offer useful information in some areas. Ease of collection and accessibility to animals should be considered: if stock are to consume at the water point, then demand assessments should consider reasonable walking distances to determine the area covered by the water point. Where water will be carried to where the animals are located, similar assessments should be made.

2. *Adequacy of the water supply.* Supplies from a water point may be inadequate for meeting demand, in which case supplementary arrangements may be necessary (for example, establishing additional water points nearby or trucking in extra supplies). In addition to satisfying current demand, assessment of the adequacy of water supplies should take into account the future utility of the water points, both generally and in the event of other emergencies. Ideally, water points should have the potential to reduce threats posed by future emergencies.

3. *Appropriate and equitable use.* The needs of humans for water are paramount during emergencies. However, water may be available that is unsuitable for human consumption but can be used for livestock. In some societies, social constraints may make it difficult for different ethnic, tribal, or caste groups to access the same water point. Such issues need to be handled with considerable sensitivity to ensure equitable access for all.

4. **Security arrangements.** People taking animals to water points may be vulnerable to livestock rustling, general robbery, and other forms of personal attack because their movements are easily predicted. The security needs of women in these situations are particularly important. Liaison with the agencies responsible for managing security in affected areas is needed at the planning stages to ensure that these dangers can be reduced as much as possible.

5. **Community leadership.** As highlighted in *Water standard 1*, local water management systems should be taken into account when siting and organizing the management of water points, whether for the rehabilitation of previous sources or the establishment of new ones. This is vital to ensure the future management and maintenance of the water source beyond the emergency and to contribute to sustainable and equitable access to water for all community members. This may be particularly important in camps because of potential competition for the resource between camp residents and the local population. In these situations, negotiation and agreement with community leaders are paramount to avoid conflict. It is recommended that women are always included on water management committees because they generally need to negotiate for domestic water use as well.

Water points standard 2: Water point rehabilitation and establishment

Rehabilitated or newly established water points represent a cost-effective and sustainable means of providing clean water in adequate quantities for the livestock that will use them.

Key actions

- Consider the rehabilitation of water points as an intervention only when demand in the affected area cannot be adequately met by extending the use of existing water points (see *Guidance note 1*).

- Undertake a full survey of degraded water points and the reasons for the degradation for all locations in the affected area where demand exists or is likely to develop (see *Guidance note 2*).

- Consider establishing new water points as an intervention only when the use of existing water points or their rehabilitation is not possible, and when the consequences have been carefully considered (see *Guidance note 3*).

- Deliver the technical inputs and materials required to implement the rehabilitation/establishment programme effectively to the selected locations (see *Guidance note 4*).

- Ensure that people are available (and trained) for the routine management and maintenance of water points (see *Guidance note 5*).

Guidance notes

1. **The need to rehabilitate water points.** Extending the use of existing water points is a cheaper option than water point rehabilitation, but the potential for introducing conflict between existing and new users should be carefully evaluated at the planning stage. In practice, it may be possible to offer some coverage of affected populations by using existing sources, but this may need to be augmented by rehabilitation as part of an integrated programme.

2. **Identification of water points suitable for rehabilitation.** A properly conducted survey is very important if a cost-effective programme of water point provision is to be established. This should include, for each water point:
   - water quality
   - resources required to operate a rehabilitation programme
   - likely capacity (quantity and persistence)
   - extent of damage and ease/cost of repairs
   - demand from users
   - knowledge of why the point has become degraded and any implications for its successful rehabilitation (issues such as conflict, water quality, and confusion over ownership may all contribute to lack of use, as well as technical and maintenance issues).

3. **The need to establish new water points.** If rehabilitation of existing water points does not offer adequate coverage of the affected population, the establishment of new ones may be considered. However, all the potential consequences of establishing a new water point (land tenure issues, modification of grazing pattern, environmental degradation, competition over resources, etc.) must be carefully analysed first.

4. **Technical feasibility.** In addition to assisting with the planning of rehabilitation schemes, an appreciation of the reasons why water points

have fallen into disuse may be of relevance when considering the technical feasibility of completing their rehabilitation. Basic requirements include:

- availability of qualified water engineers and labourers to implement programmes

- capacity to deliver required materials to the site, including adequate access roads

- continuous availability of spare parts for wells and boreholes.

These requirements apply to both rehabilitating and establishing water points, although it should be noted that the equipment required for establishing new water points is likely to be considerably heavier (for example, drilling rigs/excavation equipment for digging wells) and may therefore require higher capacity transport and better roads to allow access.

5. *Responsibilities.* Water points need routine management and maintenance as well as people (whether community members or agency staff) to conduct:

- routine checking to ensure that water quality and supplies are being maintained

- monitoring to ensure that access is maintained equitably for all users

- resolution of disputes among different user groups

- routine maintenance and ordering and replacement of damaged parts (manual wells are generally less damage-prone than boreholes)

- appropriate training of water committees for local users (taking into consideration gender and other vulnerability issues).

Water trucking standard 1: Water sources and quality

Water for trucking is obtained from sources that can maintain an adequate supply of assured quality during the period over which the intervention will operate.

Key actions

- Implement water trucking only as a short-term measure when other options are not possible (see *Guidance note 1*).

- Ensure the supply of water can be maintained throughout the lifespan of the proposed trucking operations (see *Guidance note 2*).

- Ensure that use of water sources by trucking operations does not compromise the needs of their existing users and has the approval of any relevant statutory authorities (see *Guidance notes 2* and *3*).
- Ensure that the use of water sources does not reduce the availability of water for human populations (see *Guidance notes 3* and *4*).
- Ensure that the water quality is suitable for livestock (see *Guidance note 5*).
- Ensure that tankers and other water containers are properly cleaned before use (see *Guidance note 6*).

Guidance notes

1. **Short-term measure.** Water trucking should be considered as a last-resort measure in order to save livestock lives as it is expensive and administratively complicated. Even using trucks to deliver water for human use is generally discouraged. Other options, including relocation of livestock closer to existing sources of water, should be thoroughly explored before trucking begins.

2. **Continuity of supply.** Although water trucking operations should aim to operate only in the short term, this is not always possible. Whatever the term of the operation, a realistic assessment of the continuity of water supplies needs to be made at the planning stage. This should include the following steps:

   - Assess whether water sources have the physical capacity to continue to supply during the operation. The potential for selected sources to be affected by the spread of the emergency should be considered as part of this issue.
   - Secure permission from existing users or from the relevant authorities to access the source.
   - Ascertain whether accessibility of the sources can be maintained; for example, repeated passage of trucks may degrade access routes.
   - Consider budgetary implications carefully, as water trucking is generally a high-cost operation. Operational budgets need to be adequate to handle extended trucking services if alternative interventions are delayed. Costs can be significantly reduced if water sources can be located close to the ultimate distribution points. However, this can increase the risk of conflict with existing users or threats to the continuity of supply.

3. **Considering the needs of existing users.** It is unlikely that water sources used for trucking operations will have no existing users. Conflict can seriously undermine the viability of the operation. In the worst-case scenario, it can even create a new tier of adversely affected households. Although locating water sources close to where the water will be consumed may be financially desirable, this should not extend to areas that might compromise existing users. During the planning stages of a trucking operation, managers need to engage with local leaders and other stakeholders and, where possible, use local mediation procedures to ensure that existing users' needs are properly taken into account.

4. **Conflict with the demands of human populations.** In situations where water is scarce or where resources for implementation of trucking operations are limited, the immediate needs of human populations must always be prioritized. However, meeting the demands of human and livestock populations does not have to be exclusive. In the case of a widespread emergency, the trucking infrastructure may be inadequate to service both people and animals. However, small-scale localized operations may actually be able to deliver an integrated service that supplies water to people and their livestock. Provided that the availability of trucks and staff is adequate, water for livestock may be derived from sources that are not of sufficient quality for consumption by humans.

5. **Water quality.** In cases where water trucking is for both humans and livestock, the Sphere standards for water quality will apply. However, if high-quality water sources are limited, poorer-quality water from rivers or else standing lake water that cannot feasibly or economically be purified for human consumption may be reserved for use by livestock.

6. **Cleanliness of tankers.** Tankers may have been used for transporting other types of liquid, including toxic pesticides, herbicides, solvents, fuels, and sewage. Unless their previous history is reliably known, all vessels and distribution equipment should be thoroughly cleaned and disinfected before being released for use in water trucking operations.

Water trucking standard 2: Logistics and distribution

Proper arrangements are implemented for secure transport of water and its equitable distribution on arrival in the affected area.

Key actions

- Sustain the inputs of managers and staff throughout the lifetime of the operation (see *Guidance note 1*).

- Ensure that adequate resources are available to meet the recurrent costs of fuelling and servicing the tanker fleet and associated equipment (see *Guidance note 2*).

- Where possible, select routes that will not be degraded by the frequent passage of heavily laden water trucks (see *Guidance note 3*).

- Set up distribution points in appropriate locations and accommodate any livestock movements that may occur during the course of the operation (see *Guidance notes 4* and *5*).

- Undertake proper security assessments for the proposed water distribution (see *Guidance note 6*).

Guidance notes

1. *Staffing.* Successful trucking operations require consistent and sustained staff inputs, notably competent and experienced managers and supervisors. It is also important to ensure that drivers and assistants are kept motivated through proper reimbursement and careful attention to other needs, including subsistence allowances and personal security.

2. *Maintenance and fuel supplies.* Qualified mechanics and reliable supplies of uncontaminated fuel need to be available throughout the duration of the trucking operation. This includes any material needed to operate and maintain pumps, containers, and delivery equipment. There are some major issues to consider:

    - *The cost and availability of fuel.* Ideally, it should be possible for drivers to refuel without making major detours from the trucking route. This may require fuel to be brought in separately, adding to the logistical complications of the operation. It may also be a consideration in the original selection of water sources.

    - *Spare parts.* These should be readily obtainable; locally made equipment that is easily repairable is preferred.

    These issues (particularly those relating to maintenance) may affect the decision regarding the type of transport that will be used by the trucking operation (for example, trucks or tractor trailers with bowsers or bladder tanks).

CH 7 Water

3. *Ensuring the integrity of supply routes.* These should be adequate for the passage of laden water tankers. Otherwise provision will need to be made for their maintenance and repair.

4. *Managing distribution points.* Distribution points may involve livestock keepers' collecting water to take to their livestock or bringing their animals to receive water directly from a tank or pond. In either case, a system needs to be established to ensure that the needs of all attendees are met equitably and sustainably, based where possible and appropriate on existing local water management systems (see *Water standard 1, Guidance note 3*). Where it is possible to establish storage facilities, trucking can be more efficient as tankers can decant the water quickly and return to the source to collect more, thus reducing the waiting time.

5. *Water trucking to mobile livestock.* Relocation of livestock is often an indigenous response to drought (see *Box 6.1* in *Chapter 6, Ensuring feed supplies*). Where this occurs, trucking of water may be considered to support the migration. This will add considerably to the already complex logistics of water trucking.

6. *Establishing a safe distribution network.* The risk to the personal safety of staff employed in transporting water for use in emergency programmes should always be of paramount importance (see also *Chapter 6, Ensuring feed supplies, Feed standard 4, Guidance note 5*).

Provision of water case studies

7.1 Process case study: Impact of watering stations in Ethiopia

An East African NGO, Action for Development, has built watering stations at a number of locations in the Borana rangelands of southern Ethiopia. These stations have been very successful in supplying water and have consequently helped to keep many livestock alive through the droughts that have plagued the area in recent years. However, this success has come at a price. The aggregation of livestock around watering stations sometimes leads to severe fodder shortages. Future activities in the area will seek to resolve this problem by building watering stations farther afield where rangeland is still relatively plentiful. In the meantime, other activities of the programme include the provision of feed at the water points to ensure that participating livestock can be adequately fed and watered (*Source*: IRIN News).

7.2 Process case study: Water trucking for drought relief in Somalia

VETAID received funding from the United Nations Office for the Coordination of Humanitarian Affairs (OCHA) for a water trucking project to benefit pastoralists in the Gedo, Bari, and Karkaar regions in Somalia, areas that have been severely affected by drought. In Gedo, the project trucked water to 2,500 breeding cattle and 1,100 sheep and goats to allow them to make more effective use of the pasture areas of Bardera and El Wak Districts. This intervention aimed to preserve the livelihood base of the community and allow them to recover more rapidly from the drought by maintaining at least some of their core breeding stock. The project also supplied water to 3,600 pastoralist families. In addition, with a view to the longer-term sustainability of water resources, VETAID undertook the rehabilitation of water catchment structures and the removal of livestock carcasses from wells and dams (*Sources*: VETAID project files).

7.3 Process case study: Strengthening water supply infrastructure in Pakistan

During the drought of 2000 in Pakistan, a number of initiatives involving the public, private, and NGO sectors were undertaken to reduce impacts on livestock. An initiative of the Cholistan Development Authority supported the commercial supply of water wells equipped with solar pumps. This initiative established drinking water stations over 6 million acres of the Cholistan Desert to help support the herders and cattle stranded under drought conditions. This represented a major attempt to counter the severe drought that threatened as much as 50 per cent of the livestock in parts of the country. In a similar agreement, the Punjab Rangers established six freshwater wells and 60 water supply systems with desalination capacity at a number of their border outposts. These were able to supply around 500 herders and their cattle at each of 70 water stations (*Source:* IJGlobal, 2000).

7.4 Process case study: Water provision for livestock using hafir *dams in Sudan*

North Darfur State in Sudan has a history of drought and famine. During the last decade, North Darfur experienced a complex emergency, prompting an international humanitarian response on an unprecedented scale. All livelihood systems were affected, especially those of displaced people, many of whom lost livestock when they were first displaced. Other livestock producers, including pastoralists and agro-pastoralists, were also seriously affected.

Hafirs are dam structures intended to collect surface water for cattle and other livestock. The NGO Cooperazione Internazionale (COOPI) has supported the construction of *hafirs* to address livestock water needs as part of their water sector activity. Selection of the *hafir* dam sites was based on community agreement to avoid conflict between community groups. COOPI followed a 'do no harm' and 'conflict-sensitive' approach by consulting and involving all community groups equally on site selection and the future use and management of each *hafir* dam. For example, community boundaries for animal grazing and other livelihood activities were considered when deciding on the site of the *hafir* dam. Before *hafirs* were approved for construction, an environmental impact assessment was completed and the plan for the work approved. According to the UN in Sudan, the mechanized construction of the *hafir* had to conform to basic principles (UNOPS, undated). Sudan's National Water Policy was in draft form at the time, but the National Water Supply and Sanitation Policy of 2009 was available, and that document was relevant to *hafirs*. There were also government guidelines available from the Public Water Corporation, and these provided guidance on various types of water intervention (*Source:* Gebru et al., 2013).

7.5 Impact case study: Cash for work for the provision of water in Kenya

In 2011, pastoralist households in the arid and semi-arid lands in northern Kenya were recovering from a multi-year drought compounded by post-election violence, high food and fuel prices, and El Niño-related flooding. Depletion of pastures and dry water pans led to poor animal body condition and livestock deaths. Frequent breakdown of boreholes and long queues for domestic water access increased during this period, and competing water needs both for domestic use and for livestock from limited functional water points led to conflict. To cope, out-migration of livestock intensified, reducing access to milk. Food availability and access were further strained due to continued high inflation in food prices coupled with a decline in livestock prices.

As part of the USAID-supported Arid and Marginal Lands Recovery Consortium, Action Against Hunger (ACF) USA was working in the Merti and Garbatulla districts of Isiolo County in northern Kenya, focusing on the protection of key dry-season grazing areas and improvement of access to water for livestock. Following a mapping exercise and the reactivation of dormant traditional rangeland management committees along key migratory routes, a cash-for-work (CFW) programme was established for the rehabilitation and construction of livestock water points that ensured the participation of both men and women who were highly vulnerable as a result of drought-related livestock losses. CFW activities included provision of local construction materials and labour during construction activities. Rangeland management and water committees were also supported with training, and rangeland management plans were drawn up.

According to the final evaluation of the programme, an estimated 186,440 livestock and 40,845 livestock owners benefited from rehabilitated or newly constructed water sources, including water pans, shallow wells, boreholes, water storage tanks, and access points (livestock water troughs), while 1,359 people participated in cash-for-work water point rehabilitation and construction activities. The CFW programme helped households to meet immediate needs while the rehabilitated and newly established water points ensured retention of milking herds near settlements to provide milk for the children, with the surplus taken to market for income. Additionally, the water points and pasture management contributed to continued access to livestock markets within the rangeland, ensuring consistent income to livestock keepers.

The experience of the programme shows that, even in emergency contexts, interventions can and should seek to build and develop local capacities to appropriately manage key livestock assets, such as rangelands and water, using local and indigenous structures, knowledge, and good practice; this is in addition to interventions that provide more classic short-term emergency assistance in, for example, destocking or feed and water distribution. Cash can be an important tool to achieve these ends simultaneously (*Source*: Daniel Nyabera, Muriel Calo and Charles Matemo, personal communication, 2014).

Appendix 7.1: Checklist for rapid water point assessment

This checklist summarizes the issues that need to be considered when assessing potential water points for use by livestock keepers under an emergency situation. Sources of information for answering the questions in this checklist may vary from rapid field assessments to (in principle at least) laboratory analyses for water quality. They should, however, always include some canvassing of opinion from the different stakeholder groups in the local area.

Supply of water

- Is the water point currently producing water?
- If yes:
  - Is the water point at risk of drying up over the course of the emergency response?
  - What is the capacity of the water point to support the local livestock population?
- If no:
  - Is it technically feasible (both in terms of cost and timescale) to rehabilitate the water point to meet the needs of the local livestock population?
  - Are personnel available to manage and implement rehabilitation of the water point?

Accessibility

- Is the water point within easy reach of a significant population of affected livestock?
- Are there any social, cultural, or political constraints to the use of the water point by livestock?
- Can water from the source be made available to affected livestock keepers in an equitable manner (regardless of age, gender, ethnicity, or wealth)?
- Can affected livestock make use of the water point without:
  - compromising the needs of existing users (human or animal)?
  - risk to the personal safety of the livestock keepers?
  - interfering with other aspects of the relief effort?

Water quality

- Are testing facilities (either field or laboratory) available to assess the adequacy of water quality for the source?

- If yes:

  - Is there access to laboratories that can analyse for major chemical contaminants?

  - Are water testing kits available that can be applied to the water points/sources under consideration?

  - Are suitably qualified technicians available locally to undertake assessments of microbiological contamination of water sources?

- If no, the following questions may help in making a rapid on-the-spot assessment:

  - Is water from the source clear or cloudy?

  - Is there any evidence of salinity in the area (for example formation of salt pans)?

  - Are there any local indicators of chemical contamination (for example, fertilizer and pesticide use patterns, existence of local small-scale industries such as tanneries or light industries)?

  - Have there been any reports of water-borne diseases from the source?

Appendix 7.2: Examples of monitoring and evaluation indicators for water provision

	Process indicators (measure things happening)	Impact indicators (measure the result of things happening)
Designing the system	• Number of meetings with community/community representatives and other stakeholders (including private sector suppliers where relevant)	• Meeting reports with analysis of options for water provision • Action plan including: - roles and responsibilities of different actors - approach for water supply, e.g. rehabilitation of existing sources; establishing new sources - community involvement in managing rehabilitated or new water points
Provision of water	• Number of water points rehabilitated or constructed by type and location • Delivery capacity of water points • Volume of water provided by trucking	• Accessibility of water (physical distance to water) for users and their livestock, including vulnerable groups • Availability of water – sufficient for livestock needs • Quality of water – suitability for livestock • Number of livestock-owning households using water points vs. number of livestock-owning households needing water; breakdown of figures by vulnerable group • Number of livestock using water points by livestock type; frequency of watering • Increase or decrease in women's and girls' labour burden to collect water for livestock • Influence on policy

See also the LEGS Evaluation Tool available on the LEGS website: <http://www.livestock-emergency.net/resources/general-resources-legs-specific/>.

References and further reading

Gebru, G., Yousif, H., Mohamed, A., Negesse, B. and Young, H. (2013) *Livestock, Livelihoods, and Disaster Response, Part Two: Three Case Studies of Livestock Emergency Programmes in Sudan, and Lessons Learned*, Feinstein International Center, Tufts University, Medford, MA, <http://fic.tufts.edu/publication-item/livestock-livelihoods-and-disaster-response-part-two-2/> [accessed 16 May 2014].

House, S. and Reed, R. (2004) *Emergency Water Sources – Guidelines for Selection and Treatment*, 3rd edn, Water, Engineering and Development Centre (WEDC),

Loughborough, <https://wedc-knowledge.lboro.ac.uk/details.html?id=18064> [accessed 16 May 2014].

IJGlobal (2000) 'Solar-powered pumps for drinking water provision', <http://www.ijonline.com/articles/1874>.

Markwick, G.I. (2007) *Water Requirements for Sheep and Cattle*, PrimeFact 326, New South Wales Department of Primary Industries, New South Wales. Available from: <http://www.livestock-emergency.net/resources/water-supply-2/> [accessed 16 May 2014].

Reed, R. and Shaw, R.J. (1995) 'Emergency water supply', Technical Brief No. 44, in *Waterlines*, Vol.13, No.4, IT Publications, London, <http://www.lboro.ac.uk/well/resources/technical-briefs/44-emergency-water-supply.pdf> [accessed 23 May 2014].

UNOPS (United Nations Office for Project Services) (undated) *Annex I to ITB section V Schedule 2 – Scope of Works Construction of Mechanized Hafir: Technical Specification,* UNOPS, Copenhagen, <https://www.unops.org/ApplyBO/File.aspx/Annex%20I%20to%20ITB%20Section%20V%20Schedule%202%20%E2%80%93Scope%20of%20Works.pdf?AttachmentID=18b83c9d-13e9-47b6-a127-b2c540aa54bc> [accessed 16 May 2014].

WEDC, Loughborough University (2011a) 'Cleaning and disinfecting wells in emergencies', *Technical Notes on Drinking-Water, Sanitation and Hygiene in Emergencies*, Number 1, World Health Organization (WHO), Geneva, <http://www.who.int/water_sanitation_health/hygiene/envsan/technotes/en/> [accessed 16 May 2014].

WEDC, Loughborough University (2011b) 'Cleaning and disinfecting boreholes in emergencies', *WHO Technical Notes on Drinking-Water, Sanitation and Hygiene in Emergencies*, Number 2, WHO, Geneva, <http://www.who.int/water_sanitation_health/hygiene/envsan/technotes/en/> [accessed 16 May 2014].

WEDC, Loughborough University (2011c) 'Delivering safe water by tanker', *WHO Technical Notes on Drinking-Water, Sanitation and Hygiene in Emergencies*, Number 12, WHO, Geneva, <http://www.who.int/water_sanitation_health/hygiene/envsan/technotes/en/> [accessed 16 May 2014].

Notes

1. See *Situation analysis in Assessment questions, Chapter 3.*

CHAPTER 8

Technical standards
for livestock shelter and
settlement

Livestock shelter and settlement

Standard 1
Assessment and planning

Standard 2
Livestock and settlement

Standard 3
Livestock shelter

Standard 4
Disaster risk reduction and preparedness

Introduction

This chapter discusses the importance of livestock shelter and settlement in emergency response. It presents the options for shelter interventions together with tools to determine their appropriateness. The Standards, Key actions, and Guidance notes follow each option. Case studies are found at the end of the chapter. They are followed by appendices containing checklists for assessment and monitoring and evaluation. Key references are listed at the end.

Links to the LEGS livelihoods objectives

Livestock shelter can be vital to ensuring that livestock survive an emergency. Livestock shelter therefore relates primarily to the second of the LEGS livelihoods objectives for affected communities in the emergency phase; namely, *to protect the key livestock assets of crisis-affected communities.*

The importance of livestock shelter and settlement in emergency response

The safety, security, and welfare of livestock are a primary concern of livestock keepers following a natural disaster or conflict. There are many cases of livestock keepers prioritizing the shelter needs of their livestock, irrespective of whether support is provided by intervening agencies, for example:

- Displaced livestock keepers sometimes use shelter materials distributed for their own housing to make shelter for their livestock.

- During the 1999 conflict in Kosovo, families cohabited with their animals in livestock shelters because their war-damaged houses could no longer provide suitable shelter from the cold climate. The families benefited from the body heat of the livestock during the winter nights. Co-location with their animals also helped to reduce the risk that livestock assets would be stolen (A. Porter, personal communication, 2008).

- Flooding from rivers and the sea affects many parts of Bangladesh, where a means of livestock protection is the *killa*, an extensive, flat-topped, and compacted earth mound onto which animals can be herded in response to flood warnings. Cyclone shelters, for use by the local population, are ideally located with *killas* adjacent, so that people and their animals are protected together. In the past, without this facility, some people have refused shelter protection (BUET/BIDS, 1993).

In spite of this evidence of the importance of livestock shelter to livestock keepers, it is not a common component of emergency response, and there are limited examples of effective interventions in this area.

There are a number of cases where livestock shelter interventions may be appropriate following an emergency, either to replace the structures for previously sheltered animals, or to construct new livestock shelter in response to a new context. Some examples are:

- when previously sheltered animals lose their shelter, for example, as a result of a flood or earthquake in which structures have been destroyed
- when livestock keepers are displaced because of an emergency, and their livestock lose access to their previous shelter or are placed in a context that requires new shelter, for example, when they move into camps
- when extreme weather conditions (heat or cold) or conflict and insecurity require new shelter for previously unsheltered livestock
- when livestock have been distributed as part of the response, and new shelters are required to protect them from weather, theft, or predators.

The provision of livestock shelter as part of an emergency response also contributes to one of the animal welfare 'five freedoms' described in the *Introduction*; namely, *'freedom from discomfort* – by providing an appropriate environment including shelter and a comfortable resting area'.

This chapter presents issues relating to livestock shelter and the associated settlement issues. *Livestock shelter* can be defined as the physical structures that animals need to survive, protecting them from weather, predators, and/ or theft, and can be either temporary or longer-lasting (see, for example, *Case study 8.3* at the end of this chapter). Provision for shelter is provided in the context of human settlement. *Settlement* concerns the wider environment that supports the provision of livestock shelter, in particular when populations have been displaced and simply replacing previous structures is not possible. For example, in the response to the 2005 Pakistan earthquake, animal shelters were constructed to enable livestock keepers to bring their stock down from the higher altitudes, where they were at considerable risk from the extreme cold and lack of feed. However, some livestock keepers remained in the mountains for fear of losing their houses, land, and possessions (P. Manfield, personal communication, 2008).

Settlement for humans is covered in detail in the Sphere Handbook. This chapter focuses therefore on the settlement issues that have a bearing on livestock: land rights, environmental management, and the planning and design of infrastructure such as facilities, buildings, and camps[1] (see, for example, *Case study 8.4* below).

➡ Options for livestock shelter and settlement

Livestock shelter and settlement needs vary considerably depending on the context of the affected communities. The Sphere Handbook describes human settlement scenarios that may occur following an emergency: the affected population may or may not have been displaced; they may be in temporary or in transitional shelter; their shelters may or may not require repair or reconstruction (Sphere, 2011: 245).

It is important first to understand this settlement context and its implications for livestock shelter needs. For example, if livestock keepers are in poor settlement locations (e.g. with a high risk of theft or poor access to grazing or water), then the provision of livestock shelter structures is – at least temporarily – irrelevant.

Most livestock shelter needs arise during sudden emergencies such as floods, earthquakes, or extreme cold, when previously sheltered livestock need to be protected from the weather and/or theft and predators. However, in slow-onset emergencies such as drought or ongoing conflict, particularly when livestock keepers have been displaced, shelter and settlement needs may also arise (see, for example, *Case study 8.4*).

This chapter presents two key options based on the definitions given above; namely, *settlement* interventions and *livestock shelter* interventions – which may be either *temporary* or *longer-lasting*.

Option 1: Livestock and settlement

Settlement interventions may be important to complement livestock shelter construction, particularly for displaced communities, and may include:

- support to negotiations on land rights or on access to grazing and/or shelter or other policy issues
- liaison with site planners and camp managers about the shelter needs of livestock accompanying displaced populations

- provision of infrastructure to support the livestock of displaced people (e.g. water supply)
- environmental management to address the needs of both livestock and humans in camps in order to ensure public and animal health.

Option 2: Livestock shelter

Both temporary and longer-lasting shelter interventions may take a range of forms, depending on the needs and nature of the emergency, for example:

- repair, construction, or reconstruction of livestock shelters (by contractors, agencies, or directly by beneficiaries)
- provision of materials to livestock keepers for shelter construction. This may include providing support for human shelter construction on the understanding that salvaged materials will be used for animal shelter
- incorporation of livestock shelter needs into human shelter programming (e.g. salvaging materials for livestock shelter)
- training in shelter construction
- cash or voucher distribution for livestock shelter needs.

Where there is urgent need for livestock shelter following an emergency, temporary structures may be constructed; this is often done by livestock keepers themselves with or without the support of external agencies. However, where possible, the materials and construction should be adaptable for the longer term, and settlement issues such as land rights and ownership should be taken into account.

Where possible, livestock shelter and settlement support should be provided to individual households and communities in their original homesteads. When livestock keepers have been displaced together with their livestock, shelter and settlement support should be provided collectively and in suitable large sites or enclosures within reasonable distance from grouped settlement for human populations, such as temporary planned or self-settled camps.

The advantages and disadvantages of these options are presented in *Table 8.1*.

| | Table 8.1 | Advantages and disadvantages of livestock shelter and settlement options |

Table 8.1 Advantages and disadvantages of livestock shelter and settlement options

Option	Advantages	Disadvantages/Challenges
1. Livestock and settlement interventions	• These enable design and planning of wider settlement issues to allow for livestock needs as well as those of their keepers in a range of post-emergency situations, including both camp and non-displaced contexts • They help reduce potential tension or conflict with host communities	• Depending on the nature and phase of the emergency, time is limited for discussions with host communities before immediate needs are met • Humanitarian agencies may not recognize the importance of livestock as key livelihood assets for affected communities and may therefore be reluctant to address livestock settlement issues
2.1 Temporary livestock shelter	• Responds to immediate shelter needs of livestock • Generally cheaper than longer-lasting solutions	• May need to be demolished and rebuilt in the longer term if location, accessibility, or tenure issues not carefully considered
2.2 Longer-lasting livestock shelter	• Livestock keepers remain with a long-term asset after the emergency is over • More economical use of resources in the long term	• Generally more expensive than temporary structures • Not appropriate for displaced populations who will return to their original areas after the emergency

Links to Sphere and other LEGS chapters

The provision of livestock shelter may complement the livestock interventions described in other chapters. For example, where the affected community is displaced following an emergency, livestock shelter interventions should be part of a planned response to the full range of livestock needs, including feed (*Chapter 6, Ensuring feed supplies*), water (*Chapter 7, Provision of water*), and veterinary support (*Chapter 5, Veterinary support*) in the context of a camp or camp-like setting. If livestock are distributed in situations where shelter is vital for the survival and well-being of animals, such as in cold climates, shelter needs should be addressed before distribution (*Chapter 9, Provision of livestock*). In particular, when emergency response interventions include the introduction of species to communities that are not familiar with keeping them, basic advice on the housing (and other management) needs of the animals must be provided.

Livestock shelter cannot be considered separately from human shelter and settlement. In some – but not all – instances, both animals and humans will require shelter following an emergency. Coordinated interventions that take into account the needs of both humans and their animals will have the greatest impact in the medium and long term because livelihoods are supported and lives saved (see *Core standard 8* in *Chapter 2* above). This chapter should therefore be read together with the Sphere Handbook chapter on 'Minimum standards in shelter, settlement, and non-food Items' (Sphere, 2011) and the other key references listed at the end of this chapter that deal with human shelter and settlement in detail, including UNHCR, 2007 and Corsellis and Vitale, 2005.

Timing of interventions

Livestock shelter and settlement support may be conducted at all stages of emergency response, from the emergency phase through to recovery and reconstruction and other long-term solutions.

The stage as well as the nature of the emergency will affect which options are most appropriate. After a sudden-onset emergency, there may be an urgent need to provide shelter for livestock exposed to the weather or at risk from theft or predators. For example, following the Pakistan earthquake in 2005, transitional shelters were constructed for the displaced populations that included space (based on local design) for livestock as well as people (UN-Habitat et al., 2008: 65). Such temporary measures can be made more permanent at a later stage in the emergency, when longer-term needs may be addressed. In a slow-onset emergency, there may be more time to prepare and plan for livestock shelter and settlement needs, although temporary measures may need to be put in place during the emergency itself (*Table 8.2*). For example, refugees fleeing the conflict in South Sudan arrived at Ethiopian refugee camps with thousands of livestock that needed to be accommodated immediately (UN-Habitat et al., 2012: 24–26).

Table 8.2 Possible timing of livestock shelter and settlement intervention

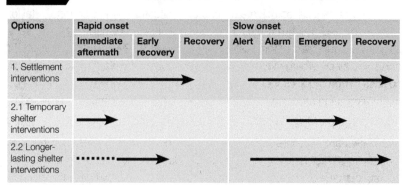

Options	Rapid onset			Slow onset			
	Immediate aftermath	Early recovery	Recovery	Alert	Alarm	Emergency	Recovery
1. Settlement interventions	──────────────►			──────────────────────►			
2.1 Temporary shelter interventions	────►			────►			
2.2 Longer-lasting shelter interventions	▪▪▪▪▪▪▪──►			──────────────────────►			

Cross-cutting themes and other issues to consider

Gender and social equity

The provision of livestock shelter and settlement following an emergency should take into account existing roles and responsibilities for animal care among the community, including gender and age divisions of labour, as well as cultural norms for animal housing regarding, for example, the proximity of livestock shelter to human accommodation. Gender roles in construction should also be taken into account and, where appropriate, form the basis for any intervention. Women as well as men should participate in shelter and settlement planning, including the design of shelter structures, as they may be key users.

The location of livestock shelters may have an impact on vulnerable groups, particularly women and children. Accessibility is an important factor affected by the distance from human dwellings, insecurity, or continuing danger from natural phenomena such as floods. This may limit access to animal products such as milk or eggs that are particularly important for some vulnerable groups, including children, older people, the sick, and people living with HIV and AIDS (PLHIV).

Protection

Settlement issues such as the location of livestock shelters or the distance to grazing/fodder can also affect the protection of livestock keepers. For example, shelters built at some distance from human habitation may expose people, particularly women or children, to risk, especially in conflict areas. The process of shelter construction may also have protection implications if women are required to look for construction materials in remote areas.

Environment

Environmental considerations should also be taken into account in the construction of animal shelters and in planning settlement infrastructure. If the construction of shelters encourages the dense concentration of livestock, this may impact on grazing availability and contribute to environmental damage. Animal waste, particularly where animals are concentrated or in close proximity to humans, can affect the health and hygiene of the human population.[2] The excessive use of local materials for construction may also have a detrimental effect on the environment. These issues may be particularly relevant in camp settings; they are discussed further under *Livestock shelter and settlement standard 2* below.

CH 8 Shelter

Local capacities

Crisis-affected communities also draw on their own capacities in response to emergencies. With regard to shelter, these may include indigenous knowledge about the most appropriate building materials and design for livestock shelters, as well as construction skills.

The Standards

Before engaging in the provision of livestock shelter and settlement, the feasibility and appropriateness of the possible interventions should be carefully considered, as highlighted in *Figure 8.1*.

Livestock shelter and settlement standard 1: Assessment and planning

Assessment and planning for livestock shelter and settlement is based on community consultation, indigenous knowledge, consideration of local environmental impact, and the potential for sustainable livelihoods.

Key actions

- Consult the affected populations, both women and men, concerning indigenous animal housing and settlement practices. These consultations should build upon the initial assessment outlined in *Chapter 3, Initial assessment and identifying responses,* (see *Guidance note 1*).

- Base the design of livestock shelter and settlement infrastructure interventions on indigenous animal housing designs (see *Guidance note 1*).

- Aim to meet the livestock shelter needs of the most vulnerable in the community (see *Guidance note 2*).

- Assess the local environmental impact of livestock shelter interventions and minimize any adverse impact (see *Guidance note 3*).

- Ensure the sustainable livelihoods needs of the community form part of the assessment and inform the emergency response (see *Guidance note 4*).

- Where appropriate, conduct a market assessment to investigate the possibility of cash or voucher transfers to support shelter and settlement interventions (see *Guidance note 5*, and *Case study 8.6* below).

Figure 8.1 Decision-making tree for livestock shelter and settlement

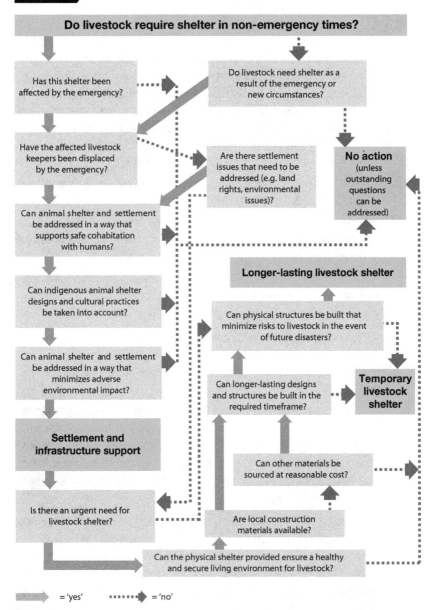

Do livestock require shelter in non-emergency times?

Has this shelter been affected by the emergency?

Do livestock need shelter as a result of the emergency or new circumstances?

Have the affected livestock keepers been displaced by the emergency?

Are there settlement issues that need to be addressed (e.g. land rights, environmental issues)?

No action (unless outstanding questions can be addressed)

Can animal shelter and settlement be addressed in a way that supports safe cohabitation with humans?

Longer-lasting livestock shelter

Can indigenous animal shelter designs and cultural practices be taken into account?

Can physical structures be built that minimize risks to livestock in the event of future disasters?

Can animal shelter and settlement be addressed in a way that minimizes adverse environmental impact?

Can longer-lasting designs and structures be built in the required timeframe?

Temporary livestock shelter

Settlement and infrastructure support

Can other materials be sourced at reasonable cost?

Is there an urgent need for livestock shelter?

Are local construction materials available?

Can the physical shelter provided ensure a healthy and secure living environment for livestock?

━━▶ = 'yes'   ┄┄┄▶ = 'no'

Note
The result *'No action (unless outstanding questions can be addressed)'* does not necessarily mean that no intervention should take place, but rather that further training or capacity building may be required in order to be able to answer 'yes' to the key questions.

- Negotiate livestock shelter and settlement interventions with all relevant stakeholders (see *Guidance note 6*).

Guidance notes

1. ***Community participation.*** An experienced livestock-owning community knows which types of animal shelter are typical for the species they keep, which shelter design options will meet these needs (materials, site selection, site access considerations, hygiene, and livestock management), and how and by whom construction can be implemented. Communities must therefore be involved at all levels of programming (assessment, design, implementation, and evaluation) with special attention to:

   - roles and responsibilities for animal care and for construction (age- and gender-based divisions of labour)
   - relevant policy issues for advocacy at the local or wider level as appropriate (see *Chapter 2, Core standards common to all livestock interventions, Core standard 7: Policy and Advocacy*)
   - involvement of host communities in the case of displaced livestock keepers in camp settings
   - use of community knowledge
   - indigenous design: cultural norms, indigenous building materials, and construction methods to adapt livestock housing technologies (only very rarely will 'shelter systems' or imported prefabricated solutions be appropriate)
   - community vs. individual shelter options, based on discussions with affected communities, local norms, and the current conditions (security, weather etc.). In most cases, it is preferable to provide livestock shelter for individual households based on practice prior to the emergency, but in some cases this may not be possible, appropriate, or affordable (see *Case studies 8.2* and *8.7*).

2. ***Vulnerability.*** Assessment and planning should examine the specific needs of potentially vulnerable groups and ascertain the need for priority assistance to the elderly, the sick, or the mobility-impaired, who may not have the labour resources to build their own livestock shelters. Those without access to construction materials may also need additional assistance (see *Appendix 8.1: Checklist for assessment of livestock shelter needs*). As with any intervention, assistance provided to vulnerable groups

should not undermine the ability of a community to provide and care for these groups using its own coping strategies.

3. *Local environmental impact.* The impact on the local environment of livestock shelters and settlement interventions must be assessed, including any unsustainable use of local materials or unsustainable concentration of livestock in confined areas. This may be particularly important in camp settings and is discussed further in *Livestock shelter and settlement standard 2*.

4. *Sustainable livelihoods.* While temporary measures to support livestock during an emergency may be required, every effort should be made to ensure that shelter and settlement interventions consider the livelihood needs of the affected population in order to ensure that these interventions are also useful in the long term. This includes careful consideration of the likely impact of anticipated changes to land use, permanent changes to community livelihoods, and changes to livestock management practices as the community recovers from the emergency.

5. *Market assessment.* Where construction materials are locally available, the possibility of providing cash or vouchers for their purchase should be assessed in order to support local markets and give greater control over the process to the affected population (see *Chapter 3, Initial assessment and identifying responses,* for more information on cash transfers).

6. *Stakeholder participation.* Livestock shelter interventions should be negotiated with stakeholders beyond the affected community, especially when livestock keepers have been displaced. Livestock shelter and settlement interventions for displaced populations should be coordinated with human shelter and settlement responses to ensure coherent planning and complementarity of activities. Stakeholders may include the local authorities that deal with agriculture, water supply, sanitation, land use, and housing. As noted in *Guidance note 1* above, it is particularly important when an affected population is displaced to consult with the host community to ensure that the location of the livestock shelter and settlement infrastructure does not cause conflict, environmental pressure, or competition for employment or natural resources.

Significant potential also exists to draw upon the experience of humanitarian actors in other sectors, such as human shelter and housing, protection, water and sanitation, and camp management. In large emergencies where the 'cluster approach' (see *Glossary*) has been implemented, these activities may be coordinated through the food security, protection, emergency shelter, camp coordination and camp management (CCCM), and early recovery clusters. Agencies providing shelter for livestock should actively participate in these clusters to promote livestock needs for shelter and settlement, particularly in the case of displaced populations, and to ensure that their own programmes are in line with agreed cluster strategies and priorities.

Livestock shelter and settlement standard 2: Livestock and settlement

Settlement supports safe and sustainable cohabitation with humans, and provides a secure, healthy, and sustainable environment for livestock

---

Key actions

- Ensure that settlement planning and implementation supports human safety and the safe cohabitation of livestock with humans (see *Guidance note 1*).

- Minimize the local environmental impact of support to settlement and livestock shelter (see *Guidance note 2*).

- Ensure that livestock shelter and settlement activities support sustainable human settlement objectives (see *Guidance note 3*).

- Ensure that settlement infrastructure enables healthy, secure, and sustainable livestock management (see *Guidance note 4*).

- Ensure that settlement infrastructure minimizes negative public health impacts (see *Guidance note 5*).

Guidance notes

1. *Human safety and cohabitation.* The location of livestock shelters can affect the safety and protection of livestock keepers. For example, shelters built at some distance from human habitation may expose people to risk, particularly women and children, especially in conflict areas. Conversely, livestock shelter and infrastructure too close to human settlement can increase the risk of spreading disease. Settlement planning should also provide for the safe cohabitation of livestock and human communities. This is particularly important to reduce the risk of transmission from animals to

humans of diseases such as avian influenza, and also prevent vector-borne disease transmission from animal faeces.

2. *Local environmental impact.* The impact of support to settlement and livestock shelter upon the local environment should be minimized. This is particularly important if livestock shelter construction requires or encourages the harvesting of locally available material that can risk permanent environmental degradation. The cutting of trees to provide construction timber for shelters and enclosures, or to fire bricks is a particular risk. Construction material should be procured from sustainable sources or harvested in a sustainable manner. The planting of 'living fences' may be a viable alternative to harvesting local material for enclosures. Dense concentrations of livestock should also be avoided to reduce the risk of overgrazing and environmental degradation.

The inclusion of livestock in camps puts significant additional pressure on the local environment and resources. Because competition for resources with local livestock populations may be a potential source of conflict, access to pasture and grazing must be negotiated with the local population.

3. *Sustainable settlement of humans and livestock.* The settlement needs of communities will always take precedence over those of livestock. It is therefore critical that interventions for livestock do not negatively affect the provision of human settlement. In many cases, settlement needs for humans and livestock are interdependent, which highlights the need for coordination and joint planning (see *Livestock shelter and settlement standard 1, Guidance note 6* above).

This coordination is particularly important when the affected communities have been displaced. Displaced settlement can be dispersed (for example, people staying with hosts or self-settled on land belonging to others). Alternatively, it can involve grouped settlement (such as families living in collective centres or camps). Displaced grouped settlement is invariably complex and expensive, with inherent barriers to reaching durable and sustainable solutions. Dense displacement camps rarely allow for the co-location of livestock, with the possible exception of poultry, because of the risk of environmental degradation and disease spread. While direct support to displaced livestock-owning communities in an emergency phase is often unavoidable, every effort should be made to support a return home.

Particularly in cases where livestock keepers have been displaced, settlement must take into account local grazing rights and management structures, accessibility, and land rights and ownership. Resolution of these issues is likely to require extensive consultation with stakeholders as well as advice from local authorities and specialists in other sectors in order to identify sustainable solutions (see *Livestock shelter and settlement standard 1, Guidance note 6* above).

4. *Secure, sustainable livestock management.* In addition to physical shelter for housing livestock (see *Livestock shelter and settlement standard 3* below), settlement infrastructure may also be needed to enable safe, sustainable livestock management. This may include advising on or providing access to water and food sources in addition to providing protection from theft and predators by means of site enclosures. Site enclosures may have implications such as the need to bring feed (see *Chapter 6, Ensuring feed supplies*) and/or water (see *Chapter 7, Provision of water*) to livestock, which may place a further burden on women, and there may be additional animal health issues such as parasite problems, increased risk of livestock disease brought about by the concentration of animals, and the need for veterinary drug storage or animal slaughter points (see *Chapter 5, Veterinary support*). All settlement infrastructure should be designed using indigenous knowledge and building practices (see *Livestock shelter and settlement standard 1* above).

5. *Public health impact.* Settlement should be designed to allow for the hygienic management and disposal of animal excreta, especially where livestock-owning communities are displaced and living in camps. Management options could include:

   • providing cash or other incentives for spreading manure

   • moving night enclosures every five to seven days in pastoral situations

   • building enclosures outside the perimeter of human settlements to limit livestock access

   • ensuring adequate distance between human dwellings and animal shelters.

The density of livestock should also remain at a safe level (see UNHCR, 2005: 30, for more details on the spatial requirements of different species).

Livestock are provided with a healthy, secure living environment appropriate to the context and for the intended use.

Key actions

- Ensure that livestock shelter provides adequate protection from prevailing climatic conditions and the extremes of daily and seasonal weather (see *Guidance note 1*).

- Design livestock shelter appropriately for the species and use; even if constructed for temporary use, the materials and structure should be capable of longer-term use or adaptation (see *Guidance note 2*).

- Ensure that livestock are afforded adequate physical protection from theft and predators (see *Guidance note 3*).

- Put measures in place to ensure that confined livestock are temporarily freed to avoid the risk of starvation before other assistance is forthcoming (see *Guidance note 4*).

Guidance notes

1. *Healthy, secure living environment.* In hot climates, shelter should provide well-ventilated shaded space. In cold climates, shelter should provide a suitably well-sealed enclosure that is free from draughts and provides insulation from the ground. Where extreme weather conditions prevail, shelter needs should be addressed before distributing livestock.

2. *Appropriate design.* Shelter for livestock should be based on local building technologies and use local materials. After a natural disaster, livestock shelter may be built using salvage material from damaged infrastructure and buildings, and efforts to maximize the potential for salvage should be encouraged, with toolkits being distributed and training provided in their use.

   Some emergencies may require urgent provision of livestock shelter in order to ensure the survival of the animals. However, these shelters may not be suitable for the long term, and communities may need support to reconstruct longer-lasting shelter. The potential to integrate emergency livestock shelters into transitional or more permanent structures is particularly important. For example, designs for livestock shelter for emergency use might incorporate long-lasting roofing and structure in anticipation of a later upgrade to permanent shelter with walls, doors, and fencing.

3. **Theft and attack.** Livestock shelters and settlement interventions should ensure that animals are protected in accordance with local norms from theft and from predators. This may include provision of suitable doors with closing mechanisms or secure enclosures around livestock accommodation. There may also be implications for site planning to ensure that livestock shelters are located near human settlements to provide security.

4. **Freeing confined animals.** Experience has shown that animals such as dairy buffaloes and cows have died where they were tethered when the families to whom they belonged were killed or injured. A simple response is to untie or release these animals so that they have a chance to find feed and water. These animals should be marked, for example, with paint, so that they can subsequently be reunited with their keepers. Emergency preparedness activities (see *Livestock shelter and settlement standard 4* below) can include encouraging livestock keepers to plan to do this in future emergencies when sufficient warning is given.

Livestock shelter and settlement standard 4: Disaster risk reduction and preparedness

Livestock shelter and settlement planning reduces the impact of future emergencies.

Key actions

- Assess the risk of future emergencies (see *Guidance note 1*).
- Ensure livestock shelter and settlement interventions minimize risks to livestock and their keepers and increase resilience in the event of future emergencies (see *Guidance note 2*).

Guidance notes

1. **Assessment of future risks.** Susceptibility to future emergencies should be assessed as part of the planning process for livestock shelter and settlement initiatives.

2. **Minimizing future livestock losses.** The construction of livestock shelters and support to settlements can mitigate the impact of future

emergencies. An assessment of future risks should therefore influence the site selection as well as the design and construction of livestock shelters and settlements to reduce the risk of livestock losses in future emergencies. Risk assessment may include:

- *Earthquakes.* Sites for livestock shelter and settlement infrastructure should be on stable ground and away from areas at risk of future landslides and other damage due to aftershocks. Structures for livestock shelter should be designed to be safe in the event of an earthquake by using seismic-resistant designs or lightweight construction. Indigenous materials and technology may be used, but it may be necessary to advise changes to local building practices to provide for increased earthquake resistance (see *Case study 8.3* below).

- *Floods.* Where possible, livestock shelters should be sited away from areas at risk of flooding, especially flash flooding. Where this is not possible, sites may need improved drainage, or livestock shelters may have to be raised above previous flood levels. Reinforced construction may be considered for foundations to reduce the risk of building failure.

- *Cyclones.* Livestock shelter construction should ensure that roofs are adequately tied and secured to the structure, and that structures are located away from the immediate coastline if there is danger of related tidal surges.

- *Tsunamis.* Animal shelters should be located away from the coastline wherever possible.

In all these cases, technical expertise from construction specialists should be sought (see *References*) to ensure that the construction adheres to best practices in disaster mitigation.

Livestock shelter and settlement
case studies

8.1 Impact case study: Preparing and responding to floods in Bangladesh

The Bangladeshi *chars* are sandy islands and low-lying flood-prone areas at the edge of rivers that are frequently eroded and redeposited. The Chars Livelihood Project (CLP), an initiative of the UK's Department for International Development (DFID), worked with *char* residents in Northern Jamuna to support livelihoods through asset transfer, homestead improvements to withstand flooding, water supply provision, and training and capacity building. The homestead improvements included a raised plinth that placed homes above the expected flood line. The plinths were designed to allow families to remain in their homes during extreme floods, prevent asset loss due to flooding, and so reduce the need to migrate to the mainland. Plinths were also intended to provide temporary shelter to other families that lacked plinths, as well as to their belongings and livestock.

In July 2007, sudden severe floods affected over 60 per cent of the country, with particular impact in Northern Jamuna. CLP responded with a relief effort that lasted for two weeks until the floods receded. The relief effort included food aid, water purification tablets, rescue operations, and livestock support. Livestock feed was provided for over 15,000 cattle over an eight-day period, sufficient for at least 90 per cent of the families in the project area. In addition, over 3,800 people were rescued, together with 3,375 cattle.

A customer satisfaction survey after the floods indicated very low levels of cattle mortality, with only 0.3 per cent of households reporting the death of cattle – a mortality rate similar to that of a normal period. Sheep and goat losses occurred in only 4.6 per cent of households, and again this was similar to a normal period. These results indicated that a combination of raised plinths to protect people and livestock, and the provision of animal feed had helped to prevent excess livestock mortality during the floods (*Source:* Marks and Islam, 2007).

8.2 Process case study: Community animal shelters in Pakistan earthquake

At the time of the 2005 Pakistan earthquake, herds of sheep and goats were migrating back from pastures, resulting in a large number of deaths. The death toll was even higher in static farming systems as buffaloes, cattle, and poultry died when the shelters in which they were kept collapsed. The surviving livestock were extremely valuable to survivors, as they provided a vital milk source for the winter and retained their value. Responding to need, the Brooke offered pastoralists community-based rather than individual shelters for animals, since resources and land for building shelters were limited and communal shelters would be able to protect the animals during the approaching winter.

People living in close proximity were encouraged to build wooden frames large enough to shelter livestock for several families (up to 30 animals). They were provided with technical support, plastic sheeting, nails, and corrugated iron sheets to complete the shelter. Beneficiaries were selected through discussions with village leaders together with surveys to find the most vulnerable and needy. If people were unable to construct a shelter within their group, the Brooke offered them support. Some were reluctant to build community animal shelters to begin with, fearing that this would cause the spread of disease, but the Brooke provided vaccination and health care before animals were put together. This project had the added benefit of sharing livestock care among women as a labour-saving measure. Following this project, the Brooke went on to provide training in animal health and husbandry to women, and then to formally train community animal health workers (CAHWs) to improve the long-term health and welfare of the animals (*Source:* Julia Macro, personal communication, 2008).

8.3 Process case study: Post-earthquake animal shelters in Pakistan

Following the 2005 Pakistan earthquake, a joint programme was initiated by Dosti Development Foundation, the Food and Agriculture Organization of the United Nations (FAO), the United Nations World Food Programme (WFP), and the Pakistan Government to provide livestock shelter and supplementary cattle feed to assist farmers in the Mansehra and Battagram Districts. The objectives of the programme were to improve livestock health and productivity and to introduce earthquake-resistant construction techniques for livestock shelter, based on the cob construction technique. Cob is a mixture of sand and clay, with long pieces of straw. The construction method is simple and the materials cheap and generally available locally. Training was provided to beneficiaries in construction methods.

A total of 3,000 shelters were built (108 by communities using their own resources), and supplementary cattle feed was provided to beneficiaries, focusing on the most vulnerable families with a high dependency on livestock (*Source:* Dosti Development Foundation and FAO, 2007).

CH 8 Shelter

8.4 Process case study: Livestock settlement interventions for Malian refugees in Mauritania

The deterioration of the humanitarian situation caused by military action in Mali in mid-January 2012 and continuing instability into the beginning of 2013 had a significant impact on large populations of civilians. By November 2012, approximately 354,000 people had been forced to flee their homes, including some 155,000 refugees hosted in Algeria, Burkina Faso, Guinea, Mauritania, Niger, and Togo. By May 2013, over 74,000 Malian refugees were located in the Bassiknou area in Mauritania.

The displaced people were living in extremely difficult conditions, dependent on humanitarian aid and the solidarity of the host families and friends. Furthermore, their arrival exacerbated the effects of the drought that already threatened the local population and their herds and put continued pressure on the livelihoods and sustainability of the local communities.

An assessment visit to the Bassiknou region by the International Organization for Migration (IOM) found that grazing rights regarding the refugees' herds were a major concern for local communities and potentially a major source of conflict. Discussions resulted in the implementation of an alternative schedule that guaranteed separate grazing areas, thus reducing the possibility of interference by other herds and reducing possible conflict between refugees and local populations. IOM Mauritania also provided intensive veterinary care to protect livestock against diseases associated with malnutrition and drought, with a target of vaccinating 2,400 animals.

IOM's experiences in Bassiknou highlighted the importance of situation analysis and needs assessment prior to intervention, as well as the need to establish discussions with host communities. The creation of discussion channels made it possible for the local population to express their fears and concerns regarding the situation with the refugees, and solutions were agreed collectively with a long-term perspective. This case study also highlights the central role of site selection as part of settlement planning for both humans and livestock (*Source:* Shelter Centre, personal communication, 2013).

8.5 Process case study: Settlement planning for Sudanese refugees and their livestock

As a result of the crisis in Darfur, Sudan, thousands of refugees moved into south-eastern Chad. Many of them were nomadic pastoralists, who crossed the border with their cattle. UNHCR, responsible for accommodating the refugees, created a new site in Abgadam, about 40 km from the Sudanese border, which housed just over 18,000 people – more than half the Sudanese refugees in Chad.

The Abgadam site was designed to allow the refugees to bring and house their livestock and to have the freedom to graze their cattle on surrounding pasture. Plans for the Abgadam site also included segregation of new livestock from the resident animals, vaccination and veterinary inspection on arrival, and other measures to prevent the spread of livestock diseases (*Source:* IRIN News, 2013).

8.6 Process case study: Mapping markets for supporting livestock shelters in Pakistan floods

In Pakistan in late July 2010, severe flooding moved southward along the Indus River through Khyber Pakhtunkhwa Province (KPK) towards western Punjab and the southern province of Sindh. In total, the National Disaster Management Authority reported that approximately 20 million people were affected, over 1.8 million houses damaged or destroyed, and 1.3 million hectares of field crops destroyed. Rapid flash floods of high erosive power damaged valley bottomlands in the north, and devastated transport infrastructure and river floodplains further south. In KPK an estimated 1.2 million livestock and 6 million poultry were lost, and more became sick due to lack of proper feed and veterinary support.

In September 2010, a multi-agency, multi-disciplinary KPK team carried out an assessment using the Emergency Market Mapping and Analysis (EMMA) methodology (see Albu, 2010).

After consultation, the EMMA team focused on critical market areas of wheat seed, livestock, agricultural labour, and timber poles (for shelter). The livestock component analysis found that livestock were a critical safety net for the key target groups of small farmers and landless labourers. Tenant farmers tended to prioritize saving/replacing animals over agricultural input purchases such as wheat seed. Livestock-related flood impacts were most severe in the agricultural plains, where there was an absence of alternatives for grazing or fodder, resulting in the deterioration of livestock condition and health. Crisis sales of diseased livestock were unprofitable due to the decline in price at village level. In the mountain areas, shelter for livestock was urgently required in preparation for winter to prevent loss of livestock livelihoods and prevent the need for animal migration into the agricultural plains. No agencies were considering livestock shelter options at that time.

Together with recommendations relating to wheat, labour, and timber supplies, the team recommended four livestock interventions:

- targeted cash-based livestock fodder/shelter programmes (fodder and shelter on plains, shelters in mountains) to start immediately and run through the winter
- livestock programmes contributing to the survival of remaining animals to start immediately for medium-term impact
- mixed fodder, timber and fuelwood, and field edge plantings to start immediately for medium-term impact
- quick shelter solutions for livestock in mountains before winter, and incorporation of livestock shelters into shelter programming (*Source:* Vetwork, 2011).

8.7 Process case study: Construction of multipurpose shelters after Myanmar cyclone

To implement a recovery project following Cyclone Nargis in Myanmar, a consortium comprising four agencies was formed in July 2009. The consortium members were ActionAid International, HelpAge International, The Leprosy Mission International and Ever Green Group. This group aimed to rebuild sustainable livelihoods and cyclone-resilient shelters for livelihood assets in 51 under-assisted villages in Bogale District. A specific focus was the inclusion of vulnerable subgroups such as landless labourers, small-scale fisherfolk, and other disadvantaged groups such as older people, people with disabilities, and female-headed households.

A rapid assessment indicated the absence of community structures where people without permanent shelters could keep their livelihood assets, such as seeds, grains, fertilizer, tools, and livestock. The recovery project therefore included the construction of multipurpose units (MPUs) to address the lack of proper storage facilities. The MPUs were designed to reduce the impact of future cyclones and thus increase the protection of livelihood assets in the future.

Once the MPUs were completed, the rules and regulations for the use and sustainability of the buildings were jointly formulated by the consortium in consultation with communities. The shelter MPUs provide serves many purposes, offering a storage facility for livelihood assets, including livestock, and also functioning as a meeting place and generating a sense of ownership among community members. Construction skills for cyclone-resistant shelters were also increased. The consortium's experience highlighted the importance of marrying existing knowledge and modern construction techniques (*Source:* Alam, 2010).

8.8 Process case study: Shelter provision in severe winter in Bolivia

In mid-2011 FAO provided supplementary feed to livestock in the Potosí region of Bolivia following snowstorms and very low temperatures (see *Case study 6.7*). FAO also provided improved shelter for the livestock. Indigenous livestock shelters, where they existed, consisted of stone and mud walls with no roof. The project provided materials and support for the construction of improved enclosures to protect the llamas and other animals against the weather and predators, using locally available materials and based on a local design. The initiative targeted households with fewer than 50 llamas, and the low-cost shelters served as a demonstration so that other community members could take up the idea and construct their own (*Source*: Einstein Tejada, personal communication, 2014).

Appendix 8.1: Assessment checklist for livestock shelter and settlement provision

Settlement issues

- What are the settlement patterns of livestock keepers?
  - Have livestock keepers been displaced from their original settlements?
  - Are they in temporary or transitional shelters, or in older shelters that require repair or reconstruction? (See Sphere Handbook, page 245.)
  - Is there potential for conflict between different livestock-keeping communities, for example, a displaced population and the host community?
  - Are there adequate grazing resources locally? Is pasture degradation a potential consequence of the presence of displaced people and their livestock after the emergency?
  - What are the existing land rights and management systems for communal or shared livestock shelters and settlement infrastructure, and will these be appropriate for any newly constructed shelters?
  - What other settlement needs do livestock keepers have?

Shelter (temporary and longer-lasting)

- Are there any practical, immediate interventions that can reduce immediate livestock mortality (such as freeing tethered animals post-earthquake)?
- Is there an immediate need for temporary livestock shelter?
- What is the estimated population of the different species of animals that may require shelter?
- What specific housing requirements do the different species have in the particular climatic and environmental conditions?
- What are the key social groups?
  - What are the roles of men and women in particular components of livestock care?
  - Who in the community is normally responsible for shelter construction?
  - Are there groups with special needs or vulnerabilities, such as PLHIV or displaced women?

- What are the local animal housing designs, construction techniques, and raw materials?
- Do these building practices adequately reduce the risk of loss in future emergencies?
- Are sufficient local materials available?
  - How are local construction materials harvested?
  - Will construction of shelters cause significant environmental destruction?
  - Would cash or voucher transfers be appropriate for supporting shelter reconstruction without negatively affecting local markets?
  - Should building materials be transported into the area?

Shelter for newly introduced species (for example, poultry and rabbits)

- Are the most vulnerable people going to benefit from the construction of shelters for species that are new to them?
- Do the beneficiaries require special training in shelter construction and management?

Appendix 8.2: Examples of monitoring and evaluation indicators for livestock shelter and settlement

	Process indicators (measure things happening)	Impact indicators (measure the result of things happening)
Designing the system	• Number of meetings with community representatives and other stakeholders, including private sector suppliers, where relevant	• Meeting reports with analysis of options for livestock shelter provision • Action plan including: - roles and responsibilities of different actors - technical approach for providing shelter - community involvement in designing, constructing, and managing shelter
Provision of shelter and settlement support	• Number of shelter structures supported by type and location • Number and type of settlement interventions	• Number of households/livestock with access to shelter vs. number of households/livestock in need of shelter • Mortality in sheltered livestock vs. mortality in livestock without shelter • Increased or decreased access to livestock products as a result of shelter interventions, particularly for vulnerable groups • Relations between displaced and host communities • Access to grazing, infrastructure, and other settlement needs by affected populations • Influence on policy

See also the LEGS Evaluation Tool available on the LEGS website:
<http://www.livestock-emergency.net/resources/general-resources-legs-specific/>.

References and further reading

Alam, K. (2010) *Joint review of the project 'Reducing the vulnerability of under-assisted Cyclone Nargis affected populations'*, implemented by the Consortium of ActionAid International (AAI), HelpAge, Ever Green Group (EGG), and The Leprosy Mission International (TLMI) and funded by the Department for International Development (DFID).

Albu, M. (2010) *Emergency Market Mapping and Analysis Toolkit* (EMMA), Practical Action Publishing, Rugby.

BUET and BIDS (Bangladesh University of Engineering & Technology and Bangladesh Institute of Development Studies) (1993) *Multipurpose Cyclone Shelter Programme*, Final Report, Part 1, July, Planning Commission, Government of Bangladesh, Dhaka.

Corsellis, T. and Vitale, A. (2005) *Transitional Settlement: Displaced Populations*, Oxfam, Oxford.

CRS (Catholic Relief Services), Emergency Operations and Emergency Response Team (Shelters and Settlements) (2013) *Managing Post-Disaster (Re)-Construction Projects*, How-To Guide, CRS, Baltimore, MD, <http://www.

crsprogramquality.org/publications/2013/1/11/managing-post-disaster-re-construction-projects.html> [accessed 16 May 2014].

Dosti Development Foundation and Food and Agriculture Organization of the United Nations (FAO) (2007) *Livestock Shelter and Supplementary Cattle Feed Project Report, 2006–2007*, Dosti Development Foundation and FAO, Pakistan.

IRIN News (2013) 'Wave of nomadic pastoral refugees hits Chad' [news report] <http://www.irinnews.org/fr/report/98657/wave-of-nomadic-pastoral-refugees-hits-chad> [accessed 25 May 2014].

Jha, A.K. with Barenstein, J.D., Phelps, P.M., Pittet, D., Sena, S. (2010) *Safer Homes, Stronger Communities: A Handbook for Reconstructing after Natural Disasters*, World Bank, Washington, D.C., <http://hdl.handle.net/10986/2409> [accessed 25 May 2014].

Marks, M. and Islam, R. (2007) *The CLP Flood Relief Activities (Aug 2007)*: *Summary of Relief Efforts and Customer Satisfaction Survey*, Innovation, Monitoring and Learning Division, Chars Livelihood Programme, Maxwell Stamp, DFID and Government of Bangladesh, London and Dhaka.

NRC/CMP (Norwegian Refugee Council/Camp Management Project) (2008) *The Camp Management Toolkit*, NRC/CMP, Oslo, <http://www.nrc.no/camp> [accessed 24 June 2014].

Shelter Centre (2012) *Transitional Shelter Guidelines*, Shelter Centre, Geneva, <http://sheltercentre.org/node/4063> [accessed 18 May 2014].

Shelter websites:
    Shelter Centre Library: <http://www.sheltercentre.org/library>
    Shelter Cluster: <http://www.sheltercluster.org/Pages/default.aspx>
    Shelter Case Studies: <www.sheltercasestudies.org> [all accessed 18 May 2014].

Sphere Project (2011) *Humanitarian Charter and Minimum Standards in Humanitarian Response* (the Sphere Handbook), The Sphere Project, Geneva, <www.sphereproject.org/> [accessed 15 May 2014].

UNDRO (United Nations Disaster Relief Organization) (1982) *Shelter after Disaster: Guidelines for Assistance*, Oxford Polytechnic Press, Oxford.

UN-Habitat, IFRC and UNHCR (International Federation of Red Cross and Red Crescent Societies and Office of the United Nations High Commissioner for Refugees), *Shelter Projects 2008, 2009, 2010 and 2011–2012* [website], <www.sheltercasestudies.org/> [accessed 18 May 2014].

UNHCR (1998) *Livestock in Refugee Situations*, UNHCR Environmental Guidelines, UNHCR, Geneva, <http://home.wfp.org/stellent/groups/public/documents/ena/wfp037503.pdf> [accessed 18 May 2014].

UNHCR (2005) *Livestock-Keeping and Animal Husbandry in Refugee and Returnee Situations: A Practical Manual of Improved Management*, UNHCR and International Union for Conservation of Nature (IUCN), Geneva, <http://www.unhcr.org/protect/PROTECTION/4385e3432.pdf> [accessed 18 May 2014].

UNHCR (2007) *Handbook for Emergencies*, 3rd edn, UNHCR, Geneva, <http://www.unhcr.org/472af2972.html> [accessed 18 May 2014].

Vetwork (2011) *The Use of Cash Transfers in Livestock Emergencies and their Incorporation into the Livestock Emergency Guidelines and Standards (LEGS)*, Animal Production and Health Working Paper No. 1, Food and Agriculture Organization of the United Nations (FAO), Rome. Available from: <http://www.livestock-emergency.net/resources/general-resources-legs-specific/> [accessed 18 May 2014].

White, C.M. (2006) *Pakistani Cob Animal Shelter (technical drawings)*, unpublished.

Notes

1. As noted in the *Introduction*, the term 'camp' is used as defined in the Camp Management Toolkit (NRC/CMP, 2008) as 'a variety of camps or camp-like settings – temporary settlements including planned or self-settled camps, collective centres and transit and return centres established for hosting displaced persons'. It also includes evacuation centres.

2. LEGS does not address issues of bio-security, which relate mainly to commercial large-scale enterprises.

Technical standards
for the provision of
livestock

Provision of livestock

| **Standard 1** |
| Assessment |

↓

| **Standard 2** |
| Definition of package |

↓

| **Standard 3** |
| Credit, procurement, transport, and delivery |

↓

| **Standard 4** |
| Additional support: training, food, vet care |

Introduction

This chapter discusses the importance of the provision of livestock in emergency response. It presents the options for intervention together with tools to determine their appropriateness. The Standards, Key actions, and Guidance notes follow each option. Case studies are found at the end of the chapter. They are followed by appendices containing checklists for assessment and monitoring and evaluation. Key references are listed at the end.

Links to the LEGS livelihoods objectives

The provision of livestock relates to the third LEGS livelihoods objective – *to rebuild the key livestock assets of crisis-affected communities* – and falls within the immediate post-emergency and recovery phases of an emergency.

The importance of livestock provision in emergency response

When disasters, particularly rapid-onset ones, result in substantial loss of livestock, the provision of livestock can be a valuable approach to rebuilding people's economic assets and providing high-quality livestock-derived foods, such as milk or eggs. In slow-onset emergencies, however, efforts to prevent massive livestock loss using other LEGS technical interventions such as destocking, veterinary support, and provision of feed and water should initially be considered.

The success of a livestock provision intervention is usually determined by the animals' ability to survive and to multiply to a level that positively contributes to beneficiaries' livelihoods. The way in which a livestock provision intervention is conducted can contribute to all of the animal welfare 'five freedoms', as described in the *Introduction*:

- *freedom from hunger and thirst*
- *freedom from discomfort*
- *freedom from pain, injury, or disease*
- *freedom to express normal behaviour*
- *freedom from fear and distress.*

If good animal welfare practice is applied, the intervention is more likely to achieve a better survival rate and improved productivity, which will contribute to a positive livelihoods impact for the initiative.

➡ Options for the provision of livestock

Based on the livelihood strategies and opportunities of the beneficiaries, livestock provision may take one of the following forms:

1. *Replacing livestock assets*: this may take different forms depending on the role of livestock in livelihoods:

    1.1 replacing herds for pastoralists and agro-pastoralists

    1.2 replacing smaller numbers of livestock for smallholder farmers or for income generation, for example, transport or draught animals

2. *Building livestock assets*: providing livestock as a new livelihood activity.

This chapter outlines these key types of livestock provision and contains four standards that apply equally to all options.

Option 1: Replacing livestock assets

1.1 Replacing herds for pastoralists and agro-pastoralists. In pastoralist or agro-pastoralist communities that rely heavily on livestock as a source of food, income, and social well-being, whole herds may be lost or decimated during an emergency, and the impact on livelihoods may be severe. Such communities range from the semi-arid lowlands of Africa to the steppes of Mongolia. Some groups keep mixed herds of sheep, goats, cattle, and camels while others rely more on single species, such as yaks or reindeer.

Given the diversity of these livelihoods, local livelihood analyses rather than broad prescriptive approaches are important for designing and implementing herd replacement activities. Communities themselves are best placed to determine how many and which type of animals make up the minimum herd size. Indigenous livestock knowledge is usually very strong in these communities, and indigenous systems for redistributing livestock may be well established, although weak or not functioning. External interventions should build on existing mechanisms and practices as much as possible (see *Appendix 9.4* at the end of this chapter; also *Core standard 1: Participation*). In these communities, training support to assist people to care for animals may not be required. The cost of herd replacement per household may be high because sufficient numbers of animals are needed to attain a minimum herd size within a defined time period.

In the post-emergency recovery phase, agencies implementing herd replacement may need to consider a broader and longer-term approach that strengthens the capacity of livestock-dependent communities and increases their resilience to face future emergencies and challenges. The challenges may relate to their changing economic and policy environment as well as to their natural resource base. In pastoral areas in particular, herd replacement should link closely with longer-term pastoral development initiatives. For example, the development of market opportunities as well as capacity building for market-oriented production could take place alongside herd replacement.

1.2 Replacing livestock assets for smallholder farmers and other income generation. For some communities, rearing a relatively small number of animals is a useful form of livelihood support. Even if these people keep only a few livestock (and perhaps rely primarily on non-livestock-derived food and income), food or income from animals may be an important supplement. For example, Thai and Vietnamese crop farmers keep a few cattle, pigs, and/or some poultry to be sold when money is needed or to be consumed during an important occasion such as a wedding. Similarly, many smallholder farmers in Africa keep a small number of cows for milk, along with chickens for eggs or income, or draught oxen for ploughing. Like pastoralists and agro-pastoralists, these communities may have significant livestock-rearing experience and skills, even though the number of livestock per household is much smaller.

In addition, some households may be highly dependent on a single animal (such as a mule or donkey used for transport) or a small number of animals for their livelihoods. Livestock may also be used to deliver humanitarian assistance. In Nepal, for example, mules carry food aid to remote mountain communities. Replacing these animals contributes to the livelihoods of crisis-affected families.

Option 2: Building livestock assets

Animal husbandry, even on a small scale, presents a significant livelihood opportunity for poor or marginalized populations in a variety of contexts:

- when conflict reduces access to cultivated fields and pasture (see, for example, *Appendix 9.3* on livestock provision in camps)
- when access to arable land is the privilege of a specific social class or clan
- as a source of income generation
- as a form of 'drought contingency fund' (see *Case study 9.2* at the end of this chapter)
- when other livelihood opportunities are scarce but natural resources abundant.

Livestock may also facilitate daily chores through transport and/or draught power, and they are a useful complement to agricultural activities (ploughing, threshing, fertilization, etc.). When livestock are provided as a new activity, the recipients may not have owned animals previously and may have limited experience of livestock rearing. In these cases, training in animal husbandry, nutrition and, as appropriate, marketing, is an important component of the intervention.

The advantages, disadvantages, and implications of these options are summarized in *Table 9.1*.

Table 9.1 Advantages and disadvantages of livestock provision options

Option	Advantages	Disadvantages	Implications
1.1 Replacing livestock assets: replacing herds for pastoralists and agro-pastoralists	• Replaces significant loss of livestock assets • Long-term response with the potential to increase livelihood assets for the future and thus strengthen livelihoods • Potential to build on indigenous herd reconstitution systems • Potential to reach additional beneficiaries whose livelihoods depend on trade and livestock production (processors, auctioneers, transporters, etc.)	• Cost per household high to reach minimum viable herd size • Requires considerable logistical management for purchase and distribution of appropriate species and breeds	• Appropriate only where beneficiary communities are chiefly dependent on livestock • Beneficiaries need sufficient assets (social relationships, access to pasture and water, technical knowledge, etc.) to maintain livestock • Other complementary livestock support (veterinary support, feed, shelter, etc.) may be needed • Other livelihood support (such as food aid) may be needed in the interim • Sources of suitable livestock need to be identified within practical distance

1.2 Replacing livestock assets: smallholder farmers/ other income-generating livestock	• Replaces lost livestock assets for:
	  - food supplement
	  - income generation (sale of livestock products; transport business)
	  - draught or transport needs
		• Costs of intervention may be high compared with other livelihood support activities	• Other complementary livestock support (veterinary support, feed, shelter, etc.) may be needed
			• Sources of suitable livestock need to be identified within practical distance

Option	Advantages	Disadvantages	Implications
2. Building livestock assets: new livelihood activity	• Provides new assets for: - food supplement - income generation (sale of livestock products; transport business) - draught or transport needs • Potential to provide livelihood opportunities when access to other livelihood options is limited through conflict, vulnerability, or other constraints	• Introduction of new livestock or species requires support and training for beneficiaries • Costs of intervention may be high compared with other livelihood support activities	• Sources of suitable livestock need to be identified within practical distance • Training in livestock management is vital for new livestock keepers

Timing of interventions

The provision of livestock – whether for herd replacement, replacing livestock assets for farming or income generation, or as a new initiative – generally takes place in the recovery phase of both rapid-onset and slow-onset emergencies. As it requires significant planning and administration, the intervention may not be possible or appropriate in the middle of an emergency. It also requires extra livestock support (feed, water, shelter, veterinary care) that may have been destroyed during the emergency. In addition, human populations may not have the immediate capacity to care for additional or replacement animals (see *Provision of livestock standard 2, Guidance note 5* below). However, for some rapid-onset emergencies in which the natural resources required by livestock are still available and the numbers of animals involved relatively small, provision may begin during the early recovery phase (*Table 9.2*). The provision of livestock should as far as possible be integrated into longer-term development planning to support the livelihoods of the beneficiary population.

Table 9.2	Possible timing of livestock provision							
Options	**Rapid onset**			**Slow onset**				
	Immediate aftermath	**Early recovery**	**Recovery**	**Alert**	**Alarm**	**Emergency**	**Recovery**
1.1 Replacing livestock assets: herd replacement		⟶					⟶
1.2 Replacing livestock assets: farmers/income generation		⟶					⟶
2. Livestock provision as a new livelihood activity		⟶					⟶

Links to Sphere and other LEGS chapters

The provision of livestock as a post-emergency response requires integration with other livestock inputs. To varying degrees, livestock may require feed, water, shelter, and veterinary care. Therefore, the Standards detailed in the LEGS Handbook for these other interventions should also be consulted (see *Chapters 5, 6, 7,* and *8*). In particular, the potential cost of veterinary care needs to be carefully considered, especially if the approach is to encourage private delivery.

When livestock is provided, it is likely that the recipient households will require other types of assistance to meet their basic needs. When pastoralist or agro-pastoralist herds are reconstituted, it may take many months or even years for the families involved to expand their herds without external assistance (see *Provision of livestock standard 4* below). Therefore, livestock provision must also be integrated with non-livestock assistance. The 'Minimum standards in food security and nutrition', as well as the 'Minimum standards in shelter, settlement, and non-food Items' in the Sphere Handbook (2011) should be consulted.

Cross-cutting themes and other issues to consider

The provision of livestock poses special challenges in terms of community vulnerabilities and capacities as well as agency capacities. Therefore, for successful livestock provision programmes, several issues need to be considered.

Gender and social equity

The roles and needs of vulnerable individuals and households should be taken into account, especially gender roles in livestock care and management. While in some communities women do not have formal ownership of livestock, they are often primary carers of animals, particularly small stock. Livestock provision initiatives should therefore build on these roles and indigenous knowledge, while taking into account any potential additional labour burden that the provision of stock may involve. Attention should also be paid to existing norms with regard to the benefits of livestock to ensure that the vulnerable continue to access these benefits as much as possible. For example, children are often involved in herding animals or trekking them to water points, and milking in the bush can be an important source of food for them. However, this work can also prevent children from attending school. Liaison with education programmes is needed to ensure that, if necessary, children can both herd animals and attend school.[1]

PLHIV

People living with HIV/AIDS are at high risk of contracting diseases transmitted by livestock. HIV-affected families may also lack sufficient labour to care for livestock. At the same time, livestock products, as noted elsewhere in this volume, can play a significant role in providing good nutrition for PLHIV.

Protection

Protection issues may affect livestock provision interventions. In insecure environments, livestock can easily be regarded as valuable and desirable items by armed militia, police, security forces, or criminals. Armed groups and governments will sometimes use livestock raiding as a specific strategic tactic for terrorizing communities and asset-stripping. Consequently, in some situations the provision of livestock can place vulnerable communities at increased risk of violence. The selection of different species may reduce vulnerability to theft – for example, goats may be less attractive to thieves than cattle. The provision of large numbers of livestock where resources are scarce may also be a potential source of conflict between farmers and livestock keepers or between livestock-owning groups. Agencies working in conflict areas may also need to ensure that animals for sale are not stolen.

Environment

The environmental implications of livestock provision should also be taken into account. The provision of large numbers of additional animals in areas that thus far have not supported livestock may contribute to degradation. However, in many cases herd replacement will take place in non-equilibrium environments with pastoralist and agro-pastoralist communities that have developed mechanisms to manage livestock in fragile and marginal areas. At the same time, herd replacement activities should ensure that livestock are provided in numbers appropriate for the survival of the family while being in balance with local environmental conditions. They should also ensure that sufficient feed and water resources exist to support them.

Targeting

There are specific targeting issues relating to herd replacement. In the case of pastoralist and agro-pastoralist communities, the provision of livestock aims to encourage a timely return to a livestock-based livelihood. In these situations, it is not necessarily the most vulnerable or destitute households that should be targeted to receive livestock, but those households that already possess some animals, that are motivated to return to a livestock-based way of life, and that possess the relevant livestock-rearing skills and knowledge. This aspect of targeting raises at least two questions. First, within a humanitarian response, is it justifiable to target households which are not the most vulnerable for livestock assistance? Second, what kinds of assistance might be appropriate for the most vulnerable households? These issues are open to debate; however, the answers remain dependent on dialogue with communities on the ground. Community involvement is the key to transparent process as well as to achieving the acceptance and understanding of non-beneficiaries.

There are also specific targeting issues relating to replacing livestock assets for smallholder farmers/income generation and for building livestock assets as a new livelihood activity. For people who do not normally rely heavily on livestock, one aim of an initial livelihoods assessment should be to identify possible livestock ownership patterns by wealth and gender and to design assistance accordingly. In general, men and wealthier people tend to own or control larger types of livestock, such as cattle, camels, or horses, whereas women and poorer people are more likely to keep poultry, goats, or sheep. In these situations, provision of the smaller types of livestock is more likely to assist the poor or vulnerable.

Disease transmission

Disease transmission from livestock to humans occurs where animals and humans live close to each other, such as in urban and peri-urban contexts or in camp settings (see *Appendix 9.3*). The numbers of animals and the amount of additional support provided should be appropriate to the local context to decrease the risk of disease transmission within and among animal herds.

Local capacities

Crisis-affected communities have their own capacities on which they draw in emergencies. Many livestock-owning communities have some form of indigenous restocking system whereby vulnerable or poor households receive stock as a gift or a loan, often passing on the original gift or the offspring to another needy recipient. Such mechanisms can form the basis of livestock provision, and building on these indigenous systems and knowledge increases the sustainability of the initiative (see *Case study 9.2* at the end of this chapter).

Agency capacities and planning

Despite the many benefits derived from livestock, the provision of livestock as a post-emergency or recovery response is technically and operationally complex, as well as expensive. The provision of livestock is not neutral as it can have positive or negative social, environmental, and economic impacts. Many aspects remain controversial, including the sustainability of the interventions due to the recurrence of emergencies, the capacity of the beneficiaries, and inappropriate planning. There is also concern about the relatively high cost of these projects per household, particularly if support inputs such as veterinary care, shelter, and training are included.

Given the complexity of designing and implementing effective livestock provision, agencies on the ground need to carefully consider their capacity to engage in such work. Many agencies need to source expertise from outside, and this process itself takes time and effort. To date, it seems that agencies with long-term development experience in a particular area are often best placed to support livestock provision because they are familiar with local uses of livestock and social systems.

Use of cash transfers

Cash transfers may be an appropriate mechanism for livestock provision when local markets are functioning and able to supply the livestock and associated inputs (see cash section in *Chapter 3, Initial assessment and identifying responses*). Cash or vouchers can be given specifically for livestock purchase, allowing beneficiaries to select their own livestock. Livestock fairs may be a useful means of facilitating this process as they bring together buyers and sellers in one place (see *Appendix 9.5* and *Case study 9.3* for livestock fairs, and *Case study 9.1* for an example of cash transfers used for herd replacement).

Camps

Appendix 9.3 below highlights some of the specific issues relating to the provision of livestock in camps, including the need to take into account the situation and potential vulnerabilities of the resident population.

The Standards

Before engaging in the provision of livestock, the feasibility and appropriateness of the intervention should be carefully considered (as highlighted in the decision-making tree in *Figure 9.1*), together with the potential impact of the activity.

> **Provision of livestock standard 1: Assessment and preparedness**
>
> An analysis is undertaken to assess the current and potential roles of livestock in livelihoods, and the potential social, economic, and environmental impact of the provision of livestock.

Key actions

- Analyse the role that livestock play in livelihoods during normal times (see *Guidance note 1*).

- Assess indigenous mechanisms for community-based redistribution of livestock (see *Guidance note 2*).

- Consider the social, physical, and natural livelihood assets of target beneficiaries to assess their suitability as recipients (see *Guidance note 3*).

- Assess the cost-effectiveness of livestock provision activities in comparison with other possible interventions, as well as any external or internal policy constraints (see *Guidance note 4*).

- Assess the probable impact of the purchase of large numbers of animals on local livestock markets (see *Guidance note 5*).

- Assess local norms for minimum viable herd size (see *Guidance note 6*).
- Assess the environmental impact of the provision of livestock (see *Guidance note 7*).
- Assess the potential risks to the welfare of livestock provided (see *Guidance note 8*).
- Assess the risk of disease outbreak (see *Guidance note 9*).
- Assess the security implications of the provision of livestock, and ensure that livestock provision only takes place when the security of the stock and the beneficiary populations can be assured (see *Guidance note 10*).

Guidance notes

1. **Livelihoods analysis.** The provision of livestock should be based on a thorough understanding of the role that livestock currently play in the livelihoods of the intended beneficiaries. If livestock keeping does not already form part of their livelihood strategy, the implications of introducing livestock must be very carefully considered before such an intervention is undertaken (see *Guidance notes 3–9* below). The assessment checklist for livestock management and the role of livestock in livelihoods can be found in *Chapter 3, Initial assessment and identifying responses*; see also *Appendix 9.1: Assessment checklist for provision of livestock*. If livestock are provided to people in camp settings, the sustainability of livestock keeping in the future must be considered (see also *Appendix 9.3: Provision of livestock in camps*).

2. **Indigenous livestock redistribution.** In many livestock-owning communities, indigenous mechanisms exist for the redistribution of livestock; for example, social support systems based on loans or gifts of livestock to specific types of poorer or more vulnerable households. Where appropriate, livestock provision interventions should be based on these mechanisms to increase community management and ownership of the process and ultimately to improve sustainability.

3. **Livelihood assets.** It is vital that the beneficiary households have sufficient livelihood assets to manage and care for any livestock that they receive. These assets may include labour, equipment, skills, social networks (particularly significant for pastoral communities where social relationships are vital for successful livestock keeping), and access to natural resources such as pasture and/or feed and water (see *Case study 9.6*). Herd

Figure 9.1 Decision-making tree for provision of livestock

Are options other than the provision of livestock impossible or not cost-effective?

Can suitable beneficiaries be identified in conjuction with the community?

Is there a supply of appropriate and good-quality local livestock for purchase in sufficient numbers (without adverse effect on local residents)?

Have roles and responsibilties regarding livestock ownership, care, and management been taken into account in planning (e.g. gender, age, and other social groupings)?

Are there sufficient natural resources (feed and water), and shelter as appropriate?

Are the environmental implications positive or at least neutral?

Can the welfare of the livestock be assured?

Can the disease risks be minimized?

Can conflict/insecurity associated with livestock provision be minimized/eliminated?

Go to next page

No action
(unless outstanding questions can be addressed)

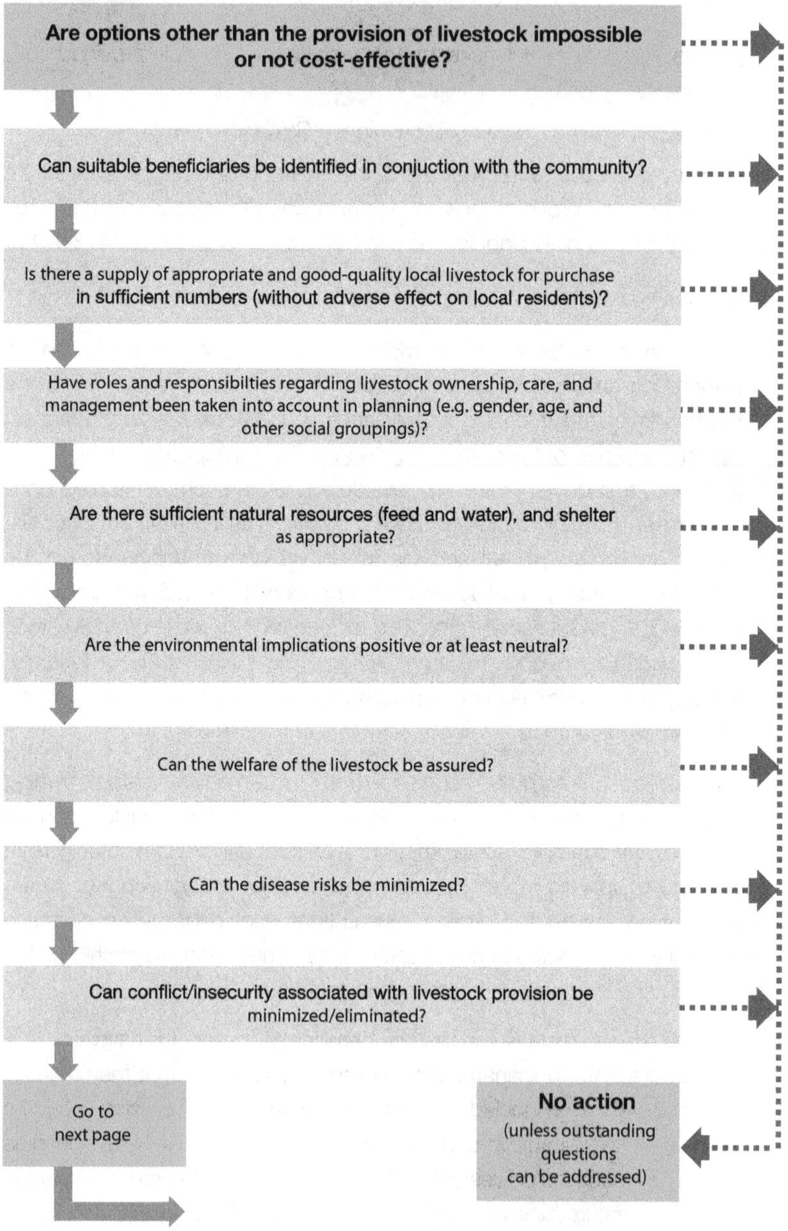

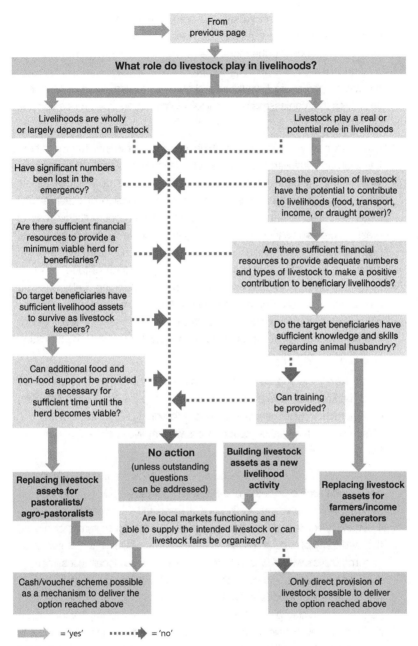

From
previous page

What role do livestock play in livelihoods?

Livelihoods are wholly
or largely dependent on livestock

Livestock play a real or
potential role in livelihoods

Have significant numbers
been lost in the
emergency?

Does the provision of livestock
have the potential to contribute
to livelihoods (food, transport,
income, or draught power)?

Are there sufficient financial
resources to provide a
minimum viable herd for
beneficiaries?

Are there sufficient financial
resources to provide adequate numbers
and types of livestock to make a positive
contribution to beneficiary livelihoods?

Do target beneficiaries have
sufficient livelihood assets
to survive as livestock
keepers?

Do the target beneficiaries have
sufficient knowledge and skills
regarding animal husbandry?

Can additional food and
non-food support be provided
as necessary for
sufficient time until the
herd becomes viable?

Can training
be provided?

No action
(unless outstanding
questions
can be addressed)

**Building livestock
assets as a new
livelihood
activity**

**Replacing livestock
assets for
pastoralists/
agro-pastoralists**

**Replacing livestock
assets for
farmers/income
generators**

Are local markets functioning and
able to supply the intended livestock or can
livestock fairs be organized?

Cash/voucher scheme possible
as a mechanism to deliver the
option reached above

Only direct provision of
livestock possible to deliver
the option reached above

= 'yes'   = 'no'

Note
The result *'No action (unless outstanding questions be addressed)'* does not necessarily mean that no
intervention should take place, but rather that further training or capacity building may be required in order
to be able to answer 'yes' to the key questions.

CH 9 Restocking

replacement for ex-pastoralists and agro-pastoralists can only succeed when the recipients have retained sufficient of these assets in spite of the loss of their stock. Furthermore, the rehabilitation of long-term destitutes is unlikely to succeed through the provision of livestock. The analysis of the most appropriate beneficiaries should be carried out by community structures that can assess potential recipients' assets and prospects most accurately.

4. *Cost-effectiveness.* Given the high costs of providing livestock (both financial and administrative), such an intervention should only be considered when other preventive measures to avoid the loss of livestock assets have failed (for example, supplementary feed, provision of water, animal health activities – see *Chapters 6, 7,* and *5*). The cost-effectiveness of livestock provision should also be set against other rehabilitation measures, particularly for communities where livestock are not the key livelihood asset. For example, other types of support in the form of food, cash, or seed may be a more cost-effective means of supporting livelihoods in a sustainable way following an emergency. Any potential policy constraints, either external (concerning the purchase or movement of livestock) or internal (purchasing protocols of the agency involved), should be assessed and should inform planning.

5. *Impact on local markets.* The purchase of large numbers of animals at local markets can have a significant impact on price, particularly following an emergency, when the availability of reproductive animals may be low. This may have a negative impact on less wealthy livestock keepers who are trying to rebuild their assets.

6. *Viable herd size.* In communities where livestock are the main livelihood asset, local communities will be able to suggest optimum viable herd sizes for herd replacement. This is based on their knowledge of suitable livestock species and breeds, productivity in relation to family size, and the availability of natural resources such as pasture/feed and water. Even in communities where livestock are less widespread, local assessment of appropriate species and numbers should be taken into account, as should the availability of feed (see *Appendix 9.4: Discussion on minimum viable herd size*). If highly productive breeds are provided to improve livestock productivity, fewer animals may be needed. However, in these cases it is important that the recipients have the capacity to support and maintain the new breeds, including the skills as well as any required resources, such as

veterinary care, fodder, etc. (see *Guidance note 3* above). The distribution of improved breeds may also contribute to the loss of traditional breeds, of genetic diversity, and of desirable traits within the livestock population. This must be weighed against the benefits that communities will receive from the provision of high-productivity breeds.

7. *Environmental impact.* Based on the viable herd size (see *Guidance note 6* above), an assessment of the environmental impact of livestock provision should be conducted (see also discussion of environmental cross-cutting issues in *Chapter 2 Core standards common to all livestock interventions*). In this context it should be noted that local purchase of livestock does not increase pressure on the range, since it is based on local circulation of stock. When the provision of livestock to people in camps is under consideration in areas where there already is a high concentration of animals, environmental impact should be carefully assessed.

8. *Livestock welfare.* Livestock should not be provided unless their welfare can be assured (see discussion of the 'five freedoms' in the *Introduction*). For example, in some cases insufficient feed may be available to support livestock in an arid area. In other cases, if adequate livestock shelter cannot be provided following an emergency in a cold climate, the animals may suffer or die.

9. *Disease risk.* Some livestock diseases are highly contagious and may have disastrous social and economic consequences. The potential risk of both local and transboundary disease outbreak should be assessed. In the recovery phase, a high burden of animal disease may be unavoidable, and project design should include actions to control disease among the livestock provided. Where cross-border purchase of animals is being considered and disease control measures may not be possible, it may be advisable not to engage in livestock provision.

10. *Security assessment.* The security implications of the provision of livestock should be assessed in detail before such an intervention is undertaken. The assessment should take into account whether beneficiary households will become a target for theft or violence, as well as the potential for conflict over natural resources (for example, between farming and livestock-keeping communities or among livestock-keeping communities). Additional support for livestock shelter may help provide more security. Nevertheless, the intervention should not take place if it is likely to increase

the vulnerability of beneficiary households and communities to violence or insecurity.

Provision of livestock standard 2: Definition of the package

Appropriate livestock species and breeds are distributed in adequate numbers and through appropriate mechanisms to provide viable and sustainable benefits to the target communities.

Key actions

- Take account of indigenous systems of stock distribution in the design of livestock provision interventions (see *Guidance note 1*).
- Base selection of beneficiaries on local participation and practice (see *Guidance note 2*).
- Where cash or voucher mechanisms are used, assess current market prices and set values accordingly (see *Guidance note 3*).
- Ensure that the types and numbers of livestock provided are appropriate to support livelihoods, and that the animals are productive, healthy, and adapted to local conditions, including patterns of climate variability (see *Guidance note 4*).
- Distribute animals at appropriate times (see *Guidance note 5*).

Guidance notes

1. *Indigenous redistribution systems.* These systems are often well developed and logical. They include provision of specific types of animals to specific types of recipient. They are based on local experience, gained over decades, in rebuilding herds in difficult environments. Livestock provision interventions should therefore be designed to complement indigenous livestock redistribution systems where these exist.

2. *Beneficiary selection.* The identification of beneficiaries should build on indigenous methods for identifying suitable recipients and be linked to a wealth-ranking exercise that takes into account the minimum livelihood assets required for successful livestock keeping in that particular context (see *Standard 1, Guidance note 3* above). As noted above, the very poorest community members, although potentially the most deserving, may not be the most appropriate beneficiaries of livestock if they lack the means to maintain

and manage the animals in the future. Livestock provision interventions based on repayment by the recipients in the form of cash or livestock offspring should also include the ability to repay as part of the selection criteria. However, this may further disadvantage the poorest in the community. Whichever criteria are used, community participation in agreeing beneficiary criteria and in selecting suitable recipients will help ensure appropriate targeting and also facilitate an open process of selection to avoid resentment.

3. *Setting cash values.* Where cash or vouchers are used as the distribution mechanism for livestock provision, local market prices and availability should be assessed and the cash values set accordingly. This assessment should also include the extent of supply and the potential implications of the programme on the market to avoid any negative impact on local traders and the future market.

4. *Type of livestock to be provided.* Selection of the type of animal includes the choice of species, breed, age, use, and sex. Livestock provision interventions should use fairly young, productive animals from local breeds adapted to local conditions, including environmental conditions, existing patterns of climate variability and extreme events, and disease. In addition, targeted communities already have knowledge and experience in the care and management of local breeds, and such breeds are also generally cheaper and more readily available for purchase than improved or exotic types. Livestock species and breed preference may vary within households; for example, women may prioritize animals that contribute most to the food supply, rather than those that generate the most income.

For herd replacement, using the analysis of the minimum viable herd size and appropriate composition (outlined in *Provision of livestock standard 1, Guidance note 6* above; see also discussion in *Appendix 9.4*), a package should be defined taking into account family size, maintenance costs, and the livestock needs of the target beneficiaries (for example, productive livestock, such as milking goats or cattle, or draught or pack animals, such as donkeys or camels). This minimum number will depend on the role of livestock in livelihoods and the anticipated contribution of livestock to the household economy.

As much as possible, recipients should be permitted to select individual animals themselves, based on an open and transparent process. Although the provision of the minimum viable herd size may be costly (particularly in livestock-dependent communities), if less than the minimum is provided, households will require additional food security support until the herd reaches sufficient size, which may take a number of years. The replacement of single or small numbers of animals requires fewer animals to achieve a positive impact on livelihood assets. Where possible, the package should be flexible to respond to the priorities of particular households, as this will increase the probability of successful repayment in those projects using credit systems, and the potential for positive livelihoods impact.

5. *Timing of distribution.* Local knowledge can be used to plan the provision of livestock to coincide with optimal availability of feed (pasture, fodder, crop residue) and water, thereby maximizing productivity and growth and minimizing negative environmental impact. This should also include consideration of climatic conditions and livestock breeding cycles as well as the disease and work calendars of the target communities.

Provision of livestock standard 3: Credit, procurement, transport, and delivery systems

Credit, procurement, transport, and delivery systems are efficient, cost-effective, and support quality provision of livestock.

Key actions

- Base procurement on local purchase where possible (see *Guidance note 1*).

- Ensure that procurement takes place according to agreed criteria and in accordance with legal procurement procedures (see *Guidance note 2*).

- Ensure that veterinary inspection takes place at the time of livestock purchase (see *Guidance note 3*).

- Only provide livestock under a credit system when this increases beneficiary commitment and does not jeopardize the productivity of the livestock provided or the capacity of the household to meet their basic needs. In all other cases, provide livestock as a gift (see *Guidance note 4*).

- Plan transport in advance to minimize risk of losses in transit, based on conditions that ensure the welfare of the stock (see *Guidance note 5*).

Guidance notes

1. *Local purchase.* Local purchase supports local markets and avoids the logistical, health-related, environmental, and financial problems associated with the movement of animals from distant areas. In particular, purchase involving cross-border movement of animals should be avoided unless appropriate disease control and certification measures can be put in place. The actual purchase of livestock should involve either the recipients themselves or their representatives, since local people usually know which types of animal best suit their situation. In a given community, recipients may appoint local experts, traders, or elders to select animals on their behalf. A livestock fair is another mechanism for enabling beneficiaries to select stock themselves (see *Appendix 9.5*). However, after an emergency it is not always possible to find sufficient young female stock locally, especially for large-scale projects requiring significant numbers of animals.

2. *Procurement procedures.* Regulations concerning livestock purchase need to be identified (taxes, quarantine, cross-border issues, etc.). Quarantine requirements can have a significant impact on implementation, as they can involve considerable extra time, resources, logistics, and management of animals before the distribution can take place. The origin, species, breed, sex, and age of the animals need to be determined before suppliers are contracted in order to ensure that agreed criteria are met. The quality of the stock should be checked by experts and community representatives before distribution. In conflict situations or areas of insecurity where looting is common, agencies should beware of purchasing looted stock.

3. *Veterinary inspection.* At the time of purchase, animals should be inspected by a veterinary surgeon or veterinary paraprofessional to minimize mortality and maximize performance. The inspector may be a local private practitioner contracted by the project, or a government official. The inspection should highlight any key disease issues.

4. *Credit systems do not jeopardize productivity.* During the design stage, the decision should be made as to whether the project will be based on credit or on gift distribution (and if credit, what form repayment should take). This should be done in close consultation with the beneficiaries and based on full understanding and commitment from all participating households. Where livestock are provided under a credit system, the

CH 9 Restocking

loan is either repaid in the form of the offspring of the livestock or in cash. Cash repayment requires a level of community integration into a market economy, and in many cases repayment in the form of stock will be more appropriate, preferably building on indigenous systems. However, the repayment arrangement (type and condition of animal, timing of repayment, etc.) must be planned carefully to ensure it does not negatively affect the quality of livelihood support received from the initial livestock provision. For example, if the animals provided are not productive, the repayment can burden the recipient with a debt. Selection of secondary beneficiaries (to receive cash or livestock offspring from primary beneficiaries) should take place at the time that primary beneficiaries are identified, and repayment should be carefully monitored.

5. *Transport planning.* Itinerary, duration, likely weather conditions, distances, opening hours of customs, staging points, and stops need to be planned in advance, as well as the equipment and supplies needed to feed, water, and milk the stock as necessary. The conditions and length of the journey should ensure the welfare of the livestock. This should include the avoidance of overloading (and the resultant risk of suffocation) and the provision of sufficient space for animals to stand and lie in their normal position, albeit packed closely (as appropriate for the species) to avoid falling. The vehicle should be disinfected before and after loading and be properly ventilated. The delivery site should also be properly prepared with sufficient water, feed, fencing, and shelter.

Provision of livestock standard 4: Additional support

Additional support (veterinary care, training, food) is provided to beneficiaries to help ensure a positive and sustainable impact on livelihoods.

Key actions

- Provide preventive veterinary care for the livestock prior to distribution (see *Guidance note 1*).

- Establish a system for the ongoing provision of veterinary care for all members of the community (see *Guidance note 2*).

- Provide training and capacity-building support to beneficiaries based on an analysis of skills and knowledge of animal husbandry (see *Guidance note 3*).

- Ensure that training and capacity building includes preparedness for future shocks and emergencies (see *Guidance note 4*).

- Identify and meet food security needs according to the Sphere 'Minimum standards in food security and nutrition' to prevent early offtake of livestock (see *Guidance note 5*).

- Identify and meet shelter and non-food needs according to the Sphere 'Minimum standards in shelter, settlement, and non-food items' (see *Guidance note 6*).

- Withdraw food security support only when herd size and/or the emergence of other economic activities enable independence from such support (see *Guidance note 7*).

Guidance notes

1. ***Preventive veterinary care.*** Prior to distribution, animals should be vaccinated, dewormed, and receive other preventive animal health care depending on the local disease situation. In most cases this service is provided as a single input, free of charge. However, attention should be paid to the issues of cost recovery outlined in *Chapter 5 (Veterinary support)*.

2. ***Long-term veterinary care.*** Beneficiary communities should have continued access to animal health-care services, both preventive and curative, according to the standards and guidelines set out in *Chapter 5 (Veterinary support)*. A system for continuing care should be established at the time the livestock are distributed to ensure they receive the treatment they need. This long-term care system may also provide an opportunity to collect monitoring and evaluation data.

3. ***Training and capacity building.*** Training in animal husbandry may not be necessary for herd replacement activities because the beneficiary communities (usually pastoralists and agro-pastoralists) may have considerable knowledge and experience in livestock management. However, communities targeted for replacing livelihood-generating livestock or else providing livestock as a new livelihood activity may have limited husbandry knowledge, or the knowledge may have been lost if the emergency has endured over a long period. In such cases, the provision of livestock should be accompanied by adequate capacity building in the care and management of the animals in order to ensure that the stock survive, are well cared for, and can provide a useful contribution to post-emergency

livelihoods. Training and/or providing information on the market economy may also be useful to secure livestock-based livelihoods in the longer term.

4. **Preparedness for future emergencies.** In communities without significant livestock management experience, it is important to develop preparedness skills to minimize the risk of losing animals in future events. Skill-building activities might include the following, for example: storage of feed; protection of pasture; optimal livestock marketing; early destocking; shelter construction; animal health care; and maintenance of water sources (all covered in other chapters of LEGS).

5. **Food security support.** Early sale and consumption of animals are common immediately following livestock provision, reflecting the urgent food security needs of beneficiary households and/or a shortage of labour and resources that can be diverted from other livelihood activities to manage the livestock. The food security needs of beneficiary households should be assessed and additional support provided until the livestock become fully productive. The Sphere Handbook provides 'Minimum standards for food security and nutrition' (Sphere, 2011). Cash or voucher mechanisms may be appropriate for providing this support.

6. **Shelter and non-food support.** Families receiving livestock may require shelter, basic household utensils, bedding, water containers, and livestock-related equipment such as carts, harnesses, and ploughs. Without this support, they may be forced to sell livestock. The use of cash or voucher mechanisms may also be considered for this support.

7. **Withdrawal of food security support.** Recipients should receive food security assistance until livestock and/or other livelihood activities can provide enough support. This avoids early and non-sustainable offtake of livestock. A well-designed participatory monitoring system can include measures of herd growth and other livelihood-based indicators to determine the best time to withdraw food aid.

Provision of livestock **case studies**

9.1 Impact case study: Herd replacement using cash transfers in Kenya

Isiolo District in Kenya suffered a severe drought in 2005 that resulted in many livestock deaths and high rates of acute malnutrition among infants. Following the long rains in April and May 2006, Save the Children Canada provided 750 households in 22 communities with a one-off cash transfer of 30,000 Kenyan shillings (approximately US$490). The cash was intended either to help families to reconstitute their herds with animals of their choice or to invest in alternative productive uses, and also to have some cash to meet pressing immediate needs.

On average, livestock prices at local markets did not change significantly as a result of the cash distribution, although sellers did attempt to charge exorbitant prices because of the sudden increase in demand. Beneficiaries adopted a variety of methods for dealing with this attempted inflation, including purchasing as groups with a representative, travelling to more distant markets, and delaying their purchases.

An evaluation conducted seven months after the distribution found that recipients appreciated the cash-based intervention because it enabled them to purchase the specific animals of their choice and to exert more quality control than is possible with in-kind restocking. It also allowed recipients to spend some of the cash on other needs. In total, 85 per cent of the cash was spent on livestock – mainly goats, sheep, and cattle, with some donkeys. The remaining 15 per cent was split between items such as shelter construction, investing in business/petty trade, debt repayments, veterinary care, health care, education, and food. Children's attendance at school, especially for girls and at the secondary level, has increased for the recipients compared to non-recipients.

The programme targeted only 11 per cent of all households, and clearly did not reach all of those in need. However, it was felt that it made sense to provide larger amounts of cash to a smaller number of people than to spread the available money more thinly across all those in need.

Seven months after the cash distribution, the impact on food security was modest. Recipients improved the diversity of their diet, particularly because of increased access to milk. However, their reliance on food aid was not significantly reduced. Based on herd growth in the first five to seven months (+3 per cent for cattle, +16 per cent for goats, and +25 per cent for sheep), it was estimated that herds should be large enough to ensure food security within two years, which is substantially faster than if there had been no intervention. However, the final impact of the programme will only be clear in the longer term – and in particular during the next drought, when the beneficiary households' resilience will be put to the test (*Sources*: O'Donnell, 2007; Croucher et al., 2006).

9.2 Process case study: Supporting traditional livestock distribution as a drought-preparedness strategy in Niger

The Pastoralist Survival and Recovery Project in Dakoro District, Niger, was run by Lutheran World Relief (LWR) with partner organization Contribution à l'Éducation de Base (CEB). The project followed LWR's emergency food relief intervention during the Niger food crisis in 2005 and aimed to increase the resilience and preparedness of affected communities to cope with future droughts and famine. In discussion with communities in Dakoro District, four key interventions were identified:

- provision of livestock
- feed banks
- water point development
- community forums to facilitate participation in all aspects of the project (addressing issues such as conflict between farming and herding communities and raising awareness on rights).

The four project components were designed and planned in a participatory planning forum. The livestock distribution activity was prioritized by pastoralists in response to the threat of future drought following the 2005 famine. In times of drought, the men travel south with the bulk of the livestock looking for pasture while the women and the elderly remain behind with the small stock. When resources are low, the first assets to be disposed of are these small stock in the care of the women. The communities identified the need to replace and build these assets, to protect the food security of the women, and also to help protect the large stock assets from sale.

This activity was a drought-preparedness intervention rather than an attempt to reconstitute herds, hence the relatively small number of stock involved. The community prioritized sheep over the mix of sheep and goats originally suggested by the project since the former had better market value.

The livestock distribution component was based on a traditional redistribution mechanism called *habbanaye*, whereby animals are given to beneficiaries who then keep the first offspring and pass on the original animals to the next beneficiary. Based on community suggestions, each initial beneficiary received one male and four female sheep. The initial 200 beneficiaries were identified by their own communities according to community criteria, based on poverty levels. To date, all the first batch of beneficiaries received offspring and passed on the original animals to the second batch.

The impact of the project thus far is that the beneficiary women, many of whom had previously had between 7 and 30 small stock of their own, which they lost in the drought, now have at least 4 animals that they can sell in case of hardship or that may reproduce during the coming year to increase their livestock assets. In other words, the distributed animals form a 'drought contingency fund' for poor women.

The livestock distribution activity is complemented by water development and feed bank initiatives (see *Case study 6.3* at the end of *Chapter 6, Ensuring feed supplies*), which also help to keep the livestock alive and thus protect assets (*Sources*: ARVIP, 2005; Burns, 2006; Evariste Karangwa, Meghan Armisted, and Mahamadou Ouhoumoudou, personal communication, 2008).

9.3 Impact case study: Livestock fairs in Niger

Between June 2005 and June 2006, the northern part of Dakoro District in Niger, a pastoralist and agro-pastoralist area, had seen livestock losses of up to 60 per cent, especially in cattle. At this level of loss, it would take nearly 30 years to rebuild the herds to their pre-crisis levels. Livestock represented the main, if not the only, source of revenue. Oxfam and its local partner, the Association pour le Renouveau de l'Elevage au Niger (AREN), took the initiative to help rebuild livestock assets via a livestock fair system.

A total of 1,500 beneficiaries received $360 worth of vouchers in order to buy the animals of their choice (such as cattle, sheep, goats, donkeys) from local traders and wealthy livestock keepers participating in eight fairs organized during January and February 2006. To avoid quick cashing-in of the distributed animals to meet immediate needs, the beneficiaries also received $30 in cash.

The fairs were held in partnership with the PROXEL project (run by VSF-Belgium and their local partner, Karkara), which oversaw both the health inspection of animals before entry to the fairs and the vaccination of the animals purchased. Oxfam also contracted PROXEL to conduct a mid-term follow-up of the distributed animals and provide technical support to beneficiaries, notably through a prophylaxis programme and awareness raising on new livestock husbandry techniques.

One year later, an evaluation of the programme highlighted the importance of this follow-up process to the success of the programme. The herd increase rate was 74 per cent. A total of 11,476 animals were purchased through the fairs, which at this rate of growth would mean a total herd of around 20,000 one year later. The offtake rate, including sales and home consumption, was very low (goats: 0.4 per cent; sheep: 0.6 per cent) in line with the objectives of the project, which focused on rebuilding herds. These positive outcomes were linked by the evaluators to the veterinary follow-up and the training provided to beneficiary communities. The target communities were also noted to have increased their demand for veterinary support for their other livestock as a result of the programme (*Sources*: Oxfam GB/VSF-B, 2007; Bernard, 2006).

9.4 Process case study: Community contributions to herd replacement in Ethiopia

In response to the 2006 drought, Save the Children USA carried out herd replacement in five districts in southern Ethiopia. The activity was designed around traditional restocking mechanisms. In Borana, traditional restocking is called *Bussa Gonifa*. Under this system, pastoralists losing their livestock due to drought, conflict, or raiding, and left with fewer than five cows are eligible for the benefit and have the right to claim a minimum of five cows from their clan to remain in the system as a pastoralist. The Degodia Somali have a similar customary livestock redistribution system.

Save the Children USA substituted sheep and goats for cows, since small stock have a faster reproduction rate and are also increasingly preferred as they are better able to withstand drought conditions. In discussion with the community, it was agreed that Save the Children would provide 15–20 sheep/goats (including one or two males) and one pack animal per beneficiary and that the community would match this number through their traditional restocking mechanism. The total number of livestock was considered a minimum herd size for the priority target households that had lost most or all of their stock in the drought.

The activity was jointly managed by Save the Children USA and representatives from the indigenous community institutions. The latter oversaw purchasing of the livestock as well as identification of beneficiary households and the management of the community contribution. Save the Children vaccinated and treated most of the livestock before distribution.

In two of the districts, the matching of the Save the Children livestock by the community worked successfully. The community contributed a total of 1,364 sheep and goats, and community members took great pride in providing livestock of better quality than the purchased animals. In the other target areas, the community contributions were less successful for two key reasons. First, in some communities the effects of the drought were more widespread, households were poorer, and the indigenous institutions were reluctant to push their clan members for contributions when all of them had suffered livestock losses in the drought. Second, the willingness of community members to make the contributions also appeared to reflect the quality and duration of the relationship with the partner agency: where there was a positive history of community-based development activity, contributions were more easily obtained than in other areas where the links with the external agency were of shorter duration or the relationship less developed.

On balance, Save the Children USA concluded that matching contributions from the community is a useful approach that may be particularly appropriate in the context of more localized droughts in the future, particularly in areas where there is a strong relationship between the operating agency and the community, and where community members have not all been equally hit by the drought (*Source*: Gebru, 2007).

9.5 Process case study: Livestock distribution following the Pakistan earthquake

Shortly after the 2005 Pakistan earthquake struck, and following initial responses such as the distribution of food, tents, and blankets, the German Red Cross initiated an activity to improve the nutritional status of children in households affected by the earthquake by providing a lactating cow with a calf to targeted households. The target beneficiaries had either lost all their animals or were vulnerable households (such as female-headed or poor households with more than four children) which may not have owned livestock in the past. Village-based committees, which included representatives from among the elders, different castes, women, religious leaders, and teachers, were established to oversee beneficiary selection. The beneficiary selection was cross-checked by field visits and community discussions.

Before the livestock were distributed, the beneficiaries received training in livestock management, including feeding, breeding, and animal health. Certain breeds and types of cattle were selected, based on agreed criteria such as adaptability to the cold climate, milk production, size, and age. Local contractors supplied the cows, which were checked by the Red Cross and treated for mastitis and ticks; they were also vaccinated and disinfected prior to distribution. A lottery system was used for the actual distribution.

Community animal health workers (CAHWs) were also trained in each village, and refresher training continued throughout the life of the project. Plans were put in place to link the CAHWs to specific government veterinary services such as artificial insemination and bull schemes (*Source*: Matthew Kinyanjui, personal communication, 2008).

9.6 Process case study: Deciding against livestock distribution following the Pakistan earthquake

On 8 October 2005, three districts in Azad Jammu and Kashmir and five districts in North-West Frontier Province (now Khyber Pakhtunkhwa) in Pakistan were struck by a severe earthquake. In support of the government's short-term recovery and rehabilitation programme, the Food and Agriculture Organization of the United Nations (FAO) undertook a review of the livestock component of the programme in May/June 2006. The objective was to formulate a strategy for the first six months of the short-term recovery phase. The review made best estimates of the post-earthquake feed supply and demand situation in the affected districts. The situation is summarized in *Table 9.3*.

Table 9.3 Post-earthquake feed supply and demand

District	Total feed demand MJME (m)	Total feed supply MJME (m)	Surplus (deficit) MJME (m)
Azad Jammu and Kashmir			
Muzaffarabad	5,361	7,560	2,199
Bagh	2,688	1,757	(931)
Rawalakot	5,092	3,306	(1,787)
North-West Frontier Province			
Mansehra	9,339	7,096	(2,242)
Battagram	4,037	1,871	(2,165)
Shangla	3,097	2,901	(197)
Abbottabad	6,339	3,336	(3,003)
Kohistan	11,962	11,103	(860)

MJME = megajoules metabolizable energy; (m) = millions

Post-earthquake, only Muzaffarabad District had a significant feed surplus although Shangla and Kohistan Districts, neither of which experienced high animal losses, had a reasonable balance between the feed demand and the associated feed resource. For the remaining districts there was a significant feed deficit.

Based on these findings, FAO changed its original plan to restock affected households and instead focused its attention on supporting the surviving livestock through the provision of winter (2006/07) feed, animal shelters, and animal health care. Despite the concerns expressed regarding the sustainability of the feed resource, of the nine implementing agencies providing livestock assistance in Azad Jammu and Kashmir and the 13 in North-West Frontier Province:

- 27 per cent indicated they would provide large ruminants.
- 33 per cent would provide small ruminants.
- 33 per cent were said to be providing both small and large ruminants.
- 7 per cent were providing support for livestock inputs only (*Source*: Simon Mack, personal communication, 2008).

9.7 Impact case study: Post-earthquake livestock distribution in Iran

In late December 2003, a major earthquake hit the region of Bam, Kerman Province, in southern Iran. In only 15 seconds, over 70 per cent of the buildings in the city and the surrounding villages collapsed, and more than 40,000 of the area's 130,000 population lost their lives. Most of the people living in the Bam area were involved in date farming or farm labouring, but many kept small numbers of animals to supplement their food supply and income – mainly cattle, sheep, and goats. Livestock keeping was particularly important for poorer farmers who owned either a small plot of land or none at all. Livestock losses in the earthquake were estimated at 31 per cent for cattle and 26 per cent for sheep and goats. Most of these animals were housed in simple shelters near their owners' homes and many were killed when the buildings collapsed. Others ran away in the panic following the earthquake, while some were stolen or sold to meet urgent cash needs.

In response to these losses, Action Against Hunger (ACF) Spain designed a livestock distribution project to provide two goats and 300 kg of feed to 1,200 vulnerable families in 17 earthquake-affected villages in the Bam area. The aim of the project was to support the target households to gain milk for their families and to provide additional income. The project targeted poor families who had lost livestock, in particular widows and other vulnerable people, but the selection criteria required that beneficiaries had experience in raising

CH 9 Restocking

sheep and goats and had adequate shelter for the animals so as to ensure the sustainability of the initiative. Selection of beneficiaries and distribution were conducted in collaboration with local councillors. The Iranian Veterinary Network was contracted to provide veterinary support to the purchased livestock before distribution; this included vaccination against enterotoxaemia, disinfection, deworming, and provision of mineral and vitamin supplements.

The 1,200 beneficiary families each received two female goats (one the local Mahali breed and the other a Rachti – local Mahali crossed with a high-quality Pakistani breed), together with 300 kg of barley for feed. The original plan was to distribute pregnant animals, but this proved logistically challenging, and it was determined that sufficient numbers of male goats had survived the earthquake to enable the distributed goats to reproduce quite quickly after distribution.

Post-distribution monitoring showed that 84 per cent of beneficiaries were satisfied with the breed selected and 87 per cent with the distribution process. Nine of the beneficiaries were already milking one goat; two households were milking both the goats they had received; and 27 had already mated their goats to a buck.

When asked about the impact of the project, beneficiaries listed economic benefits such as milk and wool production, but these were seen as potential benefits as it was too soon for the livestock to have reproduced. People also emphasized the psychological benefits – for example, entertainment for the children, and increased motivation to get involved in other activities. Most were positive about the opportunity to resume livestock activities after losing some or all of their animals in the earthquake (*Sources*: ACF-Spain, 2004; Leguene, 2004).

9.8 Impact case study: Vouchers for livestock distribution and veterinary support in Somalia

In the Hiran region of Somalia, rural households derive 50 to 60 per cent of their income from livestock. In 2011/12, a drought led to widespread loss of human lives and livestock, and poor households lost on average 54 sheep/goats. In 2012, Save the Children International initiated a livestock distribution and treatment project with support from the Norwegian Ministry of Foreign Affairs, AusAID, and the UK Department for International Development (DFID). The aim of the project was to protect and rebuild livestock assets by means of the provision of livestock and the use of veterinary support to reduce livestock disease and bolster livestock nutrition.

Baseline studies reported original herd sizes, access to veterinary services, income and food sources, and disease prevalence. The project targeted beneficiaries using vulnerability criteria such as the number of livestock losses by poor households and the level of child malnutrition. Following agreement on livestock age and types, traders were contracted to provide livestock through an open bidding system, and a standard veterinary kit was designed and procured. Local Community Animal Health Workers (CAHWs) were also given refresher training and treatment kits.

Each beneficiary household was given vouchers to procure 5–10 animals according to the specifications and livelihood zone; they were also given vouchers for treatment for 20 small stock. The livestock traders brought the animals to the villages where the beneficiaries could exchange their vouchers for livestock. A local 'livestock professionals association' provided veterinary teams who collected the medicines from contracted pharmacies and travelled to the villages where the beneficiary households could redeem their vouchers for treatment and training. A complaints mechanism was established to enable beneficiaries to give feedback on the project.

In total, 2,583 households received livestock, and 3,310 households received animal health treatment. The use of vouchers and local vendors was significant in overcoming some of the logistical challenges of transporting supplies in an insecure environment.

An external evaluation of the project reported improved access to milk, increased livestock holdings, improved animal health, and increased drought preparedness among the beneficiary households. More than two-thirds of the beneficiaries strongly agreed that their household productivity had increased, as had their resilience to future disasters. Other positive impacts included the support provided to local businesses such as pharmacies, veterinary professionals, CAHWs, and transporters, as well as the nutritional benefits brought by increased milk supplies to children of women-headed households, which constituted 35 per cent of the beneficiaries.

Key lessons included the importance of distributing pregnant or lactating animals for increasing access to milk within a short time period. Also, the use of vouchers enabled accountability to beneficiaries and ensured an audit trail; it also facilitated distribution in an insecure environment. Finally, a comprehensive package of livestock support – provision of livestock, treatment, and training – was important for increasing impact (*Source*: Save the Children International, 2013).

Appendix 9.1: Assessment checklist for provision of livestock

Options and implications

- What role did livestock play in livelihoods before the emergency?
  - Main livelihood asset?
  - Provision of supplementary food?
  - Income generation?
  - Transport or draught power?
- Which species and breeds were kept and for what purposes?
- Which species and breeds have been lost and need replacement?
- If livestock did not already form part of livelihood strategies:
  - Is there potential for the introduction of livestock to meet supplementary food or income-generation needs?
  - Which species and breeds would be most appropriate for distribution?
- Have alternative, more cost-effective options than livestock provision been considered?
- What indigenous mechanisms exist for redistributing livestock?
- What numbers of livestock would constitute the minimum viable herd per household in the local context?
- What are the implications of distributing these minimum numbers of livestock in the area?
  - Is there sufficient pasture or feed?
  - Is there sufficient water?
  - Is there adequate shelter or can this be constructed?
  - Will the livestock be secure or will the activity increase the risk to livestock keepers and/or the animals themselves?

Beneficiaries

- What social, physical, and natural livelihood assets do potential beneficiaries have to enable them to manage livestock successfully in the future?
- Can training in livestock management be provided if necessary?
- What roles do women and men play in livestock management and care, and what are the labour implications of livestock provision?

- What are the particular needs of vulnerable groups in relation to livestock management and access to livestock products?
- Are there sufficient resources to provide livestock-related support to beneficiaries (for example, veterinary care, feed, shelter) as required?
- Are there sufficient resources to provide non-livestock support to beneficiaries as required (for example, food or other livelihood support while herds rebuild)?

Procurement

- What are the implications of the purchase of significant numbers of livestock on local markets?
- Are livestock available for purchase in sufficient numbers within transporting distance of beneficiary communities?
- Is transport available, and can stock be transported safely without risk to their welfare?
- What are the risks of disease from importing stock from another area?

Appendix 9.2: Examples of monitoring and evaluation indicators for the provision of livestock

	Process indicators (measure things happening)	Impact indicators (measure the result of things happening)
Designing the system	• Number of meetings with community representatives and other stakeholders, including private sector suppliers where relevant	• Meeting reports with analysis of options for livestock provision • Action plan including: - roles and responsibilities of different actors - community process and criteria for selecting beneficiaries - community preferences for livestock species and type - procurement, transportation, and distribution plan, with beneficiary involvement - veterinary inspection and preventive care

	Process indicators (measure things happening)	Impact indicators (measure the result of things happening)
Replacing livestock assets: replacing herds for pastoralists and agro-pastoralists	• Number of livestock provided per household by livestock type[2] • Type and value of additional support to each household, e.g. food aid, utensils, etc.	• Mortality in livestock provided vs. mortality in pre-existing livestock • Number of offspring from livestock provided, and uses of offspring, e.g. sales and use of income • Human nutrition – consumption of milk by children in households receiving livestock • Herd growth and levels of reliance on external assistance over time • Influence on policy
Replacing livestock assets: smallholder farmers and other income generation	• Number of livestock provided per household by livestock type • Type and value of additional support to each household, e.g. food aid, utensils, etc. • Training, where appropriate, on livestock production and management	• Mortality in livestock provided vs. mortality in pre-existing livestock • Number of offspring from livestock provided, and uses of offspring, e.g. sales and use of income • Human nutrition – consumption of milk by children in households receiving livestock
Building livestock assets: new livelihood activity	• Number of livestock provided per household by livestock type • Training on livestock production, management, and marketing	• Mortality in livestock provided vs. mortality in pre-existing livestock • Number of offspring from livestock provided, and uses of offspring, e.g. sales and use of income • Human nutrition – consumption of milk by children in households receiving livestock

See also the LEGS Evaluation Tool available on the LEGS website:
<http://www.livestock-emergency.net/resources/general-resources-legs-specific/>.

Appendix 9.3: Provision of livestock in camps

The provision of livestock in camps and camp-like settings should be considered in discussion with the camp management agency. Together with camp residents, the camp management agency should be able to liaise with the relevant camp stakeholders, including, where relevant, the host community, to ensure that activities happen in a coordinated manner. Where appropriate, camp committees may take particular roles in supporting the intervention. For example, the watch group may ensure security of the livestock; the shelter committee may provide support for livestock shelter, and so on.

The provision of livestock in camps involves particular challenges with regard to sanitation and security because of the close proximity of humans and animals. In camps facing major overpopulation, management challenges, precarious health conditions, conflict, tensions with the host community, or shortage of key resources such as water, the provision of livestock might further exacerbate the difficulties and present additional risks to the inhabitants of the camp.

In camps where these conditions do not exist and livestock provision is possible, health and hygiene precautions should be taken in order to minimize the spreading of animal-to-human and animal-to-animal diseases. Such measures may include the following: preventing livestock from roaming within the camp; setting animal units as far as possible from human habitations; careful consideration of the type of animals to be provided (as some produce more waste than others); encouraging rapid sale of offspring; and maintaining sufficient reproductive animals to preserve stocks without massive proliferation. In addition, the following should be strictly implemented: vaccination; quarantine; biosecurity measures; and a disease surveillance system.

Access to natural and other resources necessary for the livestock should be regulated in consultation with both camp representatives and resident populations to minimize the risk of conflicts and shortage. Water availability is a key constraint, particularly in areas where water for human use is in short supply; livestock should not be provided to camps where watering the animals puts stress on the water sources of the camp or the host population.

The shelter and security needs of the livestock must be taken into account (see also *Chapter 8, Livestock shelter and settlement*), to protect the stock from bad weather and to minimize the risk of theft.

The choice of livestock types and breeds should take into account the situation of the beneficiary population. For example, small stock that require less space and feed (poultry, sheep, goats) may be more appropriate than large stock for livestock provision to camps. Livestock species with a rapid reproductive cycle and which are easy to market may be most appropriate. While camps are often planned as temporary arrangements, many last longer (particularly in conflict situations), and interventions should bear in mind the possibility that the residents may remain in the camp for some time.

Appendix 9.4: Discussion on minimum viable herd size

In herd replacement projects in pastoralist areas, the concept of 'minimum viable herd size' is often used to determine the minimum number and types of animals required to allow pastoralists to maintain a pastoralism-based livelihood. Although it might be convenient for standards and guidelines such as LEGS to indicate a specific number and type of animals to be provided, in reality this differs significantly between pastoralist groups, and there are no standard numbers of livestock that should be given. Similarly, in mixed farming communities, it is difficult to determine a global figure for livestock provision.

Field experience suggests that the best way to determine how many and which types of livestock to provide is through participatory analysis and discussion with the communities concerned. This process may include a description of the benefits and problems of different livestock species and breeds for the different wealth, gender, and age groups within the community, and an analysis of any indigenous restocking systems.

A further consideration is that although a 'minimum herd size' may be defined with communities in this way, at the same time many agencies are faced with limited budgets for the provision of livestock, and the more animals provided per household, the fewer the total number of households that will benefit from the initiative.

Save the Children UK implemented a restocking project between 2002 and 2003 for 500 internally displaced families in eastern Ethiopia as a post-drought response, providing each pastoral household with 30 breeding sheep or goats. The project was implemented in collaboration with the Ethiopian government's Disaster Preparedness and Prevention Committee and the Somali Region Livestock Bureau. The total budget was around $244,500 – equivalent to $489 per household. This budget excluded the cost of food aid and household items, which were provided by other agencies such as the Christian Relief and Development Agency and UNICEF. An evaluation concluded that although the project had provided substantial benefits through the restocking process, the package should have included at least 50 sheep and goats per household in order for the families to have a viable source of livelihood. This would have increased the project budget by 41 per cent if 500 households were still to be targeted. Alternatively, the original budget could have covered 300 households with 50 animals each. The evaluation indicated that a budget of around $690 per household was needed in order to restock the target communities in a viable way (Wekesa, 2005).

This example illustrates the challenge faced by aid agencies when deciding how many households to restock and how many animals to provide, and the importance of determining the appropriate definition of 'minimum viable herd' in each specific context.

Appendix 9.5: Livestock fairs

Livestock fairs are a way of giving livestock recipients the opportunity to choose animals from a range of species, breeds, and ages. Compared with classic distributions, livestock fairs contribute to a greater feeling of ownership and empowerment and help to stimulate the local economy. The money invested in the project goes directly into the economy of the targeted area, and the active participation of professional or occasional traders favours initiative and entrepreneurship.

Livestock fairs are specific markets dedicated to livestock where local traders and livestock keepers are invited to bring animals for sale. The preselected beneficiaries of the project receive vouchers of a monetary value that they can exchange for the animals of their choice. When the transactions are concluded, the vouchers are repaid in local currency to the traders. Livestock fairs are also a good opportunity to bring together people involved in animal husbandry to encourage sharing of information and knowledge.

Livestock fairs can be suitable for all livestock provision options. See *Case study 9.3* above for an example of livestock fairs in Niger.

References and further reading

(ACF-Spain) Action Against Hunger – Spain (2004) *Livelihoods Recovery Project (Livestock Distribution)*, ACF-Spain, Bam.

ARVIP–Lutheran World Relief Pastoralist Survival and Recovery Program (2005) *ARVIP Proposal and Baseline Survey*, Lutheran World Relief, Niamey.

Bernard, J. (2006) *Animal Fairs, an Oxfam GB Trial in the Sahel*, Oxfam, Dakoro.

Burns, J. (2006) *Mid-Term Visit Report on ARVIP*, Feinstein International Center, Tufts University, Medford, MA.

Catley, A. and Blakeway, S. (2004) 'Donkeys and the provision of livestock to returnees: lessons from Eritrea', in P. Starkey and D. Fielding (eds), *Donkeys, People and Development: A Resource Book of the Animal Traction Network for Eastern and Southern Africa* (ATNESA), pp. 86–92, Technical Centre for Agricultural and Rural Cooperation, Wageningen, The Netherlands,

<http://www.atnesa.org/donkeys/donkeys-catley-returnees-ER.pdf> [accessed 14 May 2014].

Croucher, M., Karanja, V., Wako, R., Dokata, A. and Dima, J. (2006) *Initial Impact Assessment of the Livelihoods Programme in Merti and Sericho*, Save the Children Canada, Nairobi.

Gebru, G. (2007) Project documentation from the *Save the Children-USA restocking implementation programme in Somali and Oromia regional states*, Save the Children USA, Addis Ababa.

Heffernan, C. (1999) *Livestock, Destitution and Drought: The Impact of Restocking on Food Security Post-Disaster*, Overseas Development Institute (ODI), London, <http://www.fao.org/wairdocs/LEAD/X6186E/X6186E00.HTM> [accessed 18 May 2014].

Heffernan, C. and Rushton, J. (1999) *Restocking: A Critical Evaluation*, ODI, London.

Heffernan, C., Misturelli, F. and Nielsen, L. (2004) *Restocking Pastoralists: A Manual of Best Practice and Decision Support Tools*, Practical Action Publishing, Rugby.

IFAD (International Fund for Agricultural Development) (2007) 'Issues on Restocking', in *IFAD Supporting Pastoralism: Livestock and Infrastructure* [web page], IFAD, Rome, <http://www.ifad.org/lrkm/theme/livestock.htm#issues> [accessed 18 May 2014].

INEE (Inter-Agency Network for Education in Emergencies) (2010) *Minimum Standards for Education: Preparedness, Response, Recovery*, INEE, New York, <http://toolkit.ineesite.org/toolkit/Toolkit.php?PostID=1002> [accessed 15 May 2014].

Kelly, K. (1993) *Taking Stock: Oxfam's Experience of Restocking in Kenya*, Oxfam, Oxford.

Knight-Jones, T. (2012a) *Restocking and Animal Health: A Review of Livestock Disease and Mortality in Post-Disaster and Development Restocking Programmes*, World Society for the Protection of Animals (WSPA), London.

Knight-Jones, T. (2012b) *Restocking in the Former Yugoslavia: Post-War Restocking Projects in Bosnia-Herzegovina and Kosovo,* WSPA, London.

LEGS (Livestock Emergency Guidelines and Standards) (2014), *Livestock Emergency Guidelines and Standards, 2nd Edition*, Practical Action Publishing: Rugby.

Leguene, P. (2004) *Evaluation Report: Restoration of the Livelihood and Longer-term Food Security for the Earthquake-Affected Farmers and Agricultural Labourers in Bam, South-East Iran*, project implemented by ACF-UK & ACF-Spain, London.

Lotira, R. (2004) *Rebuilding Herds by Reinforcing* Gargar/Irb among the Somali *Pastoralists of Kenya: Evaluation of Experimental Restocking Program in Wajir and Mandera Districts of Kenya*, African Union/Interafrican Bureau for Animal Resources, Nairobi, <http://sites.tufts.edu/capeipst/files/2011/03/Lotira-Restocking-evaluation.pdf> [accessed 18 May 2014].

O'Donnell, M. (2007) *Cash-based Emergency Livelihood Recovery Programme, Isiolo District, Kenya,* project evaluation draft report, Save the Children, Nairobi.

Oxby, C. (1994) *Restocking: A Guide – Herd Reconstitution for African Livestock Keepers as Part of a Strategy for Disaster Rehabilitation*, VETAID, Midlothian.

Oxfam GB/Vétérinaires sans Frontières Belgium (VSF-B) (2007) *Rapport d'activité: Opération de reconstitution du cheptel, département de Dakoro, Région de Maradi, Niger, janvier 2006–mars 2007*, Oxfam GB/VSF-B, Niamey.

Save the Children International (2012) *Contribution of Cash Programming to Resilience, Hiran*, Save the Children International, Nairobi.

Save the Children International (2013) *Drought Early Warning and FSL Needs Assessment in Hiran and Puntland*; *Livestock Baseline for Hiran, DFID Project*; *Evaluation of Livelihoods/Resilience Activities, Hiran*; and *Livestock and Cash Grants Project Baseline for Hiran*, Save the Children International, Nairobi.

Scott, M.F. and Gormley, B. (1980) 'The animal of friendship: an indigenous model of Sahelian pastoral development in Niger', in D. Brokensha, D.M. Warren and O. Werner (eds), *Indigenous Knowledge Systems and Development*, University Press of America, Lanham, MD.

Sphere Project (2011) *Humanitarian Charter and Minimum Standards in Humanitarian Response* (the Sphere Handbook), The Sphere Project, Geneva, <www.sphereproject.org/> [accessed 21 May 2014].

Toulmin, C. (1995) 'Tracking through drought: options for destocking and restocking', in I. Scoones (ed.), *Living with Uncertainty: New Directions in Pastoral Development in Africa*, pp. 95–115, Intermediate Technology Publications, London.

Vetwork (2011) *The Use of Cash Transfers in Livestock Emergencies and their Incorporation into the Livestock Emergency Guidelines and Standards (LEGS)*, Animal Production and Health Working Paper No. 1, FAO, Rome. Available from: <http://www.livestock-emergency.net/resources/general-resources-legs-specific/> [accessed 18 May 2014].

Wekesa, M. (2005) *Terminal Evaluation of the Restocking/Rehabilitation Programme for the Internally Displaced Persons in Fik Zone of the Somali Region of Ethiopia*, Save the Children UK, Addis Ababa and Acacia Consultants, Nairobi.

Notes

1. See INEE, 2010.

2. Household figures can be summated to provide total figures by area and project.

Annexes

Annex A: Glossary

acaricide	a chemical used to kill ticks, for example in a spray, pour-on, or dip solution
alarm	the second phase of a *slow-onset disaster*
alert	the first phase of a *slow-onset disaster*
anthelmintic	a drug used to kill parasitic worms
backloading	the use of trucks or other vehicles that are delivering goods to pick up and transport something else on the return journey (for example, livestock traders bringing feed to an area and then transporting livestock out of the area)
assets	see *livelihood assets*
chronic emergency	a disaster in which the phases (*alert*, *alarm*, *emergency*, *recovery*) keep repeating themselves without returning to 'normal'
cluster approach	international initiative to facilitate collaboration between humanitarian agencies in emergency response; clusters focus on particular relief sectors (such as water, sanitation, or food) and have an allocated lead agency for each cluster, accountable to the rest of the cluster membership, with which a joint strategy is developed
cold chain	a system whereby veterinary or human medicines are kept at the required temperature during storage and transportation through the use of refrigerators and mobile cold boxes
complex emergency	'a humanitarian crisis in a country, region, or society where there is total or considerable breakdown of authority resulting from internal or external conflict and which requires an international response that goes beyond the mandate or capacity of any single agency and/or the ongoing United Nations country programme' [Inter-Agency Standing Committee (IASC)]
drought cycle management	a model for drought response that divides drought into four phases (*alert*, *alarm*, *emergency*, and *recovery*); these are used by LEGS as the four phases of a *slow-onset disaster*
emergency phase	the third phase of a *slow-onset disaster*
early recovery	the second phase of a *rapid-onset disaster*
hafir	dam structure used to collect surface water for cattle and other livestock in Sudan
immediate aftermath	the first phase of a *rapid-onset disaster*: the period just after the disaster has struck, when the impact is greatest

impact indicator	point of reference for measuring the result of actions taken in terms of their effect on beneficiaries
indicators	measurements (either qualitative or quantitative) of the progress of an intervention; they are divided into *process indicators* and *impact indicators*
initial assessment	the collection and analysis of initial information about the role that livestock play in livelihoods, about the nature and impact of the emergency, and a situation analysis
intervention	a technical response in an emergency situation, i.e. destocking, veterinary services, feed, water, shelter, provision of livestock; each intervention is broken down into different *options*
key action	key step or measure that contributes to achieving the *standard*
livelihood	the capabilities, assets, and activities required to make a living
livelihood assets	the resources, equipment, skills, strengths, and relationships that are used by individuals and households to pursue their livelihoods; they are categorized as social, human, natural, financial, and physical and form part of the *livelihoods framework*
livelihoods framework	a model showing how individuals and households use their different *assets* and livelihood strategies to make a living but are also affected by their own *vulnerabilities* and the policy and institutional context in which they operate
livestock offtake	animals sold to traders or otherwise removed from the herd
minimum standard	a qualitative statement that should be applicable in any emergency situation
morbidity	incidence of ill health or disease
options	each technical *intervention* is divided into different options, which present different ways of delivering a technical response (e.g. water trucking versus borehole construction)
process indicator	(also progress indicator) point of reference for measuring the implementation of an intervention; *process indicators* are usually quantitative
purposive sampling	the selection of a 'typically' representative group based on particular characteristics (for example, livestock owners affected by drought; women livestock owners; inhabitants of a flood-affected village)
phytosanitary	relating to food safety; the 'Agreement on the Application of Sanitary and Phytosanitary Measures' sets out the basic rules for food safety and animal and plant health standards; for more information see <http://www.wto.org/english/tratop_e/sps_e/spsund_e.htm>
rapid-onset disaster	a disaster such as an earthquake, flood, or tsunami that hits very suddenly and sometimes without warning; can be divided into three key phases: *immediate aftermath*; *early recovery*; and *recovery*

real-time evaluation	the evaluation of a (generally humanitarian) operation during implementation to allow for feedback and adjustment during the life of the operation itself (see Sandison, 2003; and Herson and Mitchell, 2005 in the references to *Chapter 2, Core standards common to all livestock interventions*)
recovery	the third phase of a *rapid-onset disaster* or the fourth phase of a *slow-onset disaster*
slow-onset disaster	a disaster, such as a drought or extreme cold season, whose effects are felt gradually; divided into four phases: *alert*; *alarm*; *emergency*; and *recovery*
standard	See *minimum standard*
vulnerability	people's ability to withstand shocks and trends; the Sphere Handbook defines vulnerable people as those 'who are especially susceptible to the effects of natural or man-made disasters or of conflict … due to a combination of physical, social, environmental, and political factors' (Sphere, 2011: 54)
zoonosis	(also *zoonotic disease*) a disease that can be transmitted from animals to humans (or vice versa)

Annex B: Abbreviations and acronyms

ACF	Action Contre la Faim/Action Against Hunger
ACORD	Agency for Cooperation and Research and Development
ARV	antiretroviral
AU-IBAR	African Union – Interafrican Bureau for Animal Resources
CAHW	community-based animal health worker
CBAH	community-based animal health care
CCCM	camp coordination and camp management
CFW	cash for work
CPMS	Child Protection Minimum Standards
CPWG	Child Protection Working Group
CSO	civil society organization
DFID	Department for International Development
DRR	disaster risk reduction
EMMA	Emergency Market Mapping and Analysis
EMPRES	Emergency Prevention System (for transboundary animal and plant pests and diseases)
EWS	early warning systems
FAO	Food and Agriculture Organization of the United Nations
FEWS-NET	Famine Early Warning Systems Network
FSNAU	Food Security and Nutrition Analysis Unit for Somalia
GIEWS	Global Information and Early Warning System
HAP	Humanitarian Accountability Partnership
HEA	household economy approach

HPAI	highly pathogenic avian influenza ('bird flu')
IASC	Inter-Agency Standing Committee
ICRC	International Committee of the Red Cross
INEE	Inter-Agency Network for Education in Emergencies
IOM	International Organization for Migration
IPC	Integrated Food Security and Humanitarian Phase Classification
LEGS	Livestock Emergency Guidelines and Standards
M&E	monitoring and evaluation
MERS	Minimum Economic Recovery Standards
MPU	multipurpose unit
OCHA	United Nations Office for the Coordination of Humanitarian Affairs
OIE	World Organisation for Animal Health
PLHIV	people living with HIV and AIDS
PRA	participatory rural appraisal (also known as PLA – participatory learning and action)
PRIM	LEGS Participatory Response Identification Matrix
RDA	recommended dietary allowance
SADC	Southern Africa Development Community
SMART	Standardized Monitoring and Assessment of Relief and Transitions
UNDP	United Nations Development Programme
UNHCR	(Office of) the United Nations High Commissioner for Refugees
USAID	United States Agency for International Development
VAC	Vulnerability Assessment Committee
VSF	Vétérinaires sans Frontières (Vets without borders)
WFP	United Nations World Food Programme
WHO	World Health Organization
WSPA	World Society for the Protection of Animals

Annex C: General bibliography

Aklilu, Y., Admassu, B., Abebe, D. and Catley, A. (2006) *Guidelines for Livelihoods-Based Livestock Relief Interventions in Pastoralist Areas,* United States Agency for International Development (USAID), Addis Ababa/Feinstein International Center, Tufts University, Medford, MA.

CPWG (Child Protection Working Group) (2012) *Minimum Standards for Child Protection in Humanitarian Action,* CPWG, Geneva, <http://cpwg.net/minimum-standards> [accessed 14 May 2014].

FAO (Food and Agriculture Organization of the United Nations) (2015) *Technical Interventions for Livestock Emergencies: The How-to-do-it Guide,* Animal Production and Health Manuals Series, FAO, Rome.

Hedlund, K. (2007) *Slow-Onset Disasters: Drought and Food and Livelihoods Security – Learning from Previous Relief and Recovery Responses*, Active Learning Network for Accountability and Performance in Humanitarian Action (ALNAP) and ProVention Consortium, Geneva, <http://www.alnap.org/resource/5243.

aspx>. [Accessed: 26 May 2014]. Also available from: <http://www.livestock-emergency.net/resources/general-resources/> [accessed 17 May 2014].

Honhold, N., Douglas, I., Geering, W., Shimshoni, A. and Lubroth, J. (eds) (2011) *Good Emergency Management Practice: The Essentials,* FAO Animal Production and Health Manual No. 11, FAO, Rome, <http://www.fao.org/docrep/014/ba0137e/ba0137e00.pdf> [accessed 17 May 2014].

INEE (Inter-Agency Network for Education in Emergencies) (2010) *Minimum Standards for Education: Preparedness, Response, Recovery*, INEE, New York, <http://toolkit.ineesite.org/toolkit/Toolkit.php?PostID=1002> [accessed 15 May 2014].

Morton, J., Barton, D., Collinson, C., and Heath, B. (2002) *Comparing Drought Mitigation Interventions in the Pastoral Livestock Sector*, Natural Resources Institute (NRI), University of Greenwich at Medway, Chatham, <http://www.nri.org/projects/pastoralism/interventions.pdf> [accessed 17 May 2014].

OCHA (United Nations Office for the Coordination of Humanitarian Affairs) (1999) *OCHA Orientation Handbook on Complex Emergencies*, UN OCHA, New York, <http://reliefweb.int/report/world/ocha-orientation-handbook-complex-emergencies> [accessed 17 May 2014].

Powers, L. (2002) *Livestock Interventions: Important Principles for OFDA*, Office of US Foreign Disaster Assistance (OFDA), Washington, D.C Available from: <http://www.livestock-emergency.net/resources/general-resources/> [accessed 17 May 2014].

SEEP (Small Enterprise Education and Promotion) Network (2010) *Minimum Economic Recovery Standards,* SEEP Network, Washington, DC, <http://www.seepnetwork.org/minimum-economic-recovery-standards-resources-174.php> [accessed 15 May 2014].

Sphere Project (2011) *Humanitarian Charter and Minimum Standards in Humanitarian Response* (the Sphere Handbook), The Sphere Project, Geneva, <www.sphereproject.org/> [accessed 15 May 2014].

USAID (United States Agency for International Development) (2005) *Field Operations Guide for Disaster Assessment and Response*, USAID, Washington, DC. Available from: <http://www.livestock-emergency.net/resources/general-resources/> [accessed 26 May 2014].

Annex D: Acknowledgements and contributors

LEGS Steering Group members

Rob Allport	Food and Agriculture Organization of the United Nations
Philippe Ankers	Food and Agriculture Organization of the United Nations
Andy Catley	Feinstein International Center, Tufts University
Wendy Fenton	Humanitarian Policy Group, Overseas Development Institute
Guido Govoni	International Committee of the Red Cross
David Hadrill	Vetwork UK
Solomon Haile Mariam	PATTEC-Coordination, Department for Rural Economy and Agriculture, African Union
Serena Zanella	Independent
Cathy Watson	LEGS Coordinator

Former Steering Group members

Simon Mack	Food and Agriculture Organization of the United Nations
Ong-orn Prasarnphanich	World Animal Protection
Piers Simpkin	International Committee of the Red Cross

Coordination
Vetwork UK

Donors

The LEGS Project gratefully acknowledges the following donors for cash and in-kind support:

- African Union
- Department for International Development (UK)
- European Commission , DG Development and Cooperation – EuropeAid (DG DEVCO – EuropeAid)
- European Commission, Humanitarian Aid and Civil Protection department (ECHO)
- Feinstein International Center, Tufts University
- Food and Agriculture Organization of the United Nations
- Humanitarian Policy Group, Overseas Development Institute

- International Committee of the Red Cross
- Office for Foreign Disaster Assistance, United States Agency for International Development
- Oxfam GB
- Trócaire
- Vétérinaires Sans Frontières Belgium
- World Animal Protection
- Vetwork UK

These donors contributed to the preparation, publication, and distribution of the LEGS Handbook or to the roll-out of the related training programme.

Chapter authors

This second edition of the LEGS Handbook has been thoroughly revised. The chapter authors for the 2009 first edition are acknowledged here, together with the contributing authors of the revised chapters for the 2014 second edition:

Livestock, livelihoods, and emergencies: Cathy Watson/Andy Catley
Core standards: Andy Catley/Cathy Watson
Initial assessment and identifying responses: Cathy Watson/Andy Catley
Destocking: Yacob Aklilu/Simon Mack
Veterinary support: Andy Catley and David Ward/David Hadrill
Ensuring feed supplies: Peter Thorne/Philippe Ankers
Provision of water: Peter Thorne/Guido Govoni
Livestock shelter and settlement: David Hadrill and Peter Manfield/Cathy Watson
Provision of livestock: Hélène Berton and Andy Catley/Ong-orn Prasarnphanich
Coordinating Editor: Cathy Watson
Copy editing: Green Ink and Cordelia Lilly

Photo credits

Introduction, Chapter 4, Chapter 5, Chapter 7 and Chapter 9: Kelley Lynch/Save the Children USA
Chapter 1: Marco Longari/FAO
Chapter 2: Ana Urgoiti
Chapter 3: Astrid de Valon
Chapter 6: David Hadrill
Chapter 8: The Brooke

Briefing paper

The LEGS Project commissioned Briefing Papers to inform the Steering Group for revising and editing this book. The Briefing Paper authors were:

- Animal Welfare: Ian Dacre
- Cash Transfers: Tim Leyland
- Climate Change: John Morton
- Gender: Beth Miller
- Livestock and Camps: The Shelter Centre and Julia Ashmore

The LEGS Consultation Group and Mailing List

Interested stakeholders were invited to send feedback and comments on both the first and second editions through a consultative process via email. Both editions of the LEGS Handbook were enriched with these contributions. A wide range of people, too many to be named here, provided their support and expertise. The LEGS Project gratefully acknowledges all contributors for their valuable inputs.

Annex E: LEGS Training Programme

The LEGS Training Programme is based on regional Training of Trainers (TOT) courses, at which participants are given the skills, methodologies, and materials to run a standard three-day LEGS Training course. Graduates of the TOTs are LEGS Trainers and are encouraged to deliver the LEGS Training course in their own country on demand. 'Accredited LEGS Trainers' are those who have carried out two successful trainings within two years of their TOT, and their contact details are listed on the LEGS website. The LEGS Project does not deliver the three-day Training itself but maintains a database of LEGS Trainers and monitors the roll-out of the training courses. There are more than 300 LEGS Trainers worldwide.

The 3-day LEGS Training is based on the LEGS Handbook and is designed for practitioners and implementers of emergency response. Women are often carers and keepers of livestock (if not always the formal 'owners') and commonly the target of livestock interventions. There is therefore a need for women livestock practitioners who can reach them; hence the LEGS Training aims to include an increasing number of women participants. The Training helps participants to familiarize themselves with the key areas of the LEGS Handbook and takes them through the stages of the LEGS response and the tools for each stage:

1.   *Initial assessment,* including the role of livestock in livelihoods

2.   *Response identification,* including the PRIM

3.   Selection of the most appropriate, timely, and feasible *technical options* using participatory tools such as the decision-making trees and the Standards, Key actions, and Guidance notes for each technical intervention

4.   *Monitoring and evaluation*

Figure E.1   Stages of the LEGS Response

Stage 1	Stage 2	Stage 3	Stage 4
Initial Assessment	Response Identification	Analysis of technical interventions and options	Monitoring and Evaluation

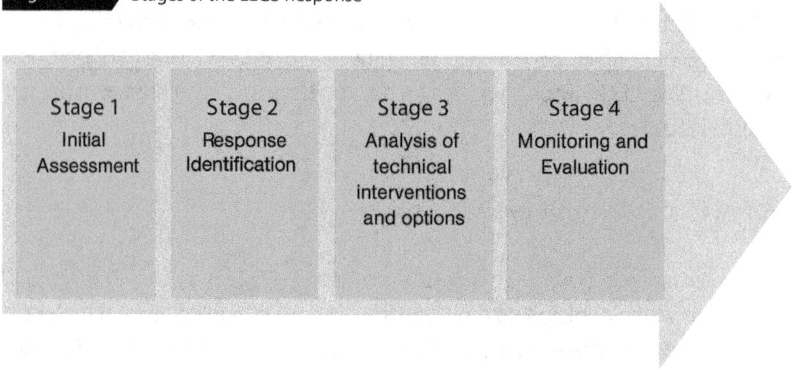

Figure E.2   Tools for the Stages of the LEGS Response

Stage 1	Stage 2	Stage 3	Stage 4
Assessment Checklists	PRIM	Advantages & Disadvantages; Timing; Decision Trees; Standards & Guidelines	Standards & Guidelines; M & E Checklists

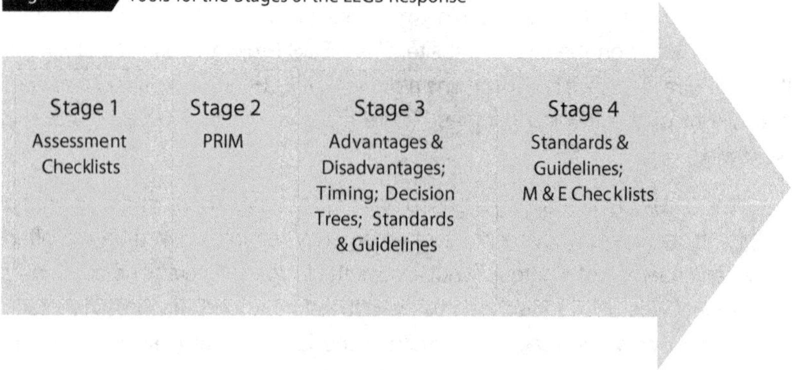

For Stage 3, the LEGS Training outlines five steps for designing a response programme using these tools (see *Box E.1*).

<table>
<tr><td>**Box E.1**</td><td>**Five steps to design a response programme**</td></tr>
</table>

1. Review the summary of options and their implications for the relevant technical intervention
2. Review the advantages and disadvantages table
3. Review the timing table
4. Work through the decision-making tree
5. Use the Standards, Key actions, and Guidance notes to design a response programme.

The LEGS Project also runs a half-day LEGS awareness session for decision-makers and donors. This presents key issues involved in livestock-based emergency response and highlights the contents of the LEGS Handbook and key decision-making tools.

For further information about the LEGS Training Programme, see the training pages of the LEGS website, or contact the LEGS Training Coordinator: <Training@livestock-emergency.net>.

To contact LEGS:

Visit the LEGS website:

Email: <Coordinator@livestock-emergency.net>

To order the LEGS Handbook:

Via the LEGS website: or direct from the publisher: <https://developmentbookshop.com/livestock-emergency-guidelines-and-standards>

Disclaimer:

Please see the disclaimer section of the LEGS website

for full details on copyright and terms of use for LEGS publications including this Handbook

Index

accountability 13, 21, 30, 32, 269
ACORD (Agency for Cooperation and
    Research in Development) 131–2
Action Against Hunger (ACF) 201
advocacy 25, 33, 34–5
Afghanistan
    case study 134
    coordination 87
    intervention areas 88
    key support 88, 89
    livestock market 87, 88
    M & E 89, 99–100
    ongoing support 89
    partnerships 88
    transaction costs 88
Agency for Cooperation and Research in
    Development (ACORD) 131–2
ALDEF (Arid Lands Development
    Focus) 94–5
animal welfare, 'five freedoms' 77, 106,
    146, 180, 210, 239, 253
anthrax 126
antiretroviral drugs (ARVs) 16, 82
Arid Lands Development Focus
    (ALDEF) 94–5
assessment, initial 27, 48–9
asset protection 9, 55t, 133
avian influenza 109, 221

Bangladesh 226
baselines 54
benchmarks 13
Benfield UCL Hazard Research Centre 49
biodiversity 83
Bolivia 170, 231
border closure 7t

CAHWs (community-based animal health
    workers)
    case studies 39, 131–2, 227, 266, 269
    female 113, 124
    importance of 107, 109
    and local capacity 114, 120
    protection 113
    resistance to 115
    supervision of 124, 125
    training 123–4
camps
    destocking 83
    feed supplies 154
    livestock provision 248

veterinary support 117
water demand 190, 192
capacity
    assessment 28
    beneficiary community 14
    building 23, 24, 67, 259, 260
    and expertise 36
    local 116box
    provision of livestock 243, 247, 252
carcass disposal 19, 79, 92, 128
    case study 134–5
CARE 49, 67, 95, 96
cash transfers 63–6, 162, 247, 248
cash-for-work (CFW) projects 65t, 66t,
    128, 135
Catholic Organization for Relief and
    Development Aid (Cordaid) 39–40
CBAH (community-based animal health-
    care) 107, 114
CE-DAT 67
CFW (cash-for-work) projects 65t, 66t,
    128, 135
child protection, minimum standards 17,
    28
climate change
    impacts on livestock 19–20
    and increased vulnerability 19
    transparency in advocacy 35
    trends 23
climate projections 25
'cluster approach' 220, 278g
commercial destocking 78, 79, 80t
    case study 93–4
    coordination 87
    decision-making 83, 84fig
    intervention areas 88
    key support 88, 89
    livestock market 87, 88
    M & E 89, 99–100
    ongoing support 89
    partnerships 88
    slow onset emergency 81
    transaction costs 88
community feed banks 157
community groups 22
community participation, case study 39
community-based animal health-care
    (CBAH) 107, 114
community-based animal health workers
    (CAHWs)
    case studies 39, 131–2, 227, 266, 269

LEGS livelihoods objectives

1 - To PROVIDE immediate benefits using livestock resources

2 - To PROTECT key livestock-related assets

3 - To REBUILD key livestock-related assets

Cross-cutting themes

1 - Gender and social equity

2 - HIV/AIDS

3 - Protection

4 - Environment and climate

Linkages to rights-based approach

- Right to food
- Right to a standard of living

Minimum standards, Key actions and Guidance notes

Minimum standards

- Describe an essential part of an emergency response
- Generally qualitative statements

Key actions

- Steps or actions that contribute to achieving the Standard

Guidance notes

- Accompany the Key actions
- Highlight particular issues to be considered when applying the Standard